Fooling with the Amish

YOUNG CENTER BOOKS IN ANABAPTIST AND PIETIST STUDIES
Steven M. Nolt, Series Editor

Fooling with the Amish

Amish Mafia, Entertaining Fakery,
and the Evolution of Reality TV

DIRK EITZEN

Johns Hopkins University Press
Baltimore

© 2022 Johns Hopkins University Press
All rights reserved. Published 2022
Printed in the United States of America on acid-free paper

2   4   6   8   9   7   5   3   1

Johns Hopkins University Press
2715 North Charles Street
Baltimore, Maryland 21218-4363
www.press.jhu.edu

Library of Congress Cataloging-in-Publication Data
Names: Eitzen, Dirk, author.
Title: Fooling with the Amish : Amish mafia, entertaining fakery, and the
evolution of reality TV / Dirk Eitzen.
Description: Baltimore : Johns Hopkins University Press, 2022. | Series:
Young Center books in Anabaptist and Pietist studies | Includes
bibliographical references and index.
Identifiers: LCCN 2021045398 | ISBN 9781421444185 (hardcover) |
ISBN 9781421444192 (ebook)
Subjects: LCSH: Amish Mafia (Television program) | Reality television programs—
Social aspects—United States. | Television viewers—Social aspects—United States. |
Deception. | Gossip.
Classification: LCC PN1992.77.A5265 E38 2022 | DDC 791.45/72—dc23/eng/20220105
LC record available at https://lccn.loc.gov/2021045398

A catalog record for this book is available from the British Library.

*Special discounts are available for bulk purchases of this book. For more information,
please contact Special Sales at specialsales@jh.edu.*

CONTENTS

Fooling with the Amish

Prologue

A Puzzle

1. Most reality TV shows—the dramatic ones, in particular, like *Survivor*, *The Bachelor*, and *Keeping Up with the Kardashians*—are full of fakery.[1] They deliberately and routinely deceive audiences about the reality status of things they show.

2. Fans of these shows know that they are being deceived. They are well aware that there is a lot of covert manipulation and sleight of hand involved in the shows' making, even though they are blind to the particulars.

3. When people find out that they have been deliberately lied to or deceived, they are typically upset or angry. It makes them feel manipulated and taken advantage of.

And yet . . .

4. Many, many people love tricked-up reality TV shows and watch them avidly.

All four of these facts seem, on their face, to be fairly self-evident. Yet they don't line up. At least one of the four propositions must be false. But which one, and why?

One could easily make reasonable guesses. For example, one might argue, with respect to the second proposition, that if you know you are being deceived, it is not really deception. But with just a little Googling, you will discover that people really are deceived by a lot of the fakery on reality TV.

Or one might suppose, with respect to the third proposition, that when people know *that* trickery is taking place but can't tell *how*, they are typically more impressed and engaged than upset or annoyed. That's true of magic shows and Hollywood special effects, for example. And yet, reality TV has little in common with magic shows and special effects. It is a totally different kind of entertainment involving a totally different kind of "fakery." Besides, viewers sometimes do complain about trickery in reality TV.

At the heart of this paradox is a familiar puzzle: What is it about the so-called reality of reality TV that fans are drawn to? What are its distinctive appeals? How do contrivance and fakery factor in? This book will explore answers to these questions, not by speculating, but by examining a great deal of evidence: other reality-based entertainments, from P. T. Barnum's "humbugs" to TV documentaries; empirical research into the psychology and sociology of deception, from cheating on exams to fake news; and audience responses, from real-time tweets to in-depth interviews.

The book's central answer—to give you a sneak preview—is that, in taking liberties with facts, reality TV works much like gossip. This is not just a metaphor—a comparison intended to help think about reality TV in a new way. I will argue that it is a psychological fact with actual explanatory utility. To get to this conclusion—to see where it comes from, to examine empirical evidence for it, to weigh its implications, and so on—requires a good bit of legwork. It will take this whole book.

An Illuminating Example

An example that the book scrutinizes closely, from many angles, is an elaborately and uniquely contrived *fake* reality TV show—*Amish Mafia*, which aired on Discovery Channel from 2012 to 2015. To say that *Amish Mafia* is a fake reality TV show requires some explaining, since everybody knows that all reality TV is somewhat fake. *Amish Mafia* was not a typical reality TV show, like *Survivor*, in which situations are pretty obviously contrived or set up. Nor was it supposed to be fictional entertainment (what reality TV producers refer to as "scripted" television). In contrast with both of those, it was deliberately and meticulously designed to dupe or at least confound viewers.

To understand the difference between typical reality TV and this instance of what I am calling fake reality TV, it helps to consider a fake documentary, *Mermaids: The Body Found*, which also aired on Discovery Channel, also in 2012, as part of the same calculated foray into fakery. *Mermaids* was not a mock documentary. A mock documentary, like Rob Reiner's famous 1984 spoof of a rockumentary about a fictional British heavy metal band, *This Is Spinal Tap*, is not fake because it deliberately, playfully foregrounds its make-believe. *Mermaids* was also not fake in the way of today's "fake news." Political documentaries and quasi-news programs that deliberately peddle half-truths or untruths might be labeled fake but are really more of a lie, inasmuch as their claims are supposed to be taken seriously, at least by those who believe them. What this means, exactly, is something we will dig into in later chapters. In the meantime, suffice it to say that *Mermaids* was very different from both mockumentaries and fake news. Indeed, it was deliberately different from any so-called documentary that Discovery Channel had ever previously aired.

Mermaids was deliberately designed to deceive and perplex audiences. It presented meticulously faked evidence, explained by actors presented as real scientists at actual universities and research organizations. It labeled some scenes as dramatizations to distinguish them from "actual" footage and cleverly chose actors for the dramatized scenes who resembled the actors playing scientists in the "actual" scenes. The producers went so far as to create fake websites for supposedly actual people and organizations presented in the program, to further mislead or confuse viewers who sought to double-check its veracity on the internet. All of this fakery was conceived as part and parcel of the show's entertainment value.

Amish Mafia pioneered the same sort of deception in the realm of reality TV. Although it was designed to look like a regular reality TV show, about a violent gang of enforcers and extortionists in a peaceful Amish community, it in fact employed non-Amish and ex-Amish people as actors in scenarios that were largely if not entirely made up. *Amish Mafia* not only deliberately disguised these sleights of hand, it expressly denied them. Just like Discovery's fake mermaid documentary, it was designed to take a partially plausible fiction and present it in a way that either deliberately confounded audiences or flat-out duped them.

To understand the specific mechanisms and effects of fakery in reality TV generally, it is helpful to look closely at a specific example. *Amish Mafia*'s extraordinary level of fakery makes it the perfect case study. Furthermore, because *Amish Mafia* takes as its subject a community that has traditionally refused to have any truck with television (the Amish), it allows us to see especially clearly the kinds of manipulation that are often involved in making reality TV and the kinds of consequences it can have for its participants.

To understand exactly how *Amish Mafia* confounded, misled, or deceived viewers, one first needs to understand exactly how its fakery was engineered.

That is the purpose of chapter 1. The chapter dissects particular examples, explains how they create the illusion of reality, discusses other more express kinds of deception in the show, and, finally, explains who the "Amish" subjects of the show really are and what is false or misleading about the way the show portrays the Amish community.

To get a better bearing on what American audiences want and expect from "reality" in their reality entertainments, the next two chapters put *Amish Mafia* into historical perspective. Chapter 2 examines the long tradition of fakery in reality-based entertainment, from P. T. Barnum's fake mermaid and early cinema to TV news and today's "fake news." Chapter 3 looks at the history of reality TV to explain how and why the conventions of trickery evolved and how Amish and ex-Amish got involved.

Chapter 4 examines the pleasures of deception in reality TV. Most people, it turns out, do not feel manipulated or taken advantage of when they learn they have been misled or lied to by *Amish Mafia*. Usually they don't care. Often they even enjoy it as something to talk about. So there is definitely a problem with the third proposition at the top of this chapter, which posits that people do not like to be deceived. Being deceived by reality TV is evidently an exception to the rule. How come? Chapter 4 gleans insights from in-depth interviews with *Amish Mafia* fans and industry insiders, from scholarly research into various kinds of reality entertainment, and from a couple of novel experiments with reality TV viewers, using clips from *Amish Mafia*.

Chapter 5 pulls the fruits of all this research together and draws conclusions. It is here that the connection to gossip is explained and teased out. The chapter discusses the evolutionary origins of gossip, its social functions for good and ill, how aspects of soap operas and documentaries serve the same social purposes, the role of deception in gossip, and how all of this is manifest in *Amish Mafia*.

Finally, chapter 6 looks at the ethics of manipulation and deception in reality TV. Again, *Amish Mafia* is a singularly useful case study. Not only did it involve an exceptional amount of trickery and deception but it also generated an exceptional amount of criticism, largely for its treatment of the Amish.

It needs to be said at the outset that this book pursues two parallel projects that touch at many points but are fairly independent. The first project, the primary one, is to dig into and attempt to explain the social and psychological appeals of reality TV in contrast to the appeal of fiction, on the one hand, and nonfiction, on the other. The second project is to discover how Amish people got involved in reality TV and what impact this involvement had on them and their community. There are some surprising connections between these two projects, so I hope the reader is sufficiently curious and engaged to read the whole book. Just the same, readers who are mainly interested in reality TV may find more information about the Amish than they need, and vice versa. Some chapters also range widely, touching on topics as diverse as the 1938 radio drama *War of the Worlds* and professional wrestling. Still, the patient reader will discover that many threads tie these diverse topics together.

So What?

Most centrally, this book is about fakery in the media, one of the defining problems of our time.

Since the mid-1990s American journalists and cultural commentators have expressed growing concern about the increasingly widespread and passionate embrace of false facts by large segments of the American public, sometimes fueled by the deliberate dissemination of disinformation, usually compounded by mistrust of mainstream journalism and science. A case in point is the deeply held conviction by some people that global climate change is nothing but a conspiracy and a hoax.

Concerns about gullible media consumers and deceptive media producers grew in the 2000s until, in 2016, they exploded into outright alarm, owing in large part to the unforeseen election to the U.S. presidency of a reality TV star with no prior political experience and a pathological propensity to lie. Media mavens and pundits in the press fretted about the problem of "post-truth" (*Oxford Dictionary*'s word of the year for 2016).[2] Politicos on the left and right accused each other of fomenting "fake news" (*Collins Dictionary*'s word of the year for 2017).[3] In 2018 the RAND Corporation, a venerable nonpartisan think tank, published a lengthy report called *Truth Decay: An Initial Exploration of the Diminishing Role of Facts and Analysis in American Public Life.*[4] What makes today's "truth decay" different and more dangerous than fake news of the past, according to the RAND report, is that Americans are having a harder and harder time even agreeing on objective facts. It is as though we each feel entitled to our own "alternative facts"—a phrase famously used by presidential advisor Kellyanne Conway in January 2017 to justify the White House press secretary's repetition of false statements made by President Donald Trump.[5]

There is general agreement about many of the causes of "truth decay." Social media play a key role. A 2019 book about recent conspiracy theories in the United States, *Republic of Lies*, opens with an epigram from Jonathan

Swift: "Falsehood flies, and truth comes limping after it, so that when men come to be undeceived, it is too late."[6] A study published in *Science* shows that this is precisely what happens on Twitter.[7] To make matters worse, social media algorithms serve up whatever users happen to like, creating political echo chambers or filter bubbles. "Bad actors" add to the problem by deliberately peddling half-truths and lies, hoping to gain income or influence or, in the case of Russian social media troll farms, just to throw sand into the gears of American democracy. On top of all that, dramatic social changes in the United States, such as a decline in middle-income jobs, the #MeToo movement, and the outcry over ongoing racial injustices, have left many Americans feeling insecure, powerless, and angry. On the one hand, this situation makes them suspicious of the establishment, including mainstream media. On the other, it makes them overly trusting of those they perceive to be on their side.

Beneath all of these proximate social causes is a more profound psychological cause: people have a natural appetite for "alternative facts." Part of this appetite is a hunger for sensation (excitement, drama, the scent of scandal, and so on). Part of it is a hunger for social and emotional validation (a sense of belonging, of moral superiority, of having access to privileged information). Note that these are two of the main ingredients of gossip. They are also two of the main ingredients of reality TV.

The study of audience responses to *Amish Mafia* clearly shows that the "reality" that interests viewers has little to do with facts. It also shows that when viewers are taken in by the show's fakery, it is by no means because they are confused about the difference between fact and fancy. They are not naive, and they are not dupes. When they are deceived, it is because they allow themselves to be. They are willing, even eager participants in a kind of mediated social transaction that revolves more around identity and illusion than around facts. This same state of affairs seems to be at work in "fake news" and close to the root of the whole "post-truth" phenomenon.

In any case, fakery in the media is rampant today and has provoked a lot of questions and concerns. Why do people so often eat it up? What do they want from it? What do they get? When do they see through it? When are they deceived? Why are they deceived? How does the fakery harm individuals? How does it harm society? How can those harms be prevented?

The best way to begin to find valid and useful answers to such questions is with close observation and careful analysis of actual cases. The main value of this book, especially in this moment of "truth decay," is that it digs deeply into one particularly fascinating, sketchy, revealing, manipulative, clever, controversial, marvelous, mind-bending example of contemporary media fakery, in a genre well known for its fakery. The plethora of interesting and useful information the book conveys along the way about Amish culture, the media business, the history of reality TV, the psychology of deception, and more is a bonus.

An Ecological Approach

Some media scholarship assumes that media texts do things to us, the viewers: they lie to us, they exploit us, they sell us things, they subtly bias us, and so on. It is true that TV shows and movies do all of these things to us, but only when we watch them, depending on how we watch them. We need to think about reality TV as a kind of interaction between viewers and media texts. We watch reality TV shows for our own reasons, and reality TV shows provide us with reasons to watch. Reality TV producers are canny matchmakers, trying to engineer a win-win outcome, in which the offerings of their shows match the interests of the greatest number of prospective viewers. Unfortunately for them, even if they could make the shows they want (constraints like budgets always get in the way), they can never really predict what will succeed, particularly in a rapidly changing media environment. So they proceed with a kind of educated guesswork, constantly trying out new tweaks of time-tested formulas. The distribution apparatus (such as ratings, marketing departments, and executive producers) provides constant feedback about which tweaks work and which ones don't. Bad guesses get culled; successful ones, copied.

This process is evolutionary, in the Darwinian sense. It proceeds through blind variation (guessing and tweaking) and selective retention (copying and culling).[8] *Amish Mafia* can be seen as the cultural equivalent of a biological phenotype: a set of physical characteristics that are the end result, through natural selection, of a long series of interactions between reality TV shows and their environment, which includes consumers, producers, and distributors. In the same way that the beaks of Darwin's finches provided clues about the environment in which they had evolved and the niches they had come to inhabit, the shape of *Amish Mafia* provides clues about its cultural environment, which includes not just other reality TV shows but also news, fake news, popular ideas about the Amish, actual Amish, and so on. A crucial job for the media scholar, in this view, is to analyze the "fit" between what consumers want from particular shows and the gratifications the shows serve up, treating the cultural environment as the primary factor in determining this outcome. That is the approach this book embodies.

This approach does not presume value judgments. It describes the fit of media texts and genres in their environment as is, without any necessary regard to what ought to be. In that sense, it is akin to ecological science. But where humans are involved, the question of "oughts" is an important one. All creatures play a role in shaping their own environment. Termites build mounds, cattle create manure, and so on. Humans have the capacity to do this deliberately. That is where "oughts" come into play.

Culture is often defined, following anthropologist Clifford Geertz, as the web of meaning that surrounds us.[9] This suggests that culture is something immaterial. I prefer a more ecological definition: culture is the material environment that human societies create for themselves, which in turn shapes them. This includes families and schools, buildings and books, automobiles and blue jeans (or buggies and buttoned breeches), courts and enacted customs, and also television shows like *Amish Mafia*.

Human creations and actions have material consequences. For example, it is not at all farfetched to suppose that Donald Trump's rise to the presidency and his followers' remarkable willingness to overlook his blatant lies had something to do with the fact that reality TV shows have helped to fashion a media environment in which sensation trumps facts. It behooves us, as creatures with the capacity to act deliberately, to try to discern and evaluate such potential consequences. That, again, is the topic of chapter 6 of this book. My analysis in that chapter is rooted not in any particular political or ideological slant (although I do not deny having such a slant); it is rooted in the ecological perspective I describe here.

The overarching purpose of this book, then, is a kind of ecological study of deception in reality TV. I initially encountered *Amish Mafia* mainly because of a scholarly interest in Amish and the media, but I quickly discovered something truly extraordinary in the show: a marvelous deceiver, exceptionally well adapted to a particular niche in the media landscape at the boundary between the factual and the fictional. That is why it continued to engage me. And that is why I hope you will find a book about it worth your while.

A Bibliographic Aside

This book is a work of cognitive cultural studies. The cognitive approach to humanities research emerged in cinema studies in the mid-1980s and expanded into literary studies and philosophical aesthetics in the following decade. The main feature of this approach was a new way of thinking about how movies and literary texts produce meanings and experiences that placed the minds of viewers and readers at the center of the process. The cognitive approach also shifted the kind of work scholars do with media and literary texts: from unpacking their hidden significations and unconscious operations to focusing on the empirical means by which they produce conscious experiences.[10]

To explain cognitive cultural studies is beyond the scope of this book. The field encompasses a wide range of topics, approaches, and methodologies. For viewers interested in knowing more, I recommend two anthologies: from cinema and media studies, Ted Nanicelli and Paul Taberham's *Cognitive Media Theory* (2014),[11] and from literary studies, Lisa Zunshine's *The Oxford Handbook of Cognitive Literary Studies* (2015).[12] Patrick Holm Cogan's *Cognitive Science, Literature, and the Arts: A Guide for Humanists* offers an accessible philosophical overview that remains relevant and useful, even though it was published nearly two decades ago, in 2003.[13] The particular ecological approach of my book, described in the previous section, was pioneered by film scholar Joe Anderson starting in the late 1990s.[14] It assumes that experiences and meanings, instead of arising from the brain alone, emerge from whole human bodies' interactions with their environment. In contemporary cognitive science and philosophy of mind, this assumption has become fairly widespread and goes by the name "embodied cognition."

For those who are especially interested in reality TV, I should mention a chapter in Lisa Zunshine's engaging "thought experiment," *Getting Inside Your Head: What Cognitive Science Can Tell Us about Popular Culture* (2012), in which she unpacks the central role that humiliation plays in the genre from a cognitive perspective.[15] Little else has been written in this vein about reality TV specifically. There is, however, an extensive and important scholarly literature that examines reality TV from other perspectives, including historical, critical, and sociological ones. I have looked at all of this literature and studied much of it closely. Still, I draw on it selectively. The reason is that, as previously stated, this is not a book about reality TV per se. It is about a particular aspect of the reality TV experience: the appeal of entertaining fakery. This topic is narrower in focus than research about reality TV in the field of media studies because it does not expressly treat other important aspects of the genre such as humiliation, class, postmodernism, and subgenres like self-improvement. At the same time, it is broader in scope because it naturally connects to a wide array of other topics, including tabloid journalism, professional wrestling, the psychology of deception, and the sociology of gossip. This scope necessitates drawing on a much wider and more diverse body of scholarship.

To readers interested in a quick overview of reality TV research in the field of media studies, I recommend Annette Hill's elegant little 2015 monograph, *Reality TV*, and Laurie Ouellette's 2014 anthology, *Companion to Reality Television*, which is particularly useful in teasing out political and ideological undercurrents in reality TV.[16]

I should also mention here two bits of autobiographical information that are relevant to my research. The first is that I was raised and remain a Mennonite, which accounts for my interest in and some of my firsthand knowledge of Amish culture and beliefs. The second is that, for many years, starting before I became a scholar, I made documentary films—about a dozen of them, including a nationally broadcast public TV documentary about the impact of tourism on the Amish. In this book, I frequently discuss the practical side of filmmaking, especially as it pertains to aesthetic and ethical decisions. My knowledge of practical filmmaking stems in large part from my own experience, which is why sometimes no external source is cited.

With this background out of the way, I will return to the central project of this book: the study of deception in reality TV, with *Amish Mafia* as a focus. If we want to understand the "lying" in *Amish Mafia*—why producers did it, why audiences enjoyed it, why critics criticized it, and what its consequences were—we need to begin by sussing out the lies. We need to separate the fact from the fancy and the reality from the make-believe. So, let us begin.

CHAPTER ONE

Enquiring Minds Want to Know

In Flagrante Delicto

The first episode of *Amish Mafia* ends with a bang: it catches an Amish leader in the act of hooking up with a prostitute. This is a marvelous piece of story engineering, worth analyzing in some detail. But before we delve into that scene, let us follow the lead of the show and begin by introducing the setting and cast of characters.

"Lancaster County, Pennsylvania," says a title. We see a farm with chickens, a buggy driving down the road, and women in Amish garb having a picnic by a stream. "It's very different in the Amish culture," says a woman narrator with a slight Pennsylvania Dutch accent. "Absolutely nothing modern. Dark dresses. Push mowers. We are very religious." Cut to a young fellow in his bedroom wearing what looks like Amish garb, with a framed kitsch-art print of the Good Shepherd on his bureau and a Bible-verse plaque on his wall. He is smartly assembling an assault rifle. The woman's voice continues over the gun sequence: "You do everything the proper way. You go to church. . . . And everything is supposed to bring you closer to God."

We then meet "Lebanon" Levi and the rest of his gang in a snappy montage of posed shots (fig. 1.1). "Levi does the dirty work that the church can't. He protects people that can't protect themselves," the narrator tells us. A little later, she explains that Levi runs the Amish communal self-insurance fund, Amish Aid. "Levi and the rest of his gang are in charge of handling the community's money. If something happens to a person and they cannot work or someone's property gets damaged, they make a claim with Levi. He often resolves things

Figure 1.1 John, Alvin, Levi, and Jolin on *Amish Mafia.*

by sending the boys out. They can resolve things that most insurance companies can't," she says. "Levi is the cops. He is the courthouse, he is the bank, and he is the insurance company."

The guy with the gun is Jolin, "Levi's foot soldier." He is Mennonite, not Amish, so he "can do things for Levi the other guys can't." (Like shoot things up. The Amish gangsters in the show confine themselves to baseball bats, sledgehammers, and firebombs.) Besides Jolin, Levi's gang consists of Levi's childhood friend Alvin ("If you want to get to Levi, you have to go through me, first") and John (who "has a good heart" but "can hold his own, too"). The narrator, we soon learn, is Esther, John's older sister and Levi's would-be sweetheart. ("Levi has always had a thing for me, so I can use that to my advantage.")

Esther continues our introduction to Amish life by taking us into her house. She shows how to light a propane lamp and explains the green roll-up window shades typical of Amish houses in Lancaster County. It seems clear that Esther is Amish, although small inconsistencies suggest that not everything is 100 percent on the level. For example, John says, "We won't have electric, won't have refrigerator, indoor plumbing except for cold water." In fact, the Amish do have modern propane-powered refrigerators, and, just moments before, we caught a glimpse of one in Esther's kitchen. For the record, the Amish of Lancaster County have indoor plumbing too, including hot water. The shot of what appears to be an outhouse that accompanies John's no-indoor-plumbing comment is actually an old telephone shanty—a small out-door shed where some Amish families or groups of families keep a telephone for occasional necessary contact with the non-Amish or "English" world, al-though nowadays cell-phone use for business is common among the Amish in much of Lancaster County.

About midway through the forty-four-minute episode, Esther informs Levi of a problem: a non-Amish acquaintance of hers who taxis Amish people around has reported to her that a certain important and powerful man in the Amish community had been using his services to visit a prostitute.

Tell the driver to see me, Levi says.

The man visits Levi, in Levi's makeshift office: a desk in the middle of a barn. The visitor's face is blurred and his voice is digitally distorted to hide his identity. He tells Levi he is concerned about the welfare of his Amish client and the client's wife and family, "because now he's telling me he's having sex without condoms." Levi asks him to write his Amish client's name and ad-dress on a piece of paper. Levi shakes his head as he reads it. In typical reality TV fashion, the sequence is broken up by short interviews in which charac-ters provide background and personal reactions to events. "This guy is a very important member of the community," Levi tells us. "He owns more than a few successful businesses. . . . I don't know why he's doing what he is, but if he gets caught, he's got a major problem on his hands."

Levi sends John and Jolin to a downtown camera store to buy a camera, to get proof of the Amish leader's philandering. This is a new experience for John. "Growing up without cameras, I don't know what I looked like when I was a baby. . . . The Amish don't believe in cameras, so I never really played with one." He is clearly delighted to experiment with the new camera.

When a call comes from the taxi driver, Jolin throws a couple of guns into the back of his pickup and he and John drive off to stake out the motel where the tryst is supposed to take place. At the motel, they wait. John tinkers with the camera. He has a nervous moment when it does not turn on immediately. Then a van pulls up and discharges a middle-aged Amishman. Although the man's face is blurred out, he is dressed in Amish garb, including a straw hat. He has the build of a middle-aged farmer. Even more convincing is the way he moves: stooped over with a slow gait, casually hitching up his pants from behind. His whole bearing seems authentic.

As soon as the Amishman enters the hotel room, Jolin and John jump out of the pickup to catch him with the prostitute. Jolin is tough and confident—clearly the man in charge. John is more timid, following along behind with the camera. "My heart, it was pounding," John says in a cut-in interview, "cause I was thinking like, What if we have the wrong guy?"

Jolin pounds on the door, waits, then pounds again. When the Amishman opens the door, still wearing his straw hat, Jolin shoulders his way past him into the room. John starts snapping pictures. We catch a couple of fleeting glimpses of a woman sitting up in bed with the sheet pulled up to her chin. "What are you doing with that camera?" the Amishman asks, trying to push Jolin out of the room. "Put that thing away! Wos isch letz?" he demands, in Pennsylvania Dutch. (A subtitle translates: "What's wrong?") "Wos isch letz mit *Dich*?" Jolin retorts. ("What's wrong with *you*?") "Geh weg!" Jolin commands the philanderer. ("Go away!")

Holding his hand in front of his face to shield it from the cameras, the Amishman retreats to the waiting van, climbs in, and closes the door. "It would be a lot worse for you if the church finds out what you're doing," Jolin calls after him. He then waits, arms crossed, as the woman in the room gathers her things. She emerges from the room wearing a halter top and a short jean skirt. Her face, too, is blurred out. "I don't want to see you around here anymore," Jolin tells her as she walks away. "And you don't want to see me, I can promise you that."

That is not quite the end of the matter or of the episode. After the motel incident, John briefly discusses with Esther the possibility of keeping the photos for himself: "If I blackmail this official, that means I'm not going to have to work for anybody."

Esther persuades him to hand over the pictures to Levi, who takes prints to the Amish leader's house. He instructs the videographers to wait outside the house, so they lurk, filming Levi's silhouette in the window and his henchman Alvin cooling his heels outside. We hear Levi's conversation, recorded on a wireless mic. "Work with us and I'll take care of you," he says. "Why don't I just make you disappear for a while . . . so you can get yourself straightened out. . . . I know you've got business going on. . . . I'll take care of it. I'll help you out, you don't have to worry about it."

However implausible this scenario may seem on the page, on screen it sweeps you right along. There are a lot of convincing elements—the spoken Pennsylvania Dutch, the actual places, the blurred-out faces, John's nervousness—plus subtler details, like the Amishman's gait. Because of the way the motel scene unfolds, the whole thing just *feels* believable. Even if you are a skeptic and presume that *Amish Mafia* is full of fakery, you are left with the question,

"How did they do that?" Even if the scene is a set piece, it presents a marvel-ous *illusion* of reality.

The Manufacture of Illusion

Illusion in art is the mastery of impressions. It is not a matter of getting all the details right; it is a matter of getting a few key details right and eliminating contrary ones. Half of the trick is to present the eye with details that the mind would expect to see in a scene were it real. The other half is to erase or elim-inate any detail that does not fit what we would expect to see.

The great art historian Ernst Gombrich published this discovery in his groundbreaking collection of essays on the psychology of art, *Art and Illu-sion*. As an illustration, he offers the painting *Artemisia* by the Dutch realist master Rembrandt van Rijn.[1] Take a look at the part of the painting repro-duced here (fig. 1.2). The woman's face is not perfect—there is something a bit plastic about it—but her sumptuous dress is wonderfully realistic. You can practically feel the texture of the gold brocade the woman is fingering and the weight of her gold chain. "We instinctively feel that glitter means, if not gold, at least smoothness, brightness, a sensual quality to which we respond with greater immediacy than we respond to outlines and which is therefore less easily analyzed," Gombrich writes. What we respond to is an impression: "the 'global' quality itself, not the elements of local color and reflection—hence the intriguing and compelling effect of the pictorial illusion."[2]

But when you step close and examine the brocade in detail (fig. 1.3), you discover that the paint on the canvas looks nothing like gold brocade, indeed nothing like a photograph: it is little dabs of white paint dotted onto yellowish-brown smears. When we step back, the dabs and smears of paint are trans-formed into something seemingly real and substantial as much by what we do *not* see as by what we do. As Gombrich puts it, "The distance from the can-vas weakens the beholder's power of discrimination and creates a blur which mobilizes his projective faculty. The indistinct parts of the canvas become a screen, provided only that certain features stand out with sufficient force and that no contradictory messages reach the eye to spoil the impression."[3]

In other words, the illusion comes from the mind, not the canvas. The painting encourages it by supplying suggestive details, like dark "shadows" and sparkling "reflections," but it permits the eye and mind to complete the picture by eliminating counterevidence, such as the surface texture of brush-strokes and canvas. The mental completion of the image is not a matter of

Figure 1.2 Rembrandt, *Artemisia (Judith at the Banquet of Holofernes)*, 1634 (detail). Museo Nacional del Prado, Madrid. Wikimedia Commons.

filling in missing details. It is simply a matter of recognition: we *see* gold brocade and it *feels* real. The impression of coherence satisfies the mind.

The same principle applies to movies. Filmmakers use it all the time to shape scenes that feel realistic. What they rely on to "weaken the beholder's power of discrimination and create a blur" is not defocusing of the image (although filmmakers often do defocus background elements); it is tempo.

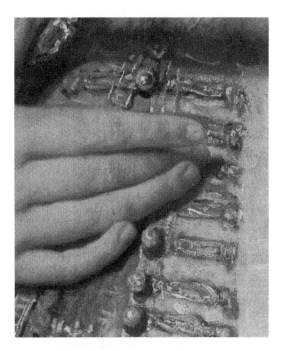

Figure 1.3 Detail of the brocade in Rembrandt's *Artemisia*.

Spectators gazing at Rembrandt's *Artemisia* in the Prado Museum can take the time to allow their gaze to wander over the image. Viewers of a movie often have barely enough time to resolve key elements of one shot before the movie cuts to the next. Skillful filmmakers know how to stitch together a sequence of shots so that spectators' minds effortlessly project a coherent scene onto it. When a filmmaker does this successfully, the cuts become invisible and viewers do not notice discrepancies between shots.

Since Gombrich made his discoveries about illusion in art in the 1950s, psychologists have learned a great deal more about the perceptual mechanisms involved. When people are engaged in some task, they are often effectively blind to things they are not looking for or expecting, even when those things are right in front of them. In one classic experiment, when people are interrupted in the middle of giving directions to a stranger by a passing obstacle, they fail to notice when a new stranger takes the place of the one they have been giving directions to. In another experiment, people counting the number of times a basketball is passed between players fail to notice when a man in a gorilla suit dances right through the middle of the action. (You can see examples of these and similar demonstrations by searching for "change blindness" and "inattentional blindness" on YouTube.[4]) By the same token, when people are paying attention to the story in a movie, they do not notice irrelevant details—even implausible ones—so long as those do not interfere with the impression of coherence. The makers of *Amish Mafia* take full advantage of that fact.

Trickery or Tradecraft?

In the scene where Jolin and John catch the philandering Amish leader at the motel, there is a moment that shot-by-shot analysis exposes as an obvious sleight of hand (fig. 1.4). Jolin and John are sitting in Jolin's pickup truck. Up to the motel rolls a black van, which they recognize as the Amishman's ride (*top left*). John starts snapping pictures (*top right*). We get a zoomed-in shot of the black van from John's vantage point (*bottom left*). With each click of John's camera, the moving image briefly flashes to a freeze-frame. Then the camera switches to a completely different vantage point, so that we can see the Amishman getting out of the van (*bottom right*). The clicks and freeze-frames continue, with intermittent shots of John and his camera, as though we are still seeing John's shots. But these cannot possibly be John's shots because, from where he sits in the pickup truck, the Amishman is completely obscured by the van.

What actually happened here? Perhaps, anticipating the need for a second angle, the reality TV crew had a second car and a second camera staking out this spot. In that case, the click/freeze-frame device is just an aesthetic nicety—a touch of style. Or perhaps this whole scene is an invention masquerading as a reenactment, and the crew shot it twice to allow for two different camera angles. In that case, the click/freeze-frame trick may be a distraction designed to draw attention away from the sleight of hand. In either case, viewers are oblivious to the change in camera angles unless it is pointed out to them. It is invisible to them.

This is an example of inattentional blindness. The show brings it about by serving up an interesting story to attend to. We have been waiting in suspense with Jolin and John to see who will get out of that van. Because the new camera angle shows us what we want to see and expect to see, we do not notice the shift in perspective. Consider what would happen without the new angle: you would not be able to see the Amishman at all, because you would be on the wrong side of the van. "If *I* can't see the Amishman," you might think, "neither can Jolin and John. Something is wrong with this picture!" Showing us the Amishman keeps the story moving forward and draws us in. It makes

Figure 1.4 Jolin and John John follow the philandering Amish leader to a motel. A shot-by-shot analysis reveals an obvious sleight of hand in the depiction of the scene.

the scene *feel* complete, even though the angle is implausible. As with Rembrandt's gold brocade, the impression of coherence satisfies the mind even though, upon close examination, the details turn out to be sketchy.

This editing technique, called continuity editing, is standard practice in narrative filmmaking. Fiction filmmakers typically accomplish it by shooting the same scene numerous times, from different angles, and cutting the various takes together. Documentary filmmakers often use the technique too, because it is so conducive to transparent storytelling, but once in a while it leads them to be accused of cheating.

An infamous example takes place near the end of Michael Moore's 2002 documentary, *Bowling for Columbine*. In an interview Moore confronts actor Charlton Heston, then president of the National Rifle Association, for leading a pro-gun-rights convention in Flint, Michigan, in the immediate aftermath of the tragic fatal shooting of a young girl. Heston tolerates Moore's increasingly aggressive questioning for some time until finally, having reached his limit, he gets up to leave. The camera shoots over Moore's shoulder as Heston walks away (fig. 1.5, *top*). "Mr. Heston, one more thing," Moore says. "This is who she is. Or was." We then see a reverse angle of Moore holding a framed photograph of the deceased girl (fig. 1.5, *bottom*). "Take a look at her. This is the girl," Moore calls after Heston.

What is controversial about this scene is that it was shot with a single cam-

Figure 1.5 Bowling for Columbine (2002). Michael Moore apparently calls after a departing Charlton Heston.

era. That means that the second shot of Moore calling after Heston—the shot with the picture of the girl—was shot after Heston had already left the scene. It was staged. Moore frequently uses this sort of technique. When he is challenged on it, he typically responds along these lines: That's not trickery; it's just good filmmaking. Indeed, we need the reverse angle to make sense of the scene I just described. We need to see Moore's face as he calls after Heston. We need to see the picture of the little girl. Without those details, the scene would lose much of its considerable impact and meaning. So it *is* good filmmaking. The same is true of the scene I described from *Amish Mafia*. But that does not necessarily mean it is not trickery.

The *Bowling for Columbine* example offers one more useful lesson about what constitutes trickery. Gun-control advocates and political progressives who look at this scene typically side with Moore. Moore is using a legitimate means to make a point, they say. There is a larger truth at stake here: a little girl died, and Heston's actions reflect callous indifference. These are actual facts. Repeating a scene for the camera in order to clearly convey these facts is tradecraft, not trickery.

Gun-rights advocates and political conservatives tend to take the opposite view. This is just another indication that Moore cannot be trusted, they say. He is so intent on grinding his axe that he will rearrange scenes, take things out of context, and even make things up. He plays fast and loose with facts. He plays fast and loose with people too. Moore took advantage of the ailing Heston in this scene (in Heston's own home, mind you, into which he had graciously been invited). That is not tradecraft; it is trickery.

This disagreement demonstrates that there is no simple litmus test to distinguish between trickery and tradecraft. The difference between them is at least in part a matter of opinion. That is true with respect to "serious" nonfiction films like *Bowling for Columbine*. It is just as true of reality TV.

The Illusion of Truth

You may have noticed that the kind of illusion I have been discussing so far—convincing details, continuity editing, a global impression of reality, and so on—applies to *Star Wars* as well as it does to *Amish Mafia*. It describes how to create the appearance of a coherent and substantial world, but that world might well be a fantasy. Nothing about the kind of illusion I have been describing necessarily has to do with the factuality or truth of what is depicted.

Decades ago, visual anthropologist Sol Worth observed that "pictures can't say ain't."[5] For example, there is no way Rembrandt could have painted a portrait that expressed, "There is no real woman named Artemisia," or "There is a real woman named Artemisia and this is not what she looks like." By the same token, there is nothing about his painting of Artemisia that declares, "There is a real woman named Artemisia, and this is what she looks like." Rembrandt could have painted the portrait from his imagination. Or he could have used his maid as a model. A picture shows you what it shows you; that's all. Any claims about the reality status of what it depicts must come from somewhere else, such as captions.

As it happens, *Amish Mafia* has captions, both at the beginning and at the end of every episode. The one at the beginning reads, "To ensure the safety of innocent Amish, select reenactments of events must be used." The one at the end says, "Re-creations are based on eyewitness accounts, testimonials, and the legend of the Amish Mafia." The legend of the Amish Mafia? To anybody with even a speck of skepticism, that says, "Don't believe a thing you see!" And still, audiences do believe what they see—an awful lot of it anyway. Even I was taken in by scene at the motel, to an extent.

I knew a thing or two about reality TV and quite a lot about the Amish before watching any of *Amish Mafia*, so I was deeply skeptical from the start. I knew from the start that Levi, Jolin, and John were pretending, even though they spoke Pennsylvania Dutch and had pretty clearly grown up in Amish and conservative Mennonite households. I did not believe that Jolin and John had caught an actual Amishman with an actual prostitute. I could not even believe that they had found an actual middle-aged Amishman who was willing to pretend to be caught with a prostitute. And yet here, before my eyes, there seemed to be incontrovertible evidence of that. Moreover, the fracas in the motel room was amazingly convincing, even when I went back later and examined it shot by shot—Jolin shoves his way in, the Amishman tries to push him back out, and John snaps away with his camera. There were none of those obvious two-angle "cheats" that I described earlier, even though there were lots of cuts. I assumed I was not seeing a real Amishman caught in flagrante delicto, but I could not figure out what I was seeing instead. "How did they do that?" I wondered. I was dumbfounded and perplexed. That is no doubt one kind of response the filmmakers were fishing for.

So somehow in this scene, on top of the impression of coherence, the filmmakers managed to layer on a second impression: the impression of reality or truth. How did they do that? How did they design this story to persuade me that it was at some level real, in spite of my disbelief? How did they manage to engineer that illusion of authenticity?

Engineering Authenticity

Engineering authenticity is an oxymoron. If something is authentic, it is not engineered. If something is engineered, it is not authentic. And yet, if the motel scene was fake, as I supposed from the start, then *Amish Mafia* had succeeded at engineering authenticity, not only in this scene but throughout the episode. When, at the start of this chapter, I described this scene as a marvelous piece of story engineering, that is what I was referring to.

It turns out that there is no second kind of sleight of hand involved, no second set of "tricks." The same mechanisms of illusion always apply: convincing details and the elimination of contrary clues. The filmmakers created the second level of illusion by adding a second level to story. The first level is the story about Jolin and John catching the philandering Amishman. It is what we might say the scene is about. The second level is the story of how a reality TV crew managed to capture this scene on camera. Were this a fictional TV show, the scene would have been scripted, rehearsed, then repeated several times, so that it could be shot from various angles to allow for transparent storytelling. The second-level story in *Amish Mafia* tells us that this is *not* how *Amish Mafia* was made. Rather, it tells how the show's producers and crew managed to get behind the scenes of Amish life, as it were, and to capture supposedly actual events, like this one, on the fly.

Some of the details of this second-level story are explicit, as when, a little later in this episode, Levi tells the reality TV crew to stay outside while he goes inside to blackmail the philanderer. As with the incongruous second camera angle in the stakeout scene, we do not even notice how oddly convenient it is that Levi allowed the crew to wire him up with a radio mic before going inside. The reason we don't notice is that the mic provides us with information that we expect and want in order to follow the story. This is another example of inattentional blindness. Other details in the second-level story are implicit and sometimes quite subtle, like the authentic-looking way the philandering Amishman hitches up his pants when he gets out of the van and stoops when he walks.

Three other details of the second-level story in this scene merit special mention. One is the fact that the Amishman's face is digitally blurred out. The second is the apparently catch-as-catch-can camerawork, particularly in moments of action. The third is that John, in particular, is a lousy actor. I'll discuss the last of these first, since it is the subtlest of the three.

Esther, the lead female character in *Amish Mafia*, clearly "gets" reality TV. Even though she grew up Amish, when she says things like, "Levi has always had a thing for me, so I can use that to my advantage," she is not just reciting her lines. She seems quite comfortable in her role. Her younger brother, John, just as clearly does *not* get reality TV. He has a perpetual deer-in-the-headlights look. Even though he tries to be a trouper, it is obvious he has no idea what he is doing in front of cameras. When he plays with the new camera that he and Jolin have bought, his exuberance looks genuine. But when he interacts with other people, even Esther, he is as wooden as a post. When he tries to improvise, he stumbles. "I got pictures . . . [cut] like, I thought about handing them into Levi, but I was debating if I should, ah . . . [cut] just keep and . . . hand them in myself . . . [cut] take it, you know, take care of it myself."

When he says directly to the camera, "If I blackmail this official, that means I'm not going to have to work for anybody," it looks like he is just repeating lines he has been fed a moment before.

Although John's bad acting makes his character feel unrealistic in terms of the first-level story (catching a philandering Amishman), it makes it feel highly realistic in terms of the second-level story (making reality TV). John's awkwardness telegraphs that he is a real person, not an actor. The fact that he is so clearly out of his element suggests that he does not know much about TV; he must be Amish. On top of that, the fact that he comes off as genuinely a bit simple and naive makes his character likable. All of this adds up to a veneer of authenticity that serves the producers well. To be clear, this outcome was not deliberate. The producers did not set out to find a bad actor. John just happened to come along with his sister. He looks like an authentic Amish kid, guileless and awkward in front of cameras, because that is what he is (or was, before *Amish Mafia*).

The camerawork has a similar effect. Interview shots are beautifully lit and well composed, usually against a barn-wall backdrop with a wagon wheel and pitchfork. Pickup shots of fields and sunsets that serve as scene transitions are gorgeous as well. But whenever action, like the confrontation at the motel, takes place, the handheld camera jerks and moves around. It shows us what we need to see to follow the story, but in bits and snatches. Upon close examination, one can find clues that the scene is contrived. Why, for example, does the Amishman caught with the prostitute focus his attention on John's rinky-dink still camera and ignore the great big movie camera? Still, the scene unfolds so fast that we do not notice this incongruity. All we have time to do is pay attention to the first-level story: Is there a prostitute in the room? What is the Amishman going to do next? But at a second level, the jiggly camera, the poorly framed shots, and the quick cuts are telling another story. They are saying that the scene was not blocked or rehearsed in advance, that it unfolded spontaneously, and that the videographer had to struggle to keep up. What makes this second story appear authentic is that, to a large degree, this is how the scene was actually shot.

The Amishman's digitally blurred-out face adds to the impression of authenticity in another way. Television news does not blur out faces. Documentaries about the Amish, like the 2012 public television documentary *The Amish*, do not blur out people's faces. Neither does reality TV, typically. There are no blurred-out faces in *The Bachelor* or *Duck Dynasty* or even the 2004 reality TV series *Amish in the City*. But from right near the start of *Amish*

Mafia, when we see a group of Amish women having a picnic by a creek, their faces are blurred out. The blurring suggests two things: it is an act of discretion on the part of the filmmakers "to ensure the safety of innocent Amish," and the women by the creek are not knowingly cooperating in any "re-creations" based on "the legend of the Amish Mafia." There are of course legal reasons too: an entertainment program is required to obtain a release from anybody who appears on camera. Disguising someone's identity is a work-around.

In any case, a pattern is quickly established: Levi, his gang, and anyone who is willing to appear on TV, are unblurred; everybody else, including non-Amish people like the taxi driver, is blurred. In one scene, Levi, Jolin, and Alvin play a gambling game called cow-patty bingo with two other Amish youths whose faces are blurred. The implication is that these two are not part of any charade: the cow-patty bingo game is real, as is the money that changes hands. The device seems farfetched in this scene, since the two fellows have obviously allowed themselves to be filmed. But when characters appear to be ignorant of being filmed (like the Amish women by the creek), reluctant to be filmed (like the taxi driver), or involved in some sort of bad behavior (like the philandering Amishman), the device seems not just plausible but logical and even necessary in terms of the second-level story about making reality TV. The believability of the device adds to the believability of those scenes.

Just as important, the device masks incongruous information that would detract from the believability of the first-level story. For example, in the cow-patty bingo scene, one of the two fellows whose face is blurred is a man we meet, face unblurred, at the start of the second season. He introduces himself to Levi as Caleb, a Brethren neighbor who wants to get in on the Amish mafia action. Had Caleb's face not been blurred when he served as an extra in the first season, viewers would have recognized him when he appeared in season two, ruining the illusion that he was a new character.

In reality, Caleb runs a tourist buggy-ride business near Strasburg, down the road from Lancaster. As he says in the show, he grew up Brethren (Old Order River Brethren, to be specific). Unlike Levi and Esther, he grew up with cars and electricity, very little Pennsylvania Dutch, and no concerns about photography, although his church banned radios and televisions. Caleb graduated from high school and went on to study business at the local community college.

As a buggy-tour operator, Caleb has worked with lots of TV crews, so when the producers of *Amish Mafia* approached him, it was nothing new. They told him they were making a documentary about Amish Aid, and he agreed to be their buggy wrangler. They wanted him to take an on-camera role too, but when he saw the kind of thing they were shooting, he said no—although he did agree to be an extra in a few scenes, like the cow-patty bingo. When the first season aired and he saw Amish neighbors watching the show at the local firehouse and yukking it up, he figured the show was harmless and agreed to play a larger role.

As for the philandering Amishman who looks so authentic: that part was played by Caleb's dad.

Faking Reality TV

Think for a moment about how you watch reality TV. Take *Survivor*. You suppose that what you are seeing is ordinary people (that is, not professional actors) reacting to extraordinary and somewhat stressful situations. You suppose that those stressful situations, while obviously contrived, are pretty much what they seem to be. So, in *Survivor*, when you see contestants put on an island, made to endure challenging ordeals, with a helicopter the only out in case of emergency, you suppose that is what is actually happening.

Now imagine, instead, that the "island" is actually a beach resort adjacent to a nice hotel where the participants sit around every evening with the producer planning what the next day's "ordeals" will look like, discussing who will be "voted off the island," and so on, before retiring for the night to comfortable suites. Imagine that the "contestants" are actually being paid to pretend to expose themselves to ordeals, to pretend to scheme and suffer, and to pretend to get emotional. Imagine, in other words, that everybody's real job—professionals and nonprofessionals alike—is to fake a compelling reality TV show.

You may be thinking, Would anybody enjoy such a show if word got out that it was fake? That is a good question. The British reality TV producer and star Bear Grylls got in hot water with fans for just such fakery in his show *Born Survivor*. He supposedly showed viewers how to survive by roughing it in the wilderness, living on "just a water bottle, a cup, and a flint for making fire," but word got out that he was actually filming his escapades in parks and retiring to nearby resort hotels between shoots. Viewers cried foul, and British Channel 4, which the aired the show, launched an investigation.[6] A spokesman for Grylls's production company stated, "*Born Survivor* is not an observational documentary series but a 'how to' guide to basic survival techniques" and "does not claim that presenter Bear Grylls's experience is one of unaided solo survival." Would such a disclaimer up front have mollified viewers of a fake *Survivor*? Or would it have turned them off? I will return to all of these questions in chapter 4; in the meantime, let us consider how this kind of fakery applies to *Amish Mafia*.

To understand how *Amish Mafia* was really made, it helps to do two things: first, think of *Amish Mafia* as *fake* reality TV, like the fake *Survivor* scenario I just described; second, try to put yourself in the producer's shoes, instead of thinking like a spectator. When you think about the scene with the philandering Amish leader in that way, the first challenge is not how to capture interesting actualities on film; it is how to come up with stories that are entertaining, unusual, and at the same time plausible: a buggy race, a barn fight, a wild Amish party, drug distribution, and the like. It helps if there are surprising or interesting facts to add credibility, such as the 1998 case of several Amish young people from Lancaster County who were convicted of joining up with members of the Pagans motorcycle gang to distribute drugs.[7]

The producer of *Amish Mafia* claims he has heard numerous stories about taxi drivers ferrying Amishmen to downtown Lancaster or Philadelphia to visit prostitutes.[8] I do not know whether these stories are true or apocryphal. In any case, the producers' challenge was not to track down facts, since those are irrelevant, but to connect this story to their characters—the group of young people, including several who grew up Amish, who had agreed to play roles in their show. So they made up a scene in which Esther says she heard the story from a taxi driver. Levi meets with the taxi driver and decides to catch the culprit in the act, and so on. These ideas were all worked out at a desk in New York by the showrunner (showbiz parlance for the head writer of a show who, in the case of reality TV, is also often the person in charge on location). Sometimes story ideas were passed down from an executive producer at Discovery Channel.

The second challenge, a potentially bigger one, was to find people willing to play the parts of the Amishman, the taxi driver, and the prostitute. The Amishman was a particular challenge since the actor needed to be middle-aged or older and look like an actual Amishman. They could not find such a person by trawling the local bars and nightclubs, which is how they found some of their younger actors. However, Caleb's dad was easy to find. Like Caleb, he runs a buggy-tour business right on the main tourist drag (Caleb got his start in the business working for his dad). He has a long grey beard so he looks the part, and for a few bucks he was happy to play a small on-camera role.

Blurring faces may have helped with the casting, since the producers were able to tell Caleb's dad that he would not be recognized. On other occasions, it allowed them to use crew members as stand-ins for Amish people. One of my college students served as a production assistant for a season. In one scene, she was asked to play the role of an Amish girl angling for Levi's affection. They dressed her up from their mobile Amish wardrobe and had her improvise the scene in English. When they blurred out her face in postproduction, it was not to hide her identity but rather to fake two details suggesting "authenticity": the appearance of protecting an "innocent" Amish person, and dialog spoken in Pennsylvania Dutch, which they added by substituting Esther's digitally altered voice for my student's.

A third challenge was keeping all of this fakery under wraps. While the producers were clearly not making an actual documentary, part of their purpose was to persuade viewers that some significant part of what they were seeing was real or at least based on reality. They also wanted to avoid a Bear Grylls episode. So, like the real Mafia, they instituted a strict code of silence, making everyone involved in the show sign a nondisclosure agreement (or NDA).[9] Instead of enforcing the NDA with gun-toting gangsters, Discovery Channel used lawyers armed with cease-and-desist letters. To be fair, NDAs are standard practice in the entertainment industry. Producers want to prevent plotlines from being leaked, and owners want to protect their creative property. Still, in this case, on account of the fakery, secrecy was particularly important. Esther got in trouble at one point for being too candid with a reporter. And when a local tour operator planned an "Amish Mafia Tour" that would show people the hotel property on which *Amish Mafia* had built sets to use as Levi's office and parts of Esther's home, Discovery Channel threatened to sue both the tour operator for trademark infringement and the hotel operator for violation of the NDA.[10]

The biggest challenge of all was to make all this fakery believable. Besides the clever editing, the use of ex-Amish people as actors, the catch-as-catch-can camera work, and the blurring of faces, there are other techniques. Producers kept the cast in the dark about what they would be doing until they showed up for a day's production (to give the impression of authenticity by creating spontaneity and genuine stress), added tension to the set by fomenting petty rivalries among cast members (one cast member told me that what was most stressful about being on *Amish Mafia* was the constant manipulation by producers), and pulled actual news events into the show (like Pennsylvania governor Tom Corbett's criticism of *Amish Mafia* in the fourth season). All of these strategies are effective largely on account of the simple psychological principle at work in all illusion: the impression of coherence satisfies the mind.

When a story is interesting and makes sense, when it works, we typically just get it, in the same way we just "see" the gold brocade in Rembrandt's painting and "feel" its texture. Getting it in this way is often enough. It serves the first purpose of the mind, which is to make sense of things. We do not pick over details in the story because we do not need to. We do not question the purpose of the story because we do not need to. A story that works is intrinsically satisfying all by itself.

In movies, the art of providing this sort of satisfaction has to do in large part with the selection and ordering of images and sounds. Mainly, this work is accomplished in post-production, although images must be gathered with post-production in mind. Editors of movies take pains to piece images and sounds together in ways that make intrinsic sense. Continuity editing plays a role (recall the example from Michael Moore's Charlton Heston interview), but three deeper principles govern how *Amish Mafia* is put together in post-production, not only within scenes but also at the structural level. These are the three Fs.

The Three Fs

The first of the three Fs is the psychological *force* of a scene. This is related to the four Fs famous among evolutionary biologists: the most basic animal instincts wired into the human brain are feeding, fighting, fleeing, and sex. (The fact that "sex" does not begin with F is a well-worn joke.) The last three of these impulses are so vital to our social well-being that just seeing other people involved in actions related to them is enough to compel our attention. That makes them easy buttons for an entertainer to push, as reality TV producers well know. The scene of the Amishman with the prostitute has all three: a fight, a flight, and a sexual impropriety. That is part of what makes the scene so interesting to viewers—part of its force, if you will.

The force of the scene is what focuses your attention on the story, blinding you to incongruous details. For example, when Jolin is introduced assembling an automatic weapon, that gun has force. It has much more story potential than, say, the green window shades that Esther shows us. We instantly feel that story potential: it commands our interest and attention. There are lots of other ways to create force: jazzy music, fast-paced editing, suspense, curiosity, humor, and surprise. Even the impression of reality described earlier has a certain force—we are curious to see how real people will react in uncomfortable situations, and such scenarios are one of the mainstays of reality TV. But in order to make sense, all such elements must fit within a larger scene.

Fit is the second F. The fit in Jolin's case is provided in part by contextual details, like the framed picture of Jesus on the bureau and the Bible-verse plaque on the wall. What makes these details work so well is their specificity. They suggest that this is not just any room: it is Jolin's room. Because they contrast with Jolin's gun, they make sense in an interesting and unusual way. So compelling is this sense that it does not even occur to us to wonder whether Jolin's bedroom is actually a set, built just for this scene. That is in fact what it is. The decorations are a set designer's, not Jolin's. So too are the guns.

The third F is *flow*. Watching a movie is a bit like riding a bike. You do not think about the bike unless the derailleur jams or you hit a pothole. For a movie to be transparent, there can be no potholes on the road to comprehension. In the scene that introduces Jolin, there are no potholes: no irrelevant details, no stray production paraphernalia like movie lights reflected in windows. In fact, apart from glimpses of Jesus and the Bible verse, the camera's focus remains firmly fixed on Jolin and his guns. And yet, as I have observed, *Amish Mafia* is full of shaky camerawork and jump cuts. This scene is full of them too. Those could be potential potholes. The reason they do not interrupt the flow in this case is that they are designed to fit perfectly with the second-level story (about making a reality TV show) without impeding our ability to make sense of the first-level story (about the Amish mafia). Plus, all those quick cuts add excitement—they have intrinsic force, particularly when combined with fast-paced rhythmic music.

The three Fs—fit, flow, and force—go a long way toward explaining many incidental untruths in *Amish Mafia*, like the Amish telephone shanty passed off as an outhouse. Here is how that particular untruth might have come about.

An assistant editor in New York had the task of logging the video footage that came in from the field, like this: "LS [long shot]—Amish kid with push mower." "LS—buggy on road—nice." "Chickens in field." Knowing little about the Amish, he had never heard of a telephone shanty, so when he got to that shot, he mistakenly noted, "Outhouse in woods."

Soon after, the principal editor started working on a short scene labeled "Esther's house," which was part of a larger sequence labeled "Introduction to Amish life" in the showrunner's outline. Reviewing all the relevant interview footage, which the assistant editor had gathered, the editor quickly found a perfect bit from an interview with John: "No electric, no refrigerator, no indoor plumbing." He laid it down in the timeline and then went looking for visuals (also known as B-roll) to accompany the line.

When the editor sorted through the footage of Esther's house (Esther's Amish parents' house, actually), he discovered a problem. The Lancaster crew had not captured any footage of the bathroom. The reason, of course, is that it was a perfectly ordinary-looking bathroom and they were interested in things that looked out of the ordinary. So the editor thumbed through the footage log, looking for other images that might relate, like John carrying a bucket perhaps, and came across the note "Outhouse in woods." Perfect! he thought. He found the shot and slotted it in.

A few days later, as the episode neared completion, the editor sat down with the producer and a member of the Lancaster production team to look at it. When they got to the shot of the "outhouse," the crew member observed, "That's actually an Amish telephone booth, you know." The producer replied, "It looks like an outhouse, so nobody will know. And Esther is going to be way more interesting to viewers if they suppose she doesn't have a toilet in her house, so keep the shot. It's perfect." In other words, it fits, it flows, and it has force. From a storytelling perspective, that is what matters. "Besides," the producer added, "we never actually say that it's an outhouse. If people assume it's an outhouse, that's on them!"

Stories, Fibs, and Whoppers

The story I just told is an illustration of how editing decisions on *Amish Mafia* got made. It is not actually true; I made up the particulars, including the conversation at the end. It's not necessarily false, though, since it is quite accurate with respect to the big picture. And it is clearly not a lie, since my purpose was not to deceive.

The producers of *Amish Mafia* might say the same thing about their phone-shanty image. The honest aim of *Amish Mafia*, they might say, is to tell a good story involving real people and real places. That phone shanty is real. So is Caleb's dad. As for the business of blurring out Caleb's dad's face: that is simply a means of making the story more engaging to viewers—giving them what they want and expect in a creative and original way. So, too, is implying that the phone shanty is an outhouse.

If you were a fan of *Amish Mafia*, you will likely accept this argument. If you think *Amish Mafia* was exploitative and demeaning of the Amish, you most certainly will not. What would be helpful here is some means of categorizing rhetorical strategies like those above that is more discriminating than true versus false and more objective than trickery versus tradecraft.

Because politicians are notorious liars, a group of political reporters from the *Tampa Bay Times* came up with a system for grading untruths in the political arena, which became the foundation for the Pulitzer Prize–winning website PolitiFact. Their Truth-O-Meter has six ratings, going from True ("the statement is accurate and there's nothing significant missing"), through Half True ("the statement is partially accurate but leaves out important details or takes things out of context") to Pants on Fire ("the statement is not accurate and makes a ridiculous claim").[11]

There is problem with applying any such scale to a reality TV show like *Amish Mafia*. How, for example, would you classify that phone shanty? Half True? (It is an actual photographic image of an actual Amish phone shanty.) Or Pants on Fire? (It appears to reinforce John's statement that the Amish have no indoor plumbing, which is in fact false.) The reason the scale does not work has to do with that word "statement" in every Truth-O-Meter rating. Politicians make express verbal assertions of fact. In reality TV, such assertions are relatively rare. As the producer says in my Mostly True scenario above, "We never actually say that it's an outhouse. If people assume it's an outhouse, that's on them."

Consider a breakdown of the kinds of truth claims made in the first episode of *Amish Mafia* (fig. 1.6). Express assertions of fact by the producers constitute only a small slice: just 5 percent, made up of intertitles, maps and diagrams, lower thirds (subtitles and labels), and credits. Most of these are true, mostly true, or sort of silly, like "The Lancaster City Police have refused to comment on Lebanon Levi." But the intertitles do include two Pants on Fire claims, both near the beginning: "The Amish Mafia is a secretive subculture that operates within its own set of rules and values" and "Lebanon Levi and his crew are in charge of collecting fees and assessing claims" for the Amish self-insurance fund Amish Aid. (I will come back to these later.)

Notably absent from this graph is anything that is transparently fictional. One short sequence showing hands and Bibles accompanies an explanation of how Amish bishops are chosen by lot, but that is an illustration, not a dramatization, so I bundled it in with pickup shots of fields and skies, Amish buggies on the road, and so on. Such illustrations make up roughly 9 percent of the episode. They serve as visual filler or local color rather than authenticating any statement of fact.

Most of what takes place in *Amish Mafia* could be called soap-opera drama.

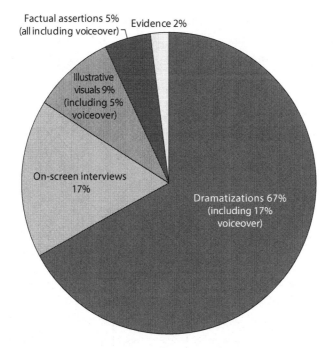

Figure 1.6 Dramatizations make up 67 percent of the first episode of *Amish Mafia*; on-screen interviews, 17 percent; illustrative visuals such as pick-up shots and graphics, 9 percent; express factual assertions, in the form of intertitles, lower-thirds, and credits, 5 percent; and evidence, such as TV news reports, 2 percent.

In the first episode, this includes the scenes I have already discussed plus a few others: Jolin shooting out the windshield of a hit-and-run driver who damaged an Amish buggy, Levi handing out charity payments, and Jolin threatening an Amishman who is pressuring an Amish widow for sex in exchange for financial support. There is nothing in any of these scenes to suggest that they are made up. In fact, most of the dramatic scenes are meticulously constructed to appear as if they are unfolding in the moment, like the scene with the prostitute. Since these scenes make no express factual claims, they are neither true nor false. Still, they are deliberately and expertly misleading. The most accurate label to give them might be "fake real-life dramas." Such scenes make up about two-thirds of the first episode.

How successful these fake scenes are naturally depends upon whether viewers see through them or not. By the end of the second season, some scenes are so silly and implausible that the fakery becomes quite obvious—like Amish mafiosos driving around Lancaster County in their buggies, blowing up Santa Claus statues because they are supposed to be idolatrous. Still, through at least the whole first season, there is little that works as an obvious giveaway or "tell" to anybody who does not already know a lot about the Amish.

A great deal of screen time is also devoted to characters talking. Much of this consists of the dialog in dramatic scenes, but 44 percent of the episode is devoted to express statements made to viewers in the form of interviews. This includes on-screen interviews (17 percent of the episode) as well as voiceover narration accompanying some of the dramatizations (another 17 percent), some of the illustrative visuals (5 percent), and all of the factual assertions made with graphics and intertitles (5 percent).

This kind of narration does much of the work of the storytelling in *Amish Mafia*, explaining what we are seeing, why it matters to characters, how it relates to Amish beliefs, and fleshing out stories that are otherwise somewhat thin. It is what screenwriters call exposition.

Screenwriters by and large avoid exposition. "Show, don't tell" is their mantra. But in *Amish Mafia* (and reality TV in general), exposition serves an important second duty as testimony to the reality of what we are seeing. In *Amish Mafia* this testimony is contrived or just plain fake. That does not necessarily make it false. In fact, a great deal of what the characters say when they describe the Amish, even when they talk about themselves, is true. But they also say outrageous things. Part of what makes *Amish Mafia* so clever is that we never know if the "real people" acting in the show are speaking as characters or as themselves. Likewise, in dramatic scenes, we never know if the actors are playing roles, being themselves, or enacting some mix of the two. Indeed, the only way we could ever know would be by gathering a lot of information from outside the show about who these people actually are and the stories they are telling.

Viewers in this situation have essentially two options. Either they can eat up all the sensational stuff without worrying about whether it is true or false— in other words, they can watch the show like a soap opera. Or they can follow their curiosity about what is going on behind the scenes—whether there actually is an Amish mafia, for example, and whether Lebanon Levi is its boss.

Is There Really an Amish Mafia?

Not even remotely. One cast member claims to have been surprised and a bit taken aback to discover at a screening of the first few episodes that he was portrayed as a member of an Amish mafia. There is probably some wishful thinking involved in this recollection, since the daily call sheets that went out to the cast included the title of the show right at the top. Anyway, he says he just went along with the pretense when he found out about it because he saw it as a lark and assumed that others would too.

It is worth looking at the brief story of the origin of the Amish mafia in the first episode because it illustrates the small sliver of the pie chart not yet discussed, the 2 percent labeled "evidence," and it helps explain why some people saw *Amish Mafia* as anything but a lark.

On Monday, October 2, 2006, in the small town of Nickel Mines in southern Lancaster County, a mentally deranged milk-truck driver walked into an Amish one-room schoolhouse armed with several guns, told the adults and boys to leave, then barricaded himself in with ten girls, ages six to thirteen. When the police arrived, he shot the girls one by one, execution style, before committing suicide. Five of the girls died; five were seriously wounded.

Amish Mafia shows clips of two TV news reports of the event. Esther says, "It changed everything for my family and for the Amish community." John adds, "The Amish believe that God protects them and watches over them, but I think sometimes he needs a little help from somebody down here." Then we see a shot of Levi, looking out his barn-office window and putting on a hat, accompanied by ominous thrumming music. The TV news reports create an implicit connection between *Amish Mafia*'s incredible stories and indisputable historical facts. *Amish Mafia* does this deliberately at other moments too, such as by showing cast members' actual police records for drunken driving in this same episode.

Here is what actually happened in the aftermath of the Nickel Mines shooting: the Amish community, including the parents of the victims, publicly forgave the shooter, gathered around his family, and included them in their grieving. The book *Amish Grace* movingly recounts this response and explains how it arises from deeply held convictions about selflessness and nonviolence that are central to who the Amish are. "When forgiveness arrived at the killer's home within hours of his crime, it did not appear out of nowhere," the authors write. "Rather, forgiveness is woven into the very fabric of Amish life, its sturdy threads having been spun from faith in God, scriptural mandates, and a history of persecution."[12]

The idea that the Amish have an armed self-protection league that arose from the Nickel Mines tragedy could not be further from the truth. Though this idea is only vaguely implied in *Amish Mafia*, some saw this suggestion as a perversion of the truth and a deliberate disparagement of the most central and precious beliefs of the Amish. In an editorial in Salon.com, Mennonite David George wrote in indignation, "It takes a complete lapse in moral and critical thinking to accept gunned-down schoolchildren . . . with your entertainment. But it takes more than that to create such content in the first place." He went on: "If the Amish really did depend upon 'a small organized group of men for protection and justice' . . . 'Amish Mafia' creator Eric Evangelista and his Hot Snakes Media production company . . . would be at the top of the group's list of items requiring attention."[13]

Producer Eric Evangelista and critic David George are clearly operating in different worlds, with different priorities and values. Evangelista's obligation is to viewers and TV executives. The bottom line in this world is the bottom line: the show needs to make money. Evangelista may find the facts recounted in *Amish Grace* interesting, attention-worthy, and even moving, but they have little to do with his job, which is to make an engaging reality TV show—one that will attract viewers' attention in an increasingly cluttered media environment. This is a difficult job, it is rarely very profitable, and Evangelista has employees who depend upon his being successful at it.

George's interests are more idealistic (or as Evangelista might put it, less practical). As a Mennonite, George identifies with and shares the values that distinguish the Amish—pacifism, in particular, and community mindedness. The notion of a gang of Amish thugs engaging in threats, extortion, and violence in pursuit of status, power, and personal enrichment is antithetical to these values in just about every way. To Evangelista, that is part of what makes *Amish Mafia* interesting to viewers. To George, it is a personal affront. In his eyes, to present such a false picture of the Amish as "reality" is a travesty; to cite the Nickel Mines tragedy to support it is a perversion.

Evangelista's and George's interests are not just incompatible, they are antagonistic. It is natural for you to gravitate toward one or the other of them. It is important to recognize, however, that which one you are drawn to depends upon your own interests. A major theme of this book is that how people engage with and respond to reality TV—indeed, to discourses of all kinds—is governed by their interests. It is legitimate and worthwhile to analyze and critique the implications and consequences of other people's interests. It is worth questioning, for example, whether the producers of *Amish Mafia* took advantage of the show's ex-Amish cast members, who had no way of knowing up front what they were getting into. (I will take up this question in chapter 6.) It is also completely fair to say, as David George more or less does, "I find this personally offensive." But what is not legitimate, particularly from a scholarly perspective, is to regard one's own interests as the only game in town.

To understand reality TV objectively and to critique it fairly, you need to understand how it works as a discourse. That requires being able to stand back and consider, from an impartial perspective, the various interests of all of the participants in the discourse. Those interests are complex, usually unconscious, typically transitory, and often at odds. Basically, most *Amish Mafia* viewers' first interest is to have a good time, Evangelista's interest is to do his job well, and George's interest is to respond to misrepresentations that he finds insulting. My own interest, in writing this book, is to peel back the facade of *Amish Mafia* in order to discover and dissect the underlying interests involved on the part of viewers, producers, and critics, not just in this show but in reality TV generally. But before continuing with this task, there are still a few important facts about *Amish Mafia* to disclose, like who Lebanon Levi and his crew really are and how they got involved in the show.

How Real Is Lebanon Levi?

The final episode of the first season of *Amish Mafia* responds head-on to critics like scholar Donald Kraybill who had the audacity to declare that the show was not real. "For the first time, Lebanon Levi and his crew respond to the allegations," says the narrator. Also, for the first time, the voiceover is narrated by a non-Amish voice. "Some critics have even questioned whether or not Levi and his group are even Amish at all," it intones. "To any Amish person, this accusation hits below the belt."

"It's insulting to hear that," John says. "You guys met our family and everything and we're not actors, and we are real Amish." Levi, Alvin, and another cast member, Alan Beiler, somewhat indignantly point to evidence that they are Amish, showing us their names in a fat book, *Descendants of Christian Fisher*, introduced by the narrator as "an official book that is in effect the directory of all the descendants of the original Amish." The book is genuine and their names are really in it but, as Levi well knows, that is completely beside the point. Like the TV reports about the Nickel Mines shooting, this scene creates the false impression of a connection between *Amish Mafia*'s made-up stories and genuine historical facts. The truth is, before *Amish Mafia*, Levi was leading an ordinary "English" (non-Amish) life, living in his own apartment, driving a car, running a roofing and siding business with his brother, and volunteering with the local fire department.

Levi grew up Old Order Amish, on a farm outside Lebanon, Pennsylvania, about twenty-five miles north of Lancaster. Starting at age sixteen, Amish young people join large interdistrict youth groups or "gangs" that get together on weekends for social activities. An important practical purpose is to allow them to expand their dating pool beyond their home district. By tradition, Amish parents give their youth considerable freedom to "run around" (*rumspringa*) during this period, sometimes permitting them to buy cars, throw dance parties in the barn, stay out all night on weekends, and go on long trips with friends. (How much freedom young folks are given varies from place to place and family to family. For more information about rumspringa, I refer you to Richard Stevick's *Growing Up Amish: The Rumspringa Years.*)

Levi had watched his many older siblings experience rumspringa, so when his turn came he was ready to cut loose. He found the Amish youth groups and girls around Lebanon boring, so he joined a wilder gang in Lancaster County, called the Souvenirs, and bought an old car to make the commute. It is in this Lancaster group that he acquired the nickname Lebanon Levi, to distinguish him from the other Levis. He also started drinking quite a lot and, regrettably, sometimes driving afterward, which accounts for the mugshot in *Amish Mafia*.

Most Amish young men settle down in their early to mid-twenties, when they find a nice Amish young woman who wants to get married and start a family (or, as Levi describes it, when a nice Amish young woman chooses them). They put away their cars and their partying and join the Amish church, which means that they are baptized as members in the particular Amish community where they live, typically near where they grew up. This path was not for Levi, who had English girlfriends and enjoyed the English lifestyle. Because he never joined the Amish church, he never had to leave it, so in spite of his non-Amish lifestyle he continued to maintain good relationships with his Amish family and friends.

At twenty-four, with the blessing of his Old Order parents, Levi was baptized into an Amish-Mennonite church that some of his buddies attended. Amish-Mennonites have church buildings and Sunday School classes, and they permit cars, electricity, and photography. They look a little like the Amish—the women wear plain dresses and wear head coverings, and married men sport beards (albeit trimmed ones). They sometimes call themselves Beachy Amish. Basically, though, they are conservative Mennonites.

There are all kinds of Mennonites in Lancaster County, from horse-and-buggy-driving Old Order Mennonites, to evangelical Mennonites, to ethnic

Latino and African American Mennonites, to worldly liberal Mennonites. Most Mennonites, by far, are outwardly indistinguishable from Catholics or Presbyterians in appearance or lifestyle, although they share a common religious heritage and certain beliefs with the Amish, including pacifism. The last season of *Amish Mafia* suggests that the Amish and Mennonites are involved in a kind of turf war in Lancaster County. That is nonsense. The Amish and Mennonites in Lancaster County are good neighbors.

Lebanon Levi published his own life story in a 2015 book, *Amish Confidential*, coauthored with freelance author and TV political commentator Ellis Henican.[14] In spite of its over-the-top blurb ("From drug runs with the help of local motorcycle gangs, to petty gossip at endless stitch-and-bitch quilting bees, to Amish-on-Amish violence, this is the book no one has ever dared to write."), the book offers an honest and illuminating account of what it is like to grow up Amish—although it is also a biased account, since like many Amish young people who drift from the church, Levi focuses on negative aspects of Amish life.

Levi had a typical Amish upbringing, a typical Amish eighth-grade education, and a not atypical rumspringa. Although he decided not to join the Amish church, he settled close to home, went into business with an Amish brother, and planned for a career doing the kind of manual labor to which Amish are accustomed, until he suddenly found himself on national TV, pretending to be a big boss in the Amish community who with a gang of ruffians "ran the finances, maintained social order, and protected their community from the dangers of the outside world," as *Amish Mafia* puts it. How that came about is another story, not told in Levi's autobiography.

Casting About

Alan Beiler is introduced in the second episode of *Amish Mafia* as the Black Amishman. The show gives us a brief biography. When he was a baby, his mother brought him from Brooklyn, New York, to Lancaster County to live for a while with an Amish-Mennonite family, the Beilers. She returned to Brooklyn, leaving him behind, and the Beilers eventually adopted him. We see photos of Alan as an infant with his mother and as a child with the Beiler family. He introduces us to his adoptive parents in their home, and we see him working with his dad on their chicken farm. In the show, he is supposed to be Levi's event planner, organizing money-making activities like Amish "hut parties."

Although Beiler has supported himself mainly through construction work, he has a creative and entrepreneurial streak. Ever since seeing the reality TV show *Amish in the City* in 2004, he had dreamed of helping produce TV shows about the Amish. He is outgoing and energetic, he speaks Pennsylvania Dutch, he has lots of Amish and Mennonite friends, and he is something of a character—in short, he is perfectly suited for such a job.

In 2010 Beiler answered a Craigslist ad seeking production assistants for *Amy*, a horror film about an Amish girl whose village becomes possessed by demons that was being shot in Lancaster County by a filmmaker from India. Beiler was hired as production manager and led a South Indian crew in finding locations, buying costumes, and rounding up extras. When, not long after, another film crew came to town to shoot a segment of a National Geographic Channel special on Amish weddings, *Amish at the Altar*, they too hired Beiler as their local fixer. Billed as a documentary, the show was actually a spin-off of *Amish in the City* and involved some of the same cast. Beiler recruited his Amish-Mennonite father to play the part of the Amish minister and friends to play the part of wedding guests.

Meanwhile, in Manhattan, Eric Evangelista opened a new office for his production company, Hot Snakes Media, "with the goal of revolutionizing the way unscripted television is produced."[15] Evangelista's first foray into reality TV, *Film Fakers*, produced for AMC in 2004, gives some indication of what he had in mind. A *New York Times* reviewer wrote, "'Film Fakers' may go down as one of the meanest reality series yet. That is because the program . . . dupes out-of-work actors into believing they have landed plum movie roles, only to reveal later that the entire production, from the crazed director to the flimsy script, is a colossal hoax."[16] Evangelista says that the show was not mean at all; it was a kind of prank show that the participant-actors all found funny when the prank was revealed at the end.[17] Regardless of one's take on the show, it is quite inspired in terms of what makes a lot of reality TV successful: "real people" in tense and awkward situations, sensational storylines, and low-budget production.

In the next half-dozen years, Evangelista notched up an impressive string of reality TV successes, including the show *Wreck Chasers*, about Philadelphia wrecking truck operators racing to collect wrecks and claim cash, which aired on Discovery Channel in 2010. When Evangelista decided to scout Lancaster County for a restaurant show he was pitching to the Food Channel, he talked to the media manager for *Wreck Chasers*, who had done location work for *Amish at the Altar* and the Indian horror movie. That person put him in touch with Alan Beiler.

Evangelista found Lancaster's restaurants boring but was fascinated by Beiler's stories about rich Amish farmers and wild Amish youth. Even in the topic of Amish Aid, he immediately saw reality TV potential. "If you did a story on how they bake pies and sew quilts, well I've heard that story before. I've heard that story a million times. But what if I told you a story about how the Amish don't have insurance and tithe all their money and this one guy collects it and it's all in cash. It's hard not to believe how it's shady."[18]

Beiler explained to Evangelista that he would never be able to cast actual Amish church members in the show but said he had lots of Pennsylvania-Dutch-speaking buddies who would be glad to play a part. So Evangelista hired Beiler as a local casting agent and production manager, brought a crew from New York to shoot a sizzle reel, and showed it to a top executive at Discovery Channel, who ordered up a full season.

Not long before shooting was to begin, the friend Beiler had found to play the main role died in a small-plane crash while visiting Mexico. Other cast members, perhaps seeing this event as a divine portent, dropped out. Beiler quickly rounded up a new cast from among his wide circle of acquaintances, inviting a long-time drinking buddy, Lebanon Levi, to take the lead.

In distant Berlin, Ohio, another young man from an Old Order household, Merlin Miller, heard about the new show from a friend involved in another one of Evangelista's Amish-themed reality TV shows, *Breaking Amish*. Like Lebanon Levi, Merlin had not returned to the church after rumspringa, and like Alan Beiler, he had entertained the idea of breaking into reality TV ever since *Amish in the City*. Merlin contacted Evangelista, who immediately saw the opportunity to create a gang to rival Lebanon Levi's and invited Merlin to play its crazy boss. Merlin brought along acquaintances to play Ohio gang members, including little person Wayne Raber and overweight Mary Troyer.[19]

In Penn Yan, New York, in the rural Finger Lakes region, the rebellious son of a Mennonite family affiliated with Lancaster County's conservative Weaverland Mennonite Conference also heard about the new show through Lancaster County friends and contacted the producers, eager to play a role. Over the strong objections of his pacifist parents, he became Levi's gun-toting enforcer, Jolin Zimmerman.

Ironically, back in Lancaster County, real trouble was brewing for Alan Beiler. Just two days after shooting began, police tried to pull him over for an expired car registration. Because he had marijuana and pills in the car, he fled, leading police on a high-speed chase. His arrest and three-month imprisonment during production of much of the first season and, due to a similar incident in nearby Perry County, much of the second season as well, were folded into *Amish Mafia* as gang-related incidents. In fact, they had the effect of relegating Beiler to a relatively minor role in the show until the end of the fourth and final season, when, with Levi discredited and his mob disbanded, Beiler emerges to take his place as Lancaster County's new Amish gang leader.

Amish Money

Amish Mafia is preoccupied with money. Levi and his crew are always trying to get it—charging admission to hut parties, running gambling operations, blackmailing Amish leaders, extorting money from shop owners, and so on. Reality TV has always been concerned with money, from the lavish living shown on *The Real World*, to the cash prizes of *Survivor* winners, to *Cribs*'s celebrity homes, to the wealthy housewives of you name it. Preoccupation with money is, arguably, a widespread American trait, but it is of particular importance in *Amish Mafia* because, along with power, it is what motivates the characters. They are gangsters, after all.

One of the main sources of Levi's wealth in *Amish Mafia* is his control of Amish Aid, the Amish self-insurance fund. He sends his boys out to collect premiums and protection money. He controls the cash that comes in. When an Amish person experiences a financial hardship or calamity, they have to ask Levi for a handout, which puts them personally in his debt. In these ways, Lebanon Levi is like Don Corleone, the Godfather.

That is of course no accident. *The Godfather* is a family drama, as is *Amish Mafia* in its own way, but both stories are driven by individual ambitions and interpersonal conflicts. There are bosses, who can be benevolent but are always trying to maintain their own power, and there are underlings, who are always angling to get a greater share of the power for themselves. In this system, money, like the threat of violence, is an instrument of social control. That is why it is so important in *Amish Mafia*—not because it represents the opportunity to buy a nice new Cadillac (although Lebanon Levi has one of those too).

In Amish society, on the whole, men have all the authority, gender roles are strict, children's options for independence are tightly controlled, and the threat of shunning keeps people in line. When bad things happen in Amish communities—like the infamous beard-cutting incident in Ohio in 2011, in which a group of renegade Amish led by Sam Mullet attacked and cut off the beards of other Amish men—it is often the result of authoritarianism gone awry. Every one of the beard-cutting attacks targeted someone who had in some way questioned Mullet's authority.[20]

By the way, that bizarre incident drew the producers of *Amish Mafia* like iron filings to a magnet, which in turn generated a surreal reality TV moment. The producers made up the story that Merlin was afraid Sam Mullet was going to turn him into the FBI in exchange for a reduced sentence. They sent Merlin to the courthouse in Cleveland where Mullet's actual sentencing hearing was taking place to see what kind of footage they could gin up. Local TV news reporters, seeing Merlin in his Amish attire, mistook him for a regular Amish person, so they interviewed him and broadcast part of the interview on the evening news. *Amish Mafia* then recycled part of that newscast in the first episode of the fourth season, where it served as evidence of the reality of the made-up scenario.

Even though the beard-cutting incident was an anomaly, Amish society is a patriarchal hierarchy. So is the Mafia. One respect in which this comparison breaks down—indeed, where it is fundamentally wrong—is its failure to capture the communitarian aspect of Amish life. That is nowhere more evident than in the real Amish Aid, which is quite different from what is depicted in *Amish Mafia*.

Amish prefer not to buy insurance and are legally exempted from having to pay into the government's Social Security system; they put their faith in God to help them out in times of need and take literally the biblical injunction to "bear one another's burdens." As a practical matter, that means they put their faith in their community. Amish Aid is a way of broadening the community of support so that, in cases of extreme need, the whole Amish church can help out, not just the local district.

Think of Amish Aid as an extension of Amish barn raising. Instead of having each barn owner pay a premium up front and get a payout to build a new barn in the event that his barn burns down, the community rallies around and rebuilds the barn. To cover the cost of materials, property owners pay a "fire tax," based on the amount of property they own, to a representative in each district, and the proceeds go into a fund managed by a cross-district committee. When the fund runs low, the committee asks district representatives to make another collection. The model is, in the words of one member, "assessment by need after the fire."[21]

The idea that Amish people go around to their neighbors to collect cash for Amish Aid astonished Eric Evangelista and sparked the idea for *Amish Mafia*. It sounded to him like a recipe for graft and extortion. The reason this system works in the Amish community is that organizations like Amish Aid are made up local volunteers in informal self-organizing committees that are set up solely to serve community needs. There are no paid employees, no professionals, and certainly no Cadillac-driving bosses. The person collecting for Amish Aid is a trusted neighbor with longstanding ties in the local community. It is these community ties that keep people honest.

In *Amish Confidential*, Lebanon Levi points out that there is a lot of money in the Amish community. The Amish are entrepreneurial, hard working, and frugal, which means some of them become quite wealthy. Levi cites harness maker Moses Smucker, who "was pulling in millions of dollars a year outfitting the Budweiser Clydesdales, the Ringling Bros. and Barnum & Bailey circus horses, and the pampered pets of Saudi princes and country-music stars."[22] (Smucker retired from that business years ago.) A big business like this would be a point of pride in the English community. For that very reason, Amish business owners are nervous about becoming too successful.[23] They avoid conspicuous consumption and strive to be good neighbors. An Amish acquaintance told me that Smucker has contributed an enormous amount of money to Amish people in need. I am sure he does not hand out cash in envelopes, as Levi does in *Amish Mafia*. The Amish donate through Amish Aid and similar funds precisely because that makes their giving anonymous—a sharing of God's blessing, passed on as part of a gift from the whole community.

On the other hand, there is the case of Monroe Beachy, the "Amish Bernie Madoff" from Ohio, convicted in 2012 of bilking Amish and Mennonite clients out of millions of dollars in a Ponzi investment scheme.[24] "You would not believe what goes on in the Amish community," several of the cast members of *Amish Mafia* have told me, defending the show and their involvement in it. Criminal defense attorney Steven Breit, who plays an exaggerated version of himself in the show told me, "All the criminal behavior you see in *Amish Mafia* is true. I've heard about child sexual abuse, drug dealing, theft, extortion . . ."[25]

"Extortion!?" I asked. Breit could not think of an actual example. Instead, he ticked off a list of the kinds of actual criminal behavior he has defended Amish for: "Drunk and disorderly, D.U.I., D.U.I. on a buggy, D.U.I. on a scooter." One thing Amish elders are clearly guilty of is failing to teach their young people about the dangers of driving drunk. Still, *Amish Mafia* is not about driving drunk. It is not even about actual Amish criminals like Sam Mullet and Monroe Beachy. It is about a made-up gang involved in made-up acts of violence, gambling, racketeering, and extortion. There is nothing intrinsically wrong with making things up—that is what fiction does. But the argument that this particular fiction is a useful corrective to the misperception that Amish society is faultless and pure is logically akin to arguing that the fiction of the man in the moon is a useful corrective to the false belief that the moon is made of cheese.

But what about shunning? The characters in *Amish Mafia* are constantly in danger of being shunned by the bishops. Does that actually happen? Is that not how Amish patriarchs maintain their authority? Is that not in fact a form of extortion?

Amish Power

Levi tells two stories in *Amish Confidential* about how power is actually exercised in the Amish community that perfectly illustrate the vast chasm between reality and the depiction in *Amish Mafia*. They also happen to resonate in interesting and surprising ways with how reality TV works.

The first of these stories is the account of Levi's older brother's shunning and eventual unshunning by his Amish community, for which Levi takes the blame and the credit. Levi's brother Chris, his partner in the roofing and siding business, has remained Old Order Amish. Old Order Amish are not supposed to drive, although they are allowed to hire English drivers. Levi and Chris got around this restriction by buying a truck together and letting Levi do all the driving. An Amish neighbor observed this practice, thought it was an unacceptable violation of the rules and a bad example for other Amish, and complained to the bishop.

A good Amish bishop's role is less to lay down the law than to mediate disputes like this one, which have the character of family squabbles, so the bishop tried to smooth things over with the neighbor. "Levi is not even baptized in the Old Order Church," Levi imagines him saying. "It's for work. This isn't the worst thing that ever happened."[26] But the neighbor was insistent, so the bishop summoned Levi's dad, a deacon in the church, and told him that for the sake of the community he needed to draw a hard line with his older son. "I guess we'll have to shun you," Levi's dad told Chris. Levi could tell that his dad did not agree with the bishop's decision but felt he had no choice but to go along with it. So Chris was shunned. Nobody in the family was supposed to talk to him directly, and when he and his wife and two small daughters joined the extended family for meals, he had to sit off to the side at a small table by himself. "Whatever the purpose of shunning," Levi writes, "the practice is still deeply humiliating. And also hugely effective. . . . It's how the Amish church keeps people in line."[27]

What is most interesting about this story is how the situation was resolved. Levi got word to the preachers that he wanted a meeting. He complained to them that Chris's shunning was not fair. If they did not find a way to lift it, he told them, "maybe we should have a big public discussion about this whole driving thing—start naming a few names." An accommodation was reached that very afternoon: "Chris went to see the preachers before church on Sunday. He told them he was very sorry for what he had done. He said he would hire a non-Amish driver, which he did—for exactly one day. No one asked what would happen the following day."[28] With that, the shunning was lifted. The nosy neighbor may not have been satisfied, but he realized that the community had made a de facto decision to turn a blind eye to Chris's riding with Levi, and there was nothing more he could do about it except grumble.

What is interesting here is the negotiation, the back and forth. That is the way Amish rules work. Certain expectations have the force of law. All around the edges, though, rules are bent, boundaries are pushed, and often accommodations are made. Expectations, boundaries, and rules in the media are formed in much the same way. Little could Levi have known, when he signed up to play a part in *Amish Mafia*, that he would be helping to bend the rules of reality TV in the same way that he helped to bend the rules of his Amish community when he drove his brother around in their truck.

The second story has to do with gossip. Gossiping happens all the time in Amish communities but especially when women get together to quilt. Levi calls Amish quilting bees stitch-and-bitch parties. He writes,

> "Did you hear?" I walked into a stitch-and-bitch party at my mother's house to hear one of her friends exclaim. "Rebecca's boy got a haircut," meaning a *barbershop haircut*—without a bowl.
>
> "That's so terrible," one of the other ladies said, commiserating. "I never thought he'd get a haircut. I feel just terrible for his mother. Unless she condoned it. You don't think she condoned it, do you?"
>
> "Well, I certainly hope not!" the first woman huffed.
>
> All that, over a silly haircut! And what next for that mother? The woman certainly risks a social shunning. Could the ladies really be seen socializing with someone who allowed her son to get a barbershop haircut?[29]

"All this stitchin' and bitchin' might sound harmless at first," Levi writes, "just a few Amish women making quilts and sharing an ancient oral tradition. But from what I've seen, these 'harmless' little get-togethers are the foundation of something much darker and more severe, the absolute, unbending refusal of the Amish to ever leave one another to their own business."[30]

Is that such a bad thing? Do we want to leave our children and loved ones to their own business if we think they are putting themselves or their community in harm's way? Levi sees only the dark side of gossip, perhaps because as a rule bender he has so often felt its sting. But gossip has a bright side too. Social psychologist Jonathan Haidt describes it this way in his book *The Happiness Hypothesis*:

> Gossip extends our moral-emotional toolkit. In a gossipy world, we don't just feel vengeance or gratitude toward those who hurt or help us; we feel pale but instructive flashes of contempt and anger toward people whom we might not even know. We feel vicarious shame and embarrassment when we hear about people whose schemes, lusts, and private failings are exposed. Gossip is a policeman and a teacher. Without it, there would be chaos and ignorance.[31]

Gossip helps to create an "ultrasocial world," Haidt goes on—"a world in which we refrain from nearly all the ways we could take advantage of those weaker than us, a world in which we often help those who are unlikely ever to be able to return a favor." That sounds a lot like the forgiving Amish described in *Amish Grace*.

For better or for worse, Levi presses our social-emotional gossip button by naming his book *Amish Confidential*. So too when he tells stories in the book about Amish shunning and backbiting and drug dealing and beard cutting. So too when he appears in a fake reality TV show as the head of a gang that exercises power in the peaceable Amish community by dispensing ill-gotten gains and threats of violence. Naturally, we are interested.

The Story So Far

As we have seen, the portrait of Amish society presented in *Amish Mafia*, while correct in many superficial details, misrepresents who and what the Amish are in terms of big-picture essentials, like their community mindedness and their rejection of violence. The reason for this distortion is not any desire to demean or denigrate the Amish on the part of producers; it is the fact that the very qualities that make for exciting TV—greed, ambition, status seeking, and other kinds of self-serving motivations and behaviors—are deliberately played down in Amish communities. Put differently, to film the Amish people as they really are, even including "scandals" such as shunning, would make for a boring reality TV show. A TV producer who wants to drum up good ratings for a show about the Amish that stretches over several seasons has no choice but to spice things up by dipping into all of the hoary conventions of soap opera and reality TV. To these, *Amish Mafia* adds conventions of the gangster drama.

Whether this makes for "good" television (fun, entertaining, provocative) or "bad" television (tawdry, exploitative, deceptive) depends upon where you are coming from. People on both sides will tell you that their view is the only reasonable one. In fact, perfectly reasonable people engage with popular entertainments for many different reasons. Furthermore, most of these "reasons" operate beneath the threshold of awareness. So, the only way to get beyond "I'm more reasonable than you" debates is to step back to consider what interests and assumptions lie beneath different kinds of "reasonableness." This does not mean withholding value judgments; it means postponing them in order to deliberately take into account how people typically watch and make sense of reality-warping TV shows like *Amish Mafia* and how such shows actually impact viewers and participants.

The biggest takeaway of this chapter lies in its explanation of the principles of illusion at work in *Amish Mafia*. One of these is a psychological principle involved in all realistic representation: the impression of coherence satisfies the mind. We tend to focus only on the details of a story that interest us. So long as these make sense and fit together neatly, with nothing to obviously contradict them, the mind purrs along on automatic pilot, content to absorb the story and blind to details that do not quite match our interests and expectations. When we do happen to stumble across a discrepancy that we cannot ignore, the mind works hard to fit it into some new or revised story. If it accomplishes that, the mind quickly slips back into autopilot.

Like *Days of Our Lives* or *Game of Thrones* or any other television drama, *Amish Mafia* is designed to tell stories that are perfectly suited to our innate capacity to easily and automatically make sense of the actions of goal-oriented characters coping with obstacles and challenges. Techniques such as continuity editing work to serve up details that advance this kind of story just when we want and expect them to. In contrast to *Days of Our Lives* and *Game of Thrones*, however, the stories we see in *Amish Mafia* are supposed to be spontaneous and unscripted. That means we expect them not to *always* serve up details just when we want and expect them. So instead of showing smoothly unfolding events, *Amish Mafia* leaves gaps and relies on voiceover narration and talking heads to fill them in. This second-level story in *Amish Mafia*—the story of its own production—is one of real people (not actors), embroiled in real conflicts, who at the same time have to deal with the challenge of being followed around by a camera crew. This is all quite typical of reality TV.

What is different about *Amish Mafia* is that the first-level story is almost entirely fictional and the second-level story therefore largely fake. *Amish Mafia* is *fake* reality TV. This is not a completely original technique, of course. Bare Grylls did it. Even *Amish in the City* did it, with worldly ex-Amish young adults pretending to be astonished by parking meters, escalators, and such. The difference in *Amish Mafia* is the boldness and bravura with which the technique is executed. *Amish Mafia* did not just contrive dramatic situations and fights as *Real World* does; it concocted a whole story world. Its cast members did not just play exaggerated versions of themselves as on *Real Housewives*; they played entirely make-believe characters who happened to share some of their actors' biographical details, which *Amish Mafia* parceled out as part of its pretense.

The pretense was never total, however. Although *Amish Mafia* deliberately deprives viewers of any reliable foothold to determine what parts of the show are fact and what parts fiction, it throws out tantalizing clues that all in the show is not as it seems, including great big ones like the provocative disclaimer about "the legend of the Amish Mafia" at the end of each episode. So, in an important sense, *Amish Mafia* is designed not to deceive viewers but rather to baffle them and arouse their curiosity—to prompt a particular kind of wonder, perhaps, akin to the wonder of a magic show or circus act. Part of the impetus for this book is the hypothesis that such curiosity or wonder is part of *Amish Mafia*'s distinctive "entertainment value."

This entertainment value comes at the cost of actual deception, of course. Many viewers wind up believing all sorts of things about the Amish and about characters in the show that are simply not true. This bothered some critics—like Mennonite writer David George—a lot, but it seems safe to assume that the millions of fans of *Amish Mafia* did not mind it at all. It is a price they were happy to pay for their entertainment—just part of the deal.

That "deal" seems totally at odds with the supposed mandate for truthfulness that characterizes TV news and most other forms of nonfiction. Is it an anomaly? Where did it come from? And how did it wind up manifesting itself in such an extreme form in a show about the distinctively non-modern and media-shy Amish, of all people? These questions are taken up in the next two chapters.

CHAPTER TWO

The Roots of Reality Entertainment

The Business of Reality TV

The previous chapter describes *Amish Mafia* as a creative enterprise. It invites you to imagine the production team as creative professionals, constantly thinking about the best way to tell stories and engage with audiences. It presents the show's clever deceptions as creative and even innovative choices.

Surprisingly, the creator and principal showrunner of the series, Eric Evangelista, does not seem to regard himself primarily as a creative innovator, even though he spends most of his time every day looking for creative solutions to problems, both aesthetic and practical.[1] Instead, judging from the way he talks about this work, much of the time he feels like a cog in a big machine that is constantly applying torque and sometimes grinding away at his teeth. No doubt part of the reason is that he is the man who minds the money for his firm in what is a highly competitive and unpredictable industry. The TV business goes like this, he said in an interview, mimicking a dolphin with his hand. With the rise of the internet and the year-after-year decline in TV viewership, the dolphin is diving deeper and deeper. An even bigger challenge, he said, is that he does not have as much control as he would like over the shows he makes.

When Evangelista launched Hot Snakes Media in 2010, he announced his intention to "revolutionize" reality TV. When I asked what he meant by that, I expected him to say something like "My goal was to bring new forms of storytelling to hackneyed reality TV formulas," which is arguably what *Amish Mafia* did. Instead, he said he just wanted to create an integrated production company so that networks would give him control over his own shows. "I wanted to be able to say, 'You have to let me shoot with Lebanon Levi because he won't work with anybody else.'"

Here's how the business works, he explained: when a network like Discovery accepts a pitch for a show, it typically hires its own pet production company to make it, often relegating the people who came up with the idea to the role of glorified office workers. With *Amish Mafia* and other recent shows, Evangelista has been allowed to bring his own team—just what he wanted. Even so, he constantly feels squeezed. At the front end, he gets a long list of menu items that networks expect, so if he wants to sell a show he needs to work to a kind of recipe. At the back end, when he delivers rough cuts, he gets minute-by-minute "notes" from network executives, which often require extensive reshooting. Since network executives hold the purse strings, their notes have the force of marching orders. And they have bosses who give them notes, too, all the way up the line.

This is a useful reminder that when we focus on the contributions of individuals in discussing how reality TV works, we may be holding the wrong end of the telescope. The production of reality TV is first and foremost a commercial enterprise. It is business, not art. Further, because of the high cost of producing and distributing mass entertainment, it is big business, with lots of bosses. And since audiences constitute the ultimate boss, no individual is really in control.

The idea of turning reality entertainment into big business dates back at least to the Roman Empire, with sporting spectacles like gladiatorial combat and chariot races. You can find direct descendants of these entertainments on TV today, such as the Ultimate Fighting Championship and NASCAR races. Roman-style reality entertainments also found their way into *Amish Mafia*, in a secret mixed-martial-arts "barn fight" in season 1, episode 3, and an illegal horse-and-buggy race in season 1, episode 4, for example. The key to the longevity of this kind of reality entertainment lies in the innate psychological appeals of contests, social spectacles, and exhibitions of prowess.

What is distinctive about reality TV in general, and *Amish Mafia* in particular, is another kind of appeal: confusion about the boundary between fact and fiction. This is different from the appeal of a sporting spectacle, different from the appeal of a story, different even from the appeal of reality-based fiction. Since confusion is something people generally try to avoid, why this particular kind of confusion should be appealing at all is difficult to fathom. It is hard even to precisely describe. It is not curiosity exactly, as we might experience at seeing a two-headed animal. Nor is it puzzlement, as we might feel while trying to figure out how a magic trick is done. Nor is it wonder, as we might experience while watching an amazing circus act. It has shades of all three of these but feels somehow different.

Experientially, what is distinctive about the appeal of *Amish Mafia* does not seem to revolve around sensation or story or spectacle but around trust and mistrust. We suspect we are being sold a bill of goods. Still, it is an appealing or at least an interesting bill of goods. We are tempted to buy it, but we do not know whether we ought to trust the seller or not. In this regard, the appeal of *Amish Mafia* seems close to the appeal of the traditional confidence game.

The Master of the Humbug

P. T. Barnum was the great pioneer of the entertaining con. Today he is best known for his circus, but that came relatively late in his career. He spent his first 35 years in the entertainment business mainly as a purveyor of "curiosities." These were unusual objects or people with faked or fluffed-up stories—like Joice Heth, supposedly a 161-year-old former slave and George Washington's nanny, billed as "The Greatest Natural & National Curiosity in the World"—or fake artifacts, like the "Feejee mermaid," the mummified torso of a monkey cleverly joined to the body of a fish (fig. 2.1).

It is worth mentioning that Barnum never invented anything. He acquired Joice Heth and the Feejee mermaid from other exhibitors. His special talent was as a huckster. And in spite of being recognized in his own time as a genius in the entertainment business, he often felt out of control, just as Evangelista sometimes does. He was forced to spend lots of time on the road, which he came to detest; he faced stiff competition from other entertainers; some of his enterprises flopped; he became embroiled in numerous lengthy litigations; and he was constantly putting out fires—sometimes literally, as his buildings kept burning down.[2]

When Barnum bought the rights to exhibit Joice Heth in 1835, he also received a dubious bill of sale, supposedly from George Washington's father to a relative, but he quickly realized that Heth's draw lay not in such "proof" of her authenticity but in its mere plausibility, which was supported by her wizened appearance and her detailed yarns about pampering the baby first president. Indeed, this worked best when coupled with a dose of doubt, fostered by criticisms both actual and planted. As Barnum biographer Neil Harris puts it, "The public was more excited by controversy than conclusiveness. The

Figure 2.1 "Feejee mermaid." Wikimedia Commons.

only requirement was to keep the issue alive and in print."[3] So when attendance at a Boston show began to fall off, Barnum wrote a letter to the editor of the newspaper suggesting that Heth was actually a fraud—a "curiously constructed automaton, made up of whalebone, india-rubber, and numberless springs, ingeniously put together, and made to move at the slightest touch, according to the will of the operator."[4] Spectators who had come a first time for the novelty came back a second time to check out the possible deception.

In 1841 Barnum acquired Scudder's American Museum in Manhattan. Museums were popular attractions at the time. In contrast to theaters, which often presented burlesque, bawdy comedy, exotic dances, and other kinds of risqué performances, museums presented mainly reality exhibits, from stuffed animals and Indian artifacts to architectural models and mechanical inventions. For this reason, they were considered more respectable than theaters and more suitable for women and children. The museums took advantage of this fact to present theatrical-style attractions in their "lecture rooms," ranging from daguerreotypists and banjo players to contortionists and "fat ladies." Facing stiff competition from other entertainments, Scudder's had fallen on hard times and was a bit down at the heels. Barnum turned the museum around by making three smart business moves: He cut costs, paying performers as little as five to ten dollars a week (roughly $150 to $300 in today's dollars). He beefed up marketing, printing posters and leaflets by the thousands, advertising heavily in newspapers, and courting newspaper editors by offering them "exclusives." And he scoured the country for new curiosities and attractions and changed them more frequently. But he also had a knack for presenting curiosities in a way that maximized their appeal to audiences: as simultaneously believable, supported by lots of actual-seeming details, and incredible, defying common sense and often surrounded by an aura of scandal. His masterpiece in this regard was the elaborately staged Feejee mermaid hoax.

Before exhibiting the creature, he hired lawyer Levi Lyman (who had also had a hand in presenting Joice Heth) to pose as Dr. Griffin, a naturalist who had supposedly brought it to America from the Lyceum of Natural History in London, which in turn had bought it from a sailor who claimed to have taken it alive in the South Sea Islands. Barnum wrote letters about the exhibit, ostensibly from people who had encountered Dr. Griffin and his marvelous creature on tour, and had them sent to New York newspaper editors by confederates in various southern cities. He then made the rounds of the editors himself, saying that he was negotiating with Dr. Griffin for permission to exhibit the mermaid and offering each of them an exclusive story, along with a woodcut of bare-breasted mermaid sirens, suitable for printing (fig. 2.2).

He put up Dr. Griffin in a hotel room and invited reporters to come and examine the curiosity firsthand. He papered the town with 10,000 flyers attesting to "the authenticity of mermaids." The first public exhibit was not the artifact itself but a lecture by the authoritative Dr. Griffin, explaining how the Great Chain of Being could explain the existence of such a curiosity. Only after all this hoopla did Barnum finally exhibit the creature to the public in his American Museum, "at no extra charge." In the following month, his receipts tripled.[5] When a bevy of scholars denounced the exhibit as a hoax,

Figure 2.2 Etching from Barnum's pamphlet promoting the "Feejee mermaid."

Barnum took advantage of that too. "Who is to decide when doctors disagree?" he wrote in an advertisement. "If it is artificial the senses of sight and touch are ineffectual—if it is natural then all concur in declaring it the greatest Curiosity in the World."[6]

Neil Harris wryly observes that all of this "raises some questions concerning his audience."[7] Why were they apparently so credulous as to flock to see something that in hindsight seems so transparently fake? And why did they continue to flock to the shows even when their obvious contrivance was pointed out? These are some of the very questions I have been asking about *Amish Mafia*'s viewers.

Harris's answer is a little surprising. It has to do not with the psychology of audiences but with the politics of the period. Americans of the time, particularly the hoi polloi who flocked to shows like Barnum's, were interested in asserting their independence, Harris says. They did not want to rely on authorities to tell them what was real or not; they wanted to judge for themselves. It was not trust that drew them to Barnum's "humbugs," but distrust of being told what to believe. The flip side of this distrust was individuals' strong belief in their own ability to figure out what was what. This self-confidence stemmed in part from rapid technological advances that suggested that anything was possible and in part from a rise in populism that led people to question authorities of all kinds. This period was marked by a remarkable burgeoning of all kinds of how-to guides and pseudo-scientific explanations, plus the invention of detective novels and what we now call procedurals. Furthermore, critics' main concern was not the exploitation of the gullible or the erosion of the public trust; it was the erosion of authority. In short, the people who flocked to Barnum's hoaxes were demonstrating not gullibility, but independence and confidence in their own judgment. Barnum's genius was that he latched onto a great democratizing impulse.

It is hard not to notice some astonishing similarities between the historical moment Harris describes and the circumstances of *Amish Mafia*. New "smart" technologies have been changing how we interact with the world. In politics, there was the rise of the populist Tea Party beginning in 2009 and presidential candidate Donald Trump's unaccountably successful appeal to anti-establishmentarians to "believe me" starting in 2015. On the cultural front, there was (and remains) the second-guessing of authorities on scientific matters such as global warming; the flood of how-to guides and behind-the-scenes reports on the internet, ranging from "How to Replace Your iPhone Screen" to "Secrets of The Bachelorette"; and a plethora of procedurals on TV, from the well-established *CSI*, which premiered in 2000, to new "true crime" serials like HBO's *The Jinx* (2015) and FX's docudrama *American Crime Story: The People v. O. J. Simpson* (2016). So it seems likely that the creation and success of *Amish Mafia* had something to do with its particular moment in America. Some of these same political and cultural forces are operating around the world, which may help to explain why *Amish Mafia* met with considerable success when Discovery aired it in Australia, England, France, and elsewhere. Likewise, Barnum had great success when he toured his curiosities in England and France.

There is one more interesting parallel between Barnum's attractions and *Amish Mafia*. Barnum's human "curiosities" included albinos and bearded ladies, "fat boys" and a famous midget, General Tom Thumb. The handful of "Amish" principals in *Amish Mafia* similarly include a black Amishman, a little person, and an extremely overweight woman. Evangelista said this casting was not deliberate; these just happened to be the ex-Amish people who turned up during the casting process.[8] Still, their presence underlines the appeal of oddities of all kinds in reality entertainment. It may also suggest that some of the ex-Amish cast members of *Amish Mafia* were eager to appear on television in part because they felt like misfits in their own society.

Framing Reality on Film

It seems sensible to suppose that the increasing popularity of photography in the second half of the nineteenth century would have had a dramatic impact on the humbug business. Imagine if Barnum had distributed daguerreotypes of his Feejee mermaid in advance of the exhibit instead of a woodcut print of bare-breasted sirens. Some people might have thought, "What a dubious and unimpressive creature. No need to see it, now that I've seen the photograph." The visual detail of photographs and the fact that they serve as evidence of the real might have worked to deflate the curiosity that Barnum was trying to pump up.

In fact, the humbug business did decline in the latter part of the century, but that decline had to do with the rise of other popular entertainments, including vaudeville, circuses like Barnum's own, amusement parks, and, from around the turn of the twentieth century, movies. It had little to do with the capacity of photography to record and present visible evidence.

One reason photography had little effect lies in the nature of the humbug. Its deception rests not so much on the thing itself as in the presentation of the thing. People did not go just to see Joice Heth; they went to hear her stories and songs. And while a fake mummified mermaid creature may be a genuine curiosity, it was the buzz around it that made it interesting and exciting. Photographs can be presented in the same way, and sometimes they were, like the "spirit photographs" that superimposed the images of dead people over the images of living ones. But for the most part, staging things for the camera was regarded not as fakery but as a matter of course, like posing people for a studio portrait.

Scientists and historians and other learned people of the time made a great deal of the power of photography to serve as evidence for all manner of things, from the appearance of important battlefields to the deviance of mental patients to the galloping pattern of horses. But the public did not buy it, which is to say that consumers of popular culture literally did not pay for photographs that purported to show such things. They were not much interested in evidence of reality; what they wanted was images that conveyed the *experience* of reality. Consider the etching of a Civil War battlefield from the popular *Frank Leslie's Illustrated Newspaper* (fig. 2.3). It was supposedly based on the drawings of eyewitnesses—so readers did care whether it illustrated an actual experience as opposed to an imaginary one—but it is obviously a creative amalgamation, capturing dying horses and exploding shells and arrayed armies all at the same time. What consumers of images of reality like this one wanted, or perhaps what they were accustomed to expect, was not evidence of the real but a sensation of the real. The same thing applied to popular photographs of the time.

CAPTURE OF McCLERNAN'S HEADQUARTERS and McAllister's and Schwartz's artillery by the Confederates, April 6, 1862 —Grant's army lay at Pittsburg Landing awaiting the arrival of Buell from Nashville. His intention was to at once march upon Corinth. On Sunday, April 6, the Confederate army opposing him, under Gen. Albert Sidney Johnson, moved forward very quietly, and completely surprised the Federals. The onslaught was so fiercely made that three brigades were caught fleeing back, with the loss of a battery, upon McClernan's division, which lay in the rear of Prentiss's force. Prentiss was surprised and surrounded, and the Confederates took possession of McClernan's camp and captured nearly half of both McAllister's and Schwartz's artillery, besides account of Prentiss's reverses and a large number of fortune. —Sketched by H. Lovie.

Figure 2.3 "Capture of McClernan's headquarters and McAllister's and Schwartz's artillery by the confederates, April 6, 1862," from *Frank Leslie's Illustrated Newspaper. Leslie's Illustrated Civil War*, 122.

The great Civil War photo entrepreneur Mathew Brady did not understand this. He was sold on the value of photographs as evidence. He sent out crews of photographers to capture soldiers in their camps, officers posing, and battlefields after battles, supposing that people would be eager to buy prints as souvenirs and historical artifacts. He was mistaken, and as a result he went bankrupt shortly after the war. A partner who went into business for himself, Alexander Gardner, is known to have deliberately staged at least one photograph, dragging the corpse of a soldier dozens of feet and artfully arranging it against a stone wall. That was a ghoulish business and probably for that reason not a common one, but Brady did have a camera assistant pose as a corpse on one proven occasion and possibly others. The author of a recent Brady biography describes these images as "deceptions, and thus difficult to defend."[9] But this is an anachronistic perspective. At the time, nobody saw such contrivance as skullduggery. As historian of photography Robert Hirsch states, "Photographic truthfulness was not only a question of picturing what chance placed before the camera, but of depicting the experience of war. Creating a field representation . . . was an inventive act."[10]

It is important to keep in mind that a faked photograph is not a fraud if nobody cares that it is faked. It is not a humbug if there is no controversy about it, no scent of scandal about its provenance. When nineteenth-century spectators engaged with photographs as a form of entertainment—when they went to see daguerreotypes of distant places at a museum, when they had portraits made, or purchased stereoscopic images—they may have been fascinated by the machinery of photography and by the optics, but whether the images were contrived, and how, was more or less beside the point. They were not looking for "truth" or "evidence"; what they were looking for was an "attraction." That became even more evident with the rise of popular cinema around the turn of the twentieth century.

Early cinema shows mixed together filmed skits, vaudeville acts, trick films, and so-called actualities, willy-nilly. Audiences might have seen a giant "Jersey skeeter" grabbing a farmer by the seat of the pants and carrying him away, followed by a fully dressed woman stripping down to a leotard while suspended on a trapeze, followed by scenes of firemen putting out a fire. Some of the "actualities" shown were authentic, like a film of workers sifting through the wreckage of the great Galveston hurricane of 1900; others were conspicuously contrived, like a 1900 film *Beheading the Chinese Prisoner*, advertised as "just received" from China but obviously a group of white actors dressed as Chinese posing in front of a painted studio backdrop while one, with the help of a special effect, chops a papier-mâché head off another.[11] Spectators could obviously tell the difference between the two kinds of "actuality." Still, in terms of entertainment value, it did not much matter. The artificial and the real were practically interchangeable. Even verisimilitude was dispensable.[12] When viewers objected to fakery—newsreel historian Raymond Fielding cites some examples—it was because they perceived it as prejudicial.[13] This is strikingly similar to criticism of the fakery in *Amish Mafia*, as we will see in chapter 6.

With the nickelodeon boom, from around 1905, actualities of all kinds went into quick decline. The reason is not that audiences lost their appetite for them. (The millions of views on YouTube of cat videos, street performers, and cell-phone recordings of police incidents proves that the appetite for actualities is strong even today.) Rather, the reason for the decline is that cinematic stories were much more profitable than cinematic sensations. Stories had several enormous economic advantages: Producers could make them up by the cartload. They could shoot dozens at a single studio or backlot. And they could stretch out a single story to the length of a whole feature, just by adding scenes. In other words, they could easily mass produce stories, making them either as sensational or as uplifting as they pleased.

In the industry that came to be known as Hollywood, "story" became virtually synonymous with "fiction." There were movies that made a big deal about looking real, like *Birth of a Nation* in 1915, with its spectacular battle scenes, but they were never supposed to *be* real—that is, until entrepreneur-explorer Robert Flaherty had the idea of marrying Hollywood storytelling with a Barnum-style reality-based attraction in what he billed as "The Screen's Greatest Novelty," *Nanook of the North*, released in 1922.

Nanook is often regarded as the first great documentary, but from a historical perspective it is perhaps better placed on a lineage with Barnum's "curiosities." Flaherty thought nothing of making things up, from the name of his Inuit hunter, to a struggle with a harpooned seal (contrived by running a rope down through a hole in the ice and up again, off camera, where it was yanked by an assistant, tug-of-war style), to a mythical struggle between primitive man and nature. It was, in short, a fake documentary, in the same sense that the Feejee mermaid was a fake creature and *Amish Mafia* is a fake reality TV show, but with one crucial difference: the question of its fakeness was not an issue with audiences. They could have seen through the fakery, had they wanted to. (The seal that Nanook eventually pulls up through the hole in the ice is pretty obviously dead and stiff.) The reason is that they did not particularly care. They were looking for something else.[14]

The something else that Flaherty supposed they were looking for was mainly sensation ("So much interest, so much heart-throb, so many pulse-quickening sensations, you'll sit as if you were hypnotized") coupled with story ("It's rare drama, great story, thrilling action—with a stupendous human punch").[15] As for faithfulness to reality: "One often has to distort a thing to catch its true spirit," Flaherty wrote.[16] The "true spirit" was the experience captured on screen: the spectacle and the feeling it conveyed—much like the sense of battle conveyed by the Civil War etching from *Frank Leslie's Illustrated Newspaper*. *Nanook* serves up the same sort of amalgamation of impressions. The primary value of cinematography in this context is not that it is authentic; it is that it is vivid. For the sake of vividness, Flaherty supposed, fakery is not only warranted, it is welcome.

The parallel to *Amish Mafia* is obvious. It is mainly sensation and story that draw viewers. The impression of authenticity is an important part of the attraction; the factuality of particular details, less so. There is also a deeper parallel that merits mention: the allure of the exotic or "Other."[17] That allure has played a key role in reality entertainments since the Romans. It is part of what drew audiences to Barnum's museum, it was an important part of the appeal of actualities in early cinema, and it has always fascinated documentary filmmakers. It is what drew Flaherty to the Inuit and Evangelista to the Amish.

In some respects, this allure is akin to simple curiosity: we wonder about people who are different from ourselves. This curiosity is part of our makeup and often one of the engines of narrative. In popular entertainments, it typically has a sensational edge: it is bound up with surface differences—visible things like buggies and bonnets. In the case of Flaherty's mythic Eskimos and the humble Amish of popular imagination, however, there are also deeper differences: these societies represent a clear alternative to the ordinariness and the grind of modern living. In *Nanook*, this alternative is heroic and self-sufficient; in the popular image of the Amish, it is simple and communitarian. In both cases, it involves vague utopian longing for something that is absent or missing from contemporary viewers' lives.

Amish Mafia flips this longing on its head. Part of its supposed reality is that it does not put forward a sentimental view of the Amish. Beneath its visible world of quaint customs and picturesque differences lies an imaginary social reality that is selfish and scabrous. Precisely because this view contradicts the popular image of the Amish, it invites suspicions of scandal and speculation about whether and what part of its depiction is actually real. That is part and parcel of its entertainment value. In this respect, *Amish Mafia* is just like Barnum's Feejee mermaid. In the same respect, it is notably different from *Nanook of the North*.

In 2014, in the midst of making *Amish Mafia*, Evangelista produced another reality TV show, about Eskimos. Called *Escaping Alaska*, it features a group of photogenic young Inuits as they move from their Alaska villages to San Diego to experience their own version of rumspringa. As they put it in an obviously scripted opening montage, "We know how to survive but we are stuck between two worlds. We are trapped in the old ways of our ancestors. We are a generation of hunters, gatherers, and survivors. We are passionate and we want more. This is the story of our escape."

Escaping Alaska is *real* reality TV, faked more along Flaherty's lines than Barnum's. Flaherty used fakery just to spice up his stories; Barnum used it for sensation but also to make people wonder about the reality status of the things he showed them. You can immediately see its difference when you compare a scene of the Inuits from *Escaping Alaska* at the beach in an online clip entitled "I'm an Eskimo at the Beach!" ("Ooh! The waves are so huge!") with a scene of Levi and his new girlfriend at the beach in episode 4 of season 4 of *Amish Mafia* ("I can't run my life in the Amish community if I have a woman with tattoos!").[18] As an executive producer of *Escaping Alaska* put it, "You look at some shows and say, 'Wow, they [the characters] are basically reading a script.' That's not the case for us."[19] It is this difference, not just its choice of subject, that makes *Escaping Alaska* a much closer descendant of *Nanook of the North* than is *Amish Mafia*.

Hearing Is Believing

In October 1938 Europe was on the brink of all-out war. American radio audiences had become accustomed to breaking-news reports routinely interrupting regular programming to describe developments. On the evening of October 30, listeners of the CBS radio network heard what sounded like a breaking-news report describing an invasion of New Jersey by creatures from Mars armed with robots and ray guns. The report included interviews with authorities, like Professor Pierson of Princeton Observatory, and frightened eyewitness reports from the field, with screams, explosions, and unearthly sounds in the background. In spite of fairly obvious inconsistencies, like an impossibly collapsed timeline, the report sounded so authentic that many listeners believed an invasion was actually taking place. Countless others did not know what to think. Police stations and newspapers received hundreds of calls from anxious listeners. In northern New Jersey, where the attack supposedly originated, telephone switchboards were flooded. Some people even took to their cars to flee.[20]

The show was a dramatization, of course—an episode of a weekly hour-long show called *Mercury Theatre on the Air*, produced and directed by Orson Welles, in which Welles and his ensemble performed dramatizations of well-known literary works. That evening's show was based on H. G. Wells's 1897 science fiction novel, *War of the Worlds*.

In a press conference the next day, Orson Welles claimed that he was surprised and taken aback that anybody was actually deceived by the show.[21] The main purpose of the show, like that of other Mercury Theatre productions, was to be artistic and original, not tricky or deceitful. Nevertheless, Welles did view this episode as something of a prank—an attempt to at least momentarily confound or frighten audiences. As he put it in the show's scripted epilogue,

War of the Worlds was "Mercury Theatre's own radio version of dressing up in a sheet and jumping out of a bush and saying Boo!"[22]

War of the Worlds's brand of trickery is fundamentally different from *Amish Mafia*'s. The radio show was straight-up fiction, for one thing: totally scripted, performed by professional actors, and clearly labeled a dramatization. It was, in this regard, more of a masquerade than a humbug. It also portrayed an entirely different genre of programming, with an entirely different purpose: "news" as opposed to entertainment. The reason it is relevant here is that it prompted the first major scientific study, led by Princeton psychologist Hadley Cantril, of what makes mass-media audiences susceptible to deceit.[23]

Most of the people who listened to *War of the Worlds* recognized it for what it was: a fantastic story, cleverly told in the form of a news report. In a national poll of several thousand adults, taken six weeks after the broadcast, of the 12 percent of the respondents who said that they listened to the show, just 28 percent said they believed it was a news bulletin.[24] (A ratings-service survey the evening of the broadcast found that just 2 percent of radio listeners were tuned to *War of the Worlds*, so the 12 percent figure seems impossibly high. It is likely that many of those surveyed were responding to newspaper hype about the show, not the show itself.[25] Be that as it may, Cantril's case studies show that some listeners really were deceived and that some of these really panicked.) Cantril and his research group wondered, Why these particular listeners? Why were they deceived? To find out, they located 135 people from northern New Jersey who said that they had been taken in and frightened by the show and interviewed them at length.

A central finding of the study, which also drew on broader surveys, is that listeners fell into four groups. Typical listeners—the largest group, by far—had background knowledge that allowed them to quickly frame the show as fiction, in spite of its novel form. For instance, they recognized Orson Welles's voice or observed the story's resemblance to familiar Buck Rogers fantasies. Because they saw the show as entertainment, they were neither frightened nor confused by it. This group included children. The other three groups all reacted to the program with confusion, consternation, and in some cases panic. Those are the groups that Cantril focused on. One group of these frightened listeners ran reality checks, like phoning the newspaper or turning the radio dial to see if other stations were reporting the same news. Those in this group eventually figured out what was what. Another group also did some checking, phoning friends or looking out the window for possible danger, for example. The purpose of these checks, however, was less to confirm or discon-firm the radio story than to figure out what to do. This kind of reaction often did more to spread anxiety and confusion than to sort it out. The last group of listeners just panicked. They took the faux news story as fact and started packing the car.

Cantril argued that, in almost every instance, what separated those who were deceived and frightened by *War of the Worlds* from those who responded to it "appropriately" was "critical ability." By that, he meant the ability to ana-lyze and correctly assess what was going on in the show. Critical ability can be influenced by personality, he noted. For example, some people are more fearful than others and therefore more prone to believe frightening stories. Critical ability can also be inhibited by circumstances, he observed. For ex-ample, in a room full of panicking people, a critically able person might not have the presence of mind to analyze and assess a radio report. But for the most part, Cantril believed, critical ability is a product of education. He sup-posed that people with PhDs, such as himself, were fairly immune to media deception, while high school dropouts were more likely to be deceived.

Cantril found substantial support for this hypothesis. For example, in his sample of people who initially thought *War of the Worlds* was an actual news report, 48 percent of high school graduates eventually realized it was a dra-matization, compared with just 30 percent of those who had completed gram-mar school only.[26] Cantril had trouble explaining, however, grammar school children who instantly recognized *War of the Worlds* as entertainment and, at the other end of the spectrum, five university-educated subjects who were completely taken in and frightened by the show. He regarded these as outliers or "deviate" cases. In fact, what they demonstrate is that little deliberate crit-ical thinking was going on at either end of his scale. The kids who perceived *War of the Worlds* as entertainment simply recognized it as such. They did not think about it. The same is true of those well-educated adults who thought they were hearing an actual news report. The folks in the middle—those who did reality checks—were not necessarily more or less thoughtful or critically sophisticated than those in the other two groups. They perceived contradic-tions in the show, were confused, and reacted by taking action of one kind or another. Nobody in any group paused to ponder.

What Cantril called critical ability is similar to what we now call media literacy, which was defined at a seminal 1992 conference as "the ability to ac-cess, analyze, evaluate and communicate messages in a variety of forms."[27] There is no doubt that listeners' prior media experience played a role in determining which ones panicked when they heard *War of the Worlds* and which ones didn't. Those who knew about Mercury Theatre or had read H. G. Wells's novel or listened to episodes of *The Shadow* on the radio were much likelier to have instantly recognized the radio broadcast as a work of fiction. That kind of media awareness tends to increase with education, for the simple reason that education exposes one to a wide range of media texts. There is also evidence that training in critical thinking can help people sort out accurate from inaccurate information in the media, if they want to—on a test, for example.[28] Still, Cantril's examples make it clear that many *War of the Worlds* listeners did not bother sifting through the show for facts and falsehoods, regardless of their level of education and critical ability. They just reacted to their immediate impressions.

Cantril supposed that critical thinking could inoculate media audiences against knee-jerk emotional reactions, like fear. His team's research findings, however, suggest just the opposite: fear can overwhelm critical thinking. That is what happened in the case of those well-educated adults who mistook *War of the Worlds* for news. It also helps explain the impact of fake news today, a great deal of which is deliberately designed to trigger fear—such as exaggerated reports, before the midterm elections of 2018, of an imminent "invasion" of the United States by "aliens" from Central America.

Critical thinking is also not a sure defense against the well-known phenomenon of confirmation bias. People naturally tend to see and hear things that reinforce their preconceptions and to ignore or discount things that don't. When confronted by facts that don't square with their preconceptions, people are prone to twist the facts rather than change their minds. For example, when confusing reports of strange machines attacking New Jersey came over the radio, fully a quarter of Cantril's frightened subjects assumed they were hearing news of a Nazi attack in spite of the show's references to Mars and meteors. One listener explained, "In the back of my head, I had the idea that the meteor was just a camouflage. It was really an airplane . . . and the Germans were attacking us with gas bombs."[29] Critical ability and media literacy education do not prevent this kind of flawed thinking. In fact, they can make the problem worse by giving people a false sense of confidence in their reasoning ability.[30]

Finally, there is the matter of social influence. Cantril's report is full of people who fell for *War of the Worlds* mainly because their friends or relatives fell for it. In a 2018 book, *The Misinformation Age: How False Beliefs Spread*, philosophers of science Cailin O'Connor and James Owen Weatherall demonstrate convincingly that what you believe depends largely upon whom you know.[31] People who read the *New York Times* do not spend a lot of time scrutinizing articles they read there for truth or accuracy; they just trust the *New York Times*, mostly because the people they associate with and hold in high regard also read and trust it. Fans of right-wing talk show host Sean Hannity are just like *New York Times* readers in that regard. They trust Hannity (and distrust the *New York Times*) because their friends and people they identify with feel the same way. Evidence, reasoning, and critical ability have relatively little to do with it.

The fakery in *Amish Mafia* is different from the trickery in *War of the Worlds* in key respects, as I have pointed out. Probably the most significant difference is that audiences do not take it seriously. The question of whether aliens are actually invading New Jersey is something to worry about. The question of whether Lebanon Levi is actually dating a girl with tattoos is not. Even the question of whether or not one "believes" that dating scenario hardly matters because it is so trivial.

In one crucial regard, however, the fakery in *Amish Mafia* works just like the trickery of *War of the Worlds*: audiences' reactions, including whether or not they fall for it, are initially based almost entirely upon impressions and preconceptions, not critical thinking or factual analysis. "Facts," such as they are, fly by largely under the radar. Reality TV fans are quite media literate, at least with respect to reality TV. They know the kind of manipulation that takes place behind the scenes. The preconception they bring to reality TV shows is not that these shows are factual or true, but rather that, in spite of (or sometimes because of) the shows' contrivance, they reveal spontaneous and authentic reactions of people to extraordinary, often stressful situations. The impressions that *Amish Mafia* serves up are deliberately designed to reinforce that preconception. But, as the previous chapter has shown, those impressions are largely false. They are illusions, carefully engineered to deceive or confound reality TV viewers whose expectations have been conditioned by other shows.

"Just the Facts, Ma'am"

In the vast landscape of American television entertainment, news stands out as an anomaly on account of its well-known injunction against fabrication and fakery. The other two notable exceptions in this regard are sporting events and game shows: sporting events, because rigging games is "unsportsmanlike"; game shows, because of a law passed in 1960 in the wake of a couple of highly publicized scandals that prohibits fixing them. News is different from these two exceptions because its standards have to do not just with fairness but also with factuality.

Two quick disclaimers are in order. First, "factual" means something different from uncontrived. Television news is obviously full of contrivance, from the selection and framing of stories, to the on-camera role of celebrity reporters, to the way footage of events is gathered, which is always dictated more by what is visual and accessible than by what is relevant and revealing.

Second, almost nobody criticizes *Amish Mafia* for its failure to be factual. When you parse all of the criticisms of the show, you find that they boil down to two: First, *Amish Mafia* is not fair to the Amish. Second, it is misleading, meaning that it is not fair to viewers. Fairness is the overriding concern of both those who accuse the show of being exploitative and those who criticize it for being made up. With respect to factuality or "truth," viewers do not hold *Amish Mafia* to the same standards as the news. Just the same, in all the chatter about fakery that surrounds not just *Amish Mafia* but reality television in general, news reporting is implicitly held up as the de facto standard of truth. In the mind of the public, TV news illustrates what a show that is not fake is supposed to be like.

In the practice of deception, humans are by no means unique. Apes deceive, crows deceive, even bugs deceive. "Truthfulness" on the other hand— that is to say, the deliberate rejection of certain kinds of deception on moral or ethical grounds—is a specifically human concern, and standards in this area are contingent and variable. What some people consider a fraud, others consider acceptable and sometimes even commendable. Think of Michael Moore's reverse-angle shot in the Charlton Heston interview described in the previous chapter. Also, standards change over time. What we now see as blatant fakery in early "actuality" movies was regarded as perfectly ordinary and acceptable by filmmakers and audiences of the time. Today such contrivances would certainly not pass muster on TV news, which is supposed to be factual. Even reality TV is sometimes accused of crossing this line, as shown by the Bear Grylls scandal mentioned in the previous chapter. These observations raise several pertinent historical questions. Where did the standard of truthfulness in TV news come from? What does it mean exactly? And how does it apply, if at all, to "standard practices" of reality TV?

In print news, the standard of truthfulness dates back to the seventeenth century. Early printers of news sheets assured readers that they printed only eyewitness reports and "matters of fact."[32] A clear distinction between fact and fiction held sway in the news in Barnum's time too—at least in theory. In 1835 the proprietor of the *New York Herald*, James Gordon Bennett, took a rival paper to task for printing a widely circulated report of a telescope that had purportedly observed a variety of living creatures, including "man-bats," on the moon. "But now," he wrote, "when that paper in order to get money out of the credulous public, seriously persists in averting its truth, it becomes highly improper, wicked, and in fact a species of impudent swindling."[33] Bennett's great cause, along with the editors of other "respectable" newspapers, was "truth, public faith, and science, against falsehood, fraud, and ignorance."[34] The guarantor of truth was "facts." As the Washington correspondent of the Associated Press put it in 1866, "My business is merely to communicate facts. My instructions do not allow me to make any comments upon the facts which I communicate."[35]

The commercial press has always been powerfully squeezed from two directions. From one side comes pressure to please political and commercial patrons; from the other comes pressure to pander to the public's taste for sensation. Responding to these constant pressures, professional societies of journalists in the 1920s established two major codes of ethics. Both of these codes enshrined "objectivity" as the norm. As a practical matter that meant three things: fairness (news was supposed to be disinterested and unbiased); independence (news was not supposed to be beholden to any patron); and factuality (news reporters were not supposed to make things up).[36] While there was some interpretive wiggle room on the first two standards, the third was iron-clad: something was either a fact or it was not.

Meanwhile, on movie screens, biweekly newsreels had become a staple. An army of cinematographers prowled the world looking for famous, sensational, or photogenic events to capture on film. These typically included sporting events, parades, shots of celebrities, and scenes from disasters and wars. Although most of the battle scenes of World War I were staged, with costumed actors and faked explosions, audiences increasingly trusted the authenticity of what they were seeing on screen. As a trade reporter wrote in 1926, "The deadly accuracy and the vivid realism of the news film has brought it to the heights of purpose and utility which it now occupies. It has reeled its way into the confidence of millions of persons."[37]

From the mid-1800s right up to the digital era, photography has often been held to epitomize objectivity, since it mechanically records what is in front of the camera. This notion ignores the important consideration of whether what is in front of the camera is staged. In newsreels, an awful lot of it was. Newsreel historian Raymond Fielding lists four kinds of commonly "manufactured" footage: setting up scenes at a news event, creating a stunt or event specifically for the camera, recreating a news event after the fact using actual participants, and recreating an event using impersonators or stand-ins.[38] The first two practices were regarded as perfectly legitimate; the latter two were sometimes seen as dubious, even by practitioners. The difference is not that they fudged facts—all four techniques did that—it is that they deliberately deceived viewers. Intent to deceive emerged as a litmus test for the violation of "factuality" in newsreels and documentaries.

The March of Time newsreel, from 1935 to 1951, is an interesting test case, since it used staged scenes and unlabeled re-creations extensively, sometimes almost exclusively, using impersonators as stand-ins for Hitler and other famous personages.[39] *The March of Time* was not really a newsreel, Fielding says.[40] It might more aptly be called a news digest, with a portentous narrator "explaining" some topic or event and with moving images gathered opportunistically from any source, from studio creations to newsreel archives, serving as illustrations. Just the same, the extremely popular series came to define what news on screen looked like from 1935 to the advent of television news.

The March of Time was in the illustration business, not the documentation business. "Looks like" was a sufficient standard of truthfulness for images. Authenticity was an additional asset when it was not too difficult to achieve, but it was by and large dispensable to filmmakers, to audiences, even to critics. The reason *The March of Time* was not regarded as a fraud is that its contrivance was frank. It even publicized its use of reenacted scenes. When episodes attracted criticism, it was not because they were not factual but because they were perceived as biased. On that score, *The March of Time* and other newsreels came under increasing suspicion, especially after people saw the effectiveness of the Nazi propaganda machine. As one critic wrote in 1945, "News has divorced Truth and eloped with Politics. Their offspring is Propaganda. . . . Film lends itself to skillful shaping. It is dangerous."[41] Still, *The March of Time* remained immune to criticism for its contrived images.

Television news was a game changer when it began streaming into American homes in the late 1940s and early 1950s because it introduced a new standard: immediacy. It was not enough for news images to be factual; they needed to be current. What that meant, as a practical matter, is that most of the news consisted of a reporter-host, like Walter Cronkite, sitting behind his desk in the newsroom reading written reports. Two kinds of on-location reporting were cut into this newsroom narration: interviews or on-camera reports by reporters outside the studio, and spontaneous footage, filmed and quickly spliced together on location or on rare occasions broadcast live, narrated by a reporter.

All of these images tended to be static and dull. In lieu of spectacle and story, images of the news anchor at his desk gave an impression of authority and presence; images from the field conveyed authenticity and immediacy. In this context, footage that appeared spontaneous was supposed to actually be spontaneous. The reporter in the field was supposed to be the guarantee of that.

When visual illustrations on television news have generated controversy, it has invariably been the result of a breach of this implicit trust. One infamous example is *Dateline*'s rigged demonstration of the explosion-prone gas tank of a GM pickup truck in 1992.[42] Far more often, though, when TV reporters get in trouble, it is not on account of images but because of factually incorrect verbal statements—especially self-serving ones. An example is newscaster Brian Williams's 2015 dismissal from *NBC Nightly News* for making up a story about having come under fire while reporting in Iraq.[43] Williams was brought back six months later as an anchor for MSNBC news, showing that ultimately it is more important today for a TV news reporter to be winsome and popular than to be absolutely factual.

What does this history of news reporting have to do with *Amish Mafia*? First, it demonstrates that the idea of a clean boundary between fact and fiction is a myth. The line has never been particularly neat. The practical boundary that emerged along with standards of "objectivity" in the 1920s meant that depictions of circumstances and events are supposed to actually be what they appear to viewers to be. In other words, a re-creation is perfectly acceptable so long as it looks like a re-creation, is contextualized as a re-creation, or, in cases where it appears to be authentic, is labeled as a re-creation. It is this boundary that *Amish Mafia* deliberately crosses.

All reality TV breaches this boundary, to be sure, but in a way that audiences have come to understand and expect. For example, in *Escaping Alaska*, it is obvious that the young Inuit woman at the beach is no primitive aboriginal. She appears to be a typical American young adult. Her trip to San Diego looks like an escape only in the figurative sense, in spite of the show's attempt to blow it out of proportion. It is also obvious that the scene at the beach is a set piece from start to finish. Nevertheless, when the young woman whoops and dances in the waves, even though her behavior is artificially over the top, she appears to be expressing emotions that are genuine. That is what the scene looks like because that is what it is. It that regard, at least, it is real. In contrast, in *Amish Mafia*, when Levi says his girlfriend's tattoo is going to be a problem for him in the Amish community, that is fiction plain and simple. Levi is not Amish, and the girl is not his girlfriend. Yet the characters and their relationship are presented as actual, and the scene is deliberately contrived to appear spontaneous and unscripted. This pretense goes considerably deeper than the pretense in *Escaping Alaska*.

Second, the history of news reporting demonstrates that there is a double standard for factuality in images and factuality in words. A deliberately faked image may be considered an illustration; a deliberately false statement is usually considered a lie. With this in mind, it is worth reviewing those "Pants on Fire" claims made with intertitles in the first episode of *Amish Mafia*: "The Amish Mafia is a secretive subculture that operates within its own set of rules and values" and "Lebanon Levi and his crew are in charge of collecting fees and assessing claims" for the Amish self-insurance fund Amish Aid. By news standards, those statements are outright lies and therefore impermissible. In the context of *Amish Mafia*, they are something else, which is revealing.

There is a crucial exception to the rule of thumb that a deliberately false statement is a lie: that is when it is considered a fiction. If Lebanon Levi is playing a make-believe character and makes some outrageous statement while in that role, it is not a violation of the standard of factuality; it is just part of a story. Those intertitles are different because they represent the voice of the filmmakers. They are making statements about the characters. They appear to be stepping back from the story and commenting on it. This puts them squarely in the realm of what would ordinarily be regarded as factual claims. But here is the trick: what happens if the intertitles themselves are part of the make-believe, if the filmmakers we catch glimpses of throughout the series are themselves part of the fiction? If we knew that for sure—if there were another title up front that clearly explained the subterfuge—then we would be in the realm of the mockumentary or parody, like *This is Spinal Tap* or the clever IFC series *Documentary Now!* If we watch such a movie and assume that it is actual—not a fiction, in other words—then it is we who are in the wrong, not the filmmakers. We are credulous and uninformed.

But what happens if the filmmakers leave us hanging? What happens if they put scenes in their show that are just about impossible to believe, like Amish men going around in buggies blowing up storefront Santa Clauses, and at the same time repeatedly step back from the story with misleading intertitles and even interviews with executive producers on the internet, saying in effect, Hey, believe it! This is all true! Then the filmmakers are not exactly lying; they are involved in an elaborate ruse. We, the audience, are left in limbo: on the one hand, we are skeptical; on the other, we never know what to believe. If we happen to be taken in by something, it is not because the filmmakers are liars; it is because we are dupes. At least, that is what the filmmakers can say. The question of why this should be entertaining will be taken up in chapters 4 and 5; the question of its ethical implications, in chapter 6. What we can definitely say now is that this technique puts us outside the realm of "factual" discourses like TV news, or even openly fake factual discourses like mockumentaries. It lands us back in the realm of what Barnum called the humbug—a realm that, thanks in part to a century-long tradition of "just the facts, ma'am" news reporting, people do not quite know how to navigate (if they ever did).

CHAPTER THREE

A Chronicle of Contrivance

The Invention of Reality TV

In the late 1950s and early 1960s, "objectivity" got a new look: a fly-on-the-wall style of documentary filmmaking emerged, pioneered by Robert Drew with cameraman Ricky Leacock and others, made possible by new lightweight synchronized sound recording gear and fueled by an interest in more nonfiction programming for television. The new approach involved embedding a filmmaker in some institution or event, shooting copious amounts of observational footage, then editing the footage to construct a largely chronological story, keeping narrated explanation to a minimum. Because of the long production schedule this approach required, it was not suited to news reporting. Instead, it became a new form of nonfiction storytelling variously called cinéma vérité, direct cinema, or living cinema.

A culmination of this movement was the television series *An American Family*, which aired on PBS in 1973. Over the course of twelve weekly episodes, upwards of 10 million Americans peered into the lives of a "typical" upper-middle-class American family as the parents, Bill and Pat Loud, separated and got divorced, a gay son moved to New York and came out of the closet, and four other teenaged children went about their daily business. The series offered an unprecedented experience of televisual voyeurism that viewers and critics responded to with fascination. At the same time, the strategy of merely following family members around with cameras did not exactly yield scintillating drama. On the contrary: One of the dramatic high points of the series is when Bill gets home from a business trip and Pat immediately tells him to move out. "That's a fair deal," Bill responds with equanimity. The two chat casually for a bit about business, including which hotel he will be staying at, then he calmly picks up his suitcase and leaves.[1] In televisual terms, this socially fraught moment is awfully dull.

What producer Craig Gilbert counted on to compensate for the slowness of *An American Family* was its high-mindedness. He hoped that the series would launch a national conversation about men's and women's roles in society. Instead, the conversation that took place revolved largely around judgments about the family and family members. In other words, it was gossip, much of which was scathing. Pat complained vigorously in newspaper and talk show interviews, blaming the producers after the fact for sensationalism and cruelty.[2] Some critics also raised the issue of pretense, pointing out that the fly-on-the-wall style disguised the filmmakers' editorial choices and the subjects' complicity. Gilbert responded that all of these criticisms missed the point not just of *An American Family* but of documentaries generally, which is to prompt us to reflect upon ourselves and our world. He concluded that, in a television industry ruled by ratings and advertisers' dollars, the observational documentary was doomed.[3] He was right. There have been many subsequent observational documentaries, including important films by Frederick Wiseman and D. A. Pennebaker, but Wiseman's films, like *State Legislature* (2007), reach a tiny niche audience, and Pennebaker's, like *Startup.com* (2001), have put aside the strict observational format.

An American Family illustrates the quandary that faces all reality TV producers: real life tends to be pretty boring, at least when observed through a camera lens. It consists mostly of mundane and routine business. But if you try to spice it up, to make it more interesting and dramatic for TV viewers, you risk departing from the very reality that is supposed to make it worthwhile in the first place.

One solution to this dilemma is to seek out naturally dramatic and stressful situations. Robert Drew and his associates tried this technique at ABC in the early years of observational cinema, filming politicians on the campaign trail, a race-car driver preparing for a big race, an international piano competition, and the like, but network executives quickly gave up on the commercial potential of the whole approach, which is why *An American Family* wound up on public television.[4] Two decades later, however, thanks in part to new lightweight video cameras and the proliferation of police surveillance, Fox made the technique work with *Cops*. *Cops* followed a simple formula: show a policeman telling you about a potential action; show a sequence of rough action footage of policemen breaking down doors, handcuffing suspects, and so on, interspersed with brief interviews; then come back to a policeman explaining what happened. In spite of the repetitiveness of this formula, audiences liked it. *Cops* remains on the air today, more than a quarter-century later.

A different solution to the boring-reality conundrum, at the other end of the contrivance scale, is to stage pranks and film people's reactions to them. Pranking people had been popular on TV since the 1948 debut of *Candid Camera*. This formula has also proven hardy, generating countless spin-offs and knockoffs right up to today, like the YouTube Red series *Prank Academy*. The main appeal of this kind of show lies in observing people's spontaneous reactions to awkward or stressful situations. In that respect, these shows reveal reality. The situations they depict, however, are anything but real.

The Real World, which premiered on MTV in 1992, pioneered a middle way between tagalong observation and full-blown contrivance. Producers Mary-Ellis Bunim and Jonathan Murray chose seven young adults and paid them each $2,600 to live together in a New York loft for three months, with cameras rolling. Their original aim had been to write and produce a fictional series for MTV, like Fox's popular youth series *Beverly Hills 90210*, but when it became clear that MTV could not give them the budget they needed for such a show, they decided to film a real-world social experiment instead, loosely modeled on *An American Family*.[5] Instead of finding a family to film, they concocted a pseudo-family of attractive young people with big personalities, representing different races, religions, and worldviews, chosen with the expectation that they would not get along. Instead of waiting for events to occur, the producers planned activities for cast members, pairing them up for "dates"; sending them out in groups to dance parties, sporting events, and political rallies; and inviting family members and old flames to visit. Instead of simply filming conversations as they happened, the producers invented the on-camera "confessional," so they could milk every conflict for all it was worth. Every season, they cast a new batch of young folks and put them in a different city. This formula proved successful in balancing "reality" and drama in a way that viewers found satisfying, launching a series that has now lasted for thirty seasons, with no end in sight.

The most important ingredient in the success of all of these reality-based TV shows is economic: they cost a fraction of what scripted television shows do to produce. The first goal of TV executives has always been to maximize the ratio of viewers to dollars spent. In the cable era, with channels multiplying and audiences dividing, this imperative has become critical. In the age of YouTube and the internet, it has become more urgent still. Cheap TV has therefore become increasingly appealing to TV executives. This factor is the main reason for the proliferation of reality TV in recent years. But cheap is just half of the equation. To succeed, a reality TV show must also consistently attract lots of eyeballs, which means it must find ways to out-entertain the competition, including scripted shows.

In purely dramatic terms, no reality TV show can touch scripted TV. Scripted television employs carefully crafted stories, professional actors, artful sets, omniscient camerawork, and transparent editing. Reality TV sacrifices all of these elements. The only attraction it offers in exchange is "reality," whatever that means. Some have suggested that it means, essentially, something to gossip about. *The Real World* producer Jonathan Murray holds this view. To peek behind the curtains of other people's lives, he says, is why viewers tuned into *The Real World* in the first place.[6] That supposes that reality TV needs to present something to gossip about—some scandal or sensation. Indeed, since the early years of *The Real World*, the pursuit of scandal and sensation has continually upped the ante for bad behavior on reality TV, resulting in what Murray and others refer to as "train-wreck TV."

The opportunity to observe scandalous and sensational behavior is a big part of what draws people to reality TV. But that is not what makes reality TV "real," since the same thing also draws people to scripted soap operas and other TV fiction. Furthermore, when supposedly real behavior is artificial or trumped up, as is often the case on train-wreck TV, viewers get wise and it loses some of its appeal.[7] Besides, in the early years of *The Real World*, cast members tended to be remarkably polite to each other, in spite of the show's tagline, "Find out what happens when people stop being polite . . . and start getting real." So, the "reality" that distinguishes and defines reality TV is not scandal or sensation; it is something else.

That something else consists largely of *risk*: risk of embarrassment, conflict, emotional stress, sometimes even physical harm.[8] People do not tune into reality TV just to see people act up or act out; they tune in to observe the consequences of such behavior. What sustains their interest is less the momentary "train wreck" itself than the ever-present possibility of a train wreck and fascination with its emotional aftermath. Viewers watch reality TV not just to see people perform, as at a concert or play, but to see them perform without a net, as it were. That is why star Simon Cowell was so important to the early success of the performance competition show *American Idol*—because he was not afraid to humiliate contestants.

Reality TV scholar Misha Kavka has argued that intimacy is key: "It is the promise of intimate interaction—whether positive or negative or merely banal—that underlies the shows' claims to the real."[9] But intimacy is just as much a part of fictional soap opera. What makes reality TV "real" is rather the impression of *vulnerability*. This is created in large part by the expression of emotions that appear spontaneous and raw, like outbursts of anger or tears. Such scenes are the Holy Grail of reality TV—"the moment's moment," as some producers call them. Gary Carter, former head of FremantleMedia and Endemol Shine, two of the largest international producers of reality TV, has said that such moments are "faux and stagey and utterly illegitimate."[10] What he means is that producers engage in all sorts of manipulation to create them. Just the same, they work. The reason is not that viewers mistake the emotions displayed or the scenarios in which they are embedded as totally genuine; it is that such scenes, whether or not they are contrived, create the impression of actual (as opposed to merely enacted) risk. That impression is what sustains a great deal of nonfiction storytelling.[11]

The Second and Third Generations

Since the start of *The Real World*, two major transformations have reshaped the reality TV landscape. Reality TV scholar Misha Kavka has labeled these transformations the second and third generations of reality TV.[12] The second generation was launched in the United States by spectacular success of CBS's *Survivor*, which drew an astonishing 51.7 million viewers to its first-season finale in 2000.[13] *Survivor* introduced two major innovations—one formal, the other commercial—that define the second generation of reality TV.

The formal innovation was a nifty way of dramatically raising the stakes. In some ways, *Survivor* is just like *The Real World*: it takes a disparate group of strangers and forces them to live together, fishing for "moment's moments" and using "confessionals" to tease those out. In addition, it divides cast members into teams, sets up competitive challenges and ordeals to test them, requires the losing team to eliminate a member every episode, and gives a huge cash prize to the solo winner, all of which naturally lead to a great deal of scheming. What this competition-elimination formula does, essentially, is multiply and magnify elements of risk. The fact that the risk is entirely manufactured is completely irrelevant to viewers, demonstrating again that the "reality" of reality TV has little to do with the absence of artifice and a lot to do with the impression of vulnerability.

The commercial innovation that *Survivor* introduced was the so-called format—a template for a reality TV show that could be copyrighted and licensed as a franchise for production and distribution in other languages and countries. This development brought about the rise of international reality TV mega-producers, like FremantleMedia and Endemol Shine, which are able to license, produce, and distribute shows with demonstrated mass appeal and high production values at relatively low cost.[14] As a result smaller producers, like Eric Evangelista, were pushed into smaller corners of the market, and cable distributors, like the Discovery network, were forced to be more creative and sometimes more outrageous in distinguishing their reality TV fare in order to attract the attention of viewers.

The other major transformation in the reality TV landscape in recent years—Miska's third generation—has been an increasing focus on celebrity. Fascination with celebrity has been part of reality TV since the first season of *The Real World*, in which all seven cast members were performers with show-business aspirations. Many *Survivor* competitors have gone on to become minor celebrities, featured in other reality TV shows. Performance-competition shows like *American Idol* are all about acquiring fame. But a new kind of show has emerged in which celebrity has switched from a secondary theme to the main attraction. The first of this breed was the *The Osbournes*, about the domestic life of heavy-metal rocker Ozzy Osbourne and his family, which played on MTV from 2002 to 2005. In its premiere season *The Osbournes* became the highest-rated regular series in the history of MTV, with more than 6 million viewers weekly.[15]

Superficially, *The Osbournes* seems similar to *The Real World*, with cameras following subjects around the house and on informal outings, filming their petty conflicts. But the show is deliberately comical, billed by MTV as "the first reality sitcom."[16] The role of producers and writers changed from contriving situations and outings, as on *The Real World*, to mapping out themes and throughlines, more like conventional screenwriters. While producers did not script scenes, they planned and planted them, saying things like, "I would love to have a scene in which you talk to your kids about what you find in their room."[17] Moreover, mom Sharon Osbourne was the show's executive producer, very much in charge of her family's image, and the whole family was clearly not only complicit but quite involved in its own self-presentation.

Scholar Jennifer Gillan has made the fascinating observation that, in spite of Ozzy Osbourne's constant bleeped-out swearing and apparently drug-addled behavior, *The Osbournes* more closely resembles scripted family sitcoms of the 1950s, like *The Adventures of Ozzie and Harriet*, than it does its reality TV precursors.[18] She suggests that this turn back toward a traditional generic form brought with it a whole series of subtle substitutions. In place of social drama, revolving around big themes like race and religion, the show offers family drama around issues such as parental style. In place of spontaneity, the show offers the feeling of familiarity—we recognize the Osbournes as a regular family, just like ours, in spite of being famous and odd. And most important, in lieu of "reality" (which is to say, the impression of genuine risk, of which there is little), the show offers the appearance of "truth" (familiar and culturally resonant themes and values). In sum, the show swaps out the appeal of seeing ordinary people in vulnerable moments for the appeal of seeing celebrities in silly and sometimes sentimental moments. *The Osbournes* looks a lot like train-wreck TV, but it is a cartoon train wreck—over the top, lots of fun, and nobody gets hurt.

Audience researcher Annette Hill argues that celebrity-based reality TV invites a different kind of viewing stance. To illustrate, she makes a comparison to professional wrestling.[19] Connoisseurs of professional wrestling speak of themselves as "smart fans," capable of distinguishing between the showmanship and the actual athleticism and risk. They speak of those who are taken in by the apparent violence as "marks." The difference is not a matter of seeing through the artificial facade—even marks do that. It is a matter of appreciating it. Connoisseurs enjoy the show, including its posturing and fakery. Anybody who does not—anybody who finds the pretend violence distasteful, for instance—can be dismissed as a mark.

The Osbournes invites spectators to think of themselves as "smart fans" who recognize and enjoy the contrivance of the show. The fact remains, however, that there is a big difference between recognizing contrivance and knowing what is contrived. Fans of professional wrestling know the tricks of the trade; viewers of *The Osbournes*, in contrast, had no way of knowing what part of what they were seeing was made up. This opened the door to charges of deception.[20] Even some viewers who enjoyed the playful performances felt put out when, at the end of the second season finale, the entire episode, including the death of the family dog, was revealed to be a gag. On an online bulletin board one viewer complained, "Ozzy's outtakes at the end, I think, ruined my ability to watch the show anymore. I had to call into question the past couple of years worth of the show, 'were they staging this stuff the whole time?' Maybe MTV is once again on the cutting edge and killing off reality TV."[21]

Faking It

This brings us back to *Amish Mafia*, which took a big stride further even than *The Osbournes* in fictionalizing "reality." Perhaps *Amish Mafia* was the leading edge of another new generation of reality TV. Or perhaps it marked an outside boundary that reality TV approaches at its peril: a form of manipulation that if revealed ruins viewers' pleasure and makes them feel like marks. The future of reality TV is impossible to predict. But looking at its precursors helps clarify how *Amish Mafia* was different from other reality TV.

From *Candid Camera* and *Cops* to *Cutthroat Kitchen* and *Keeping Up with the Kardashians*, all reality TV shows are involved in the balancing act between spontaneous and unscripted (but also potentially boring) reality on one side and controlled and contrived (but also more intrinsically engaging) forms of entertainment such as stories on the other. The rule of thumb, from a business standpoint, is that if you have a tight production schedule, you lean toward the controlled, although that requires a healthy production budget; if you do not have much money to work with, you need to go the more spontaneous route, although that takes more time.[22] What audiences want is *both* the impression of genuine spontaneity *and* tightly crafted stories. That is an eat-your-cake-and-have-it-too scenario, of course, but it is what reality TV producers are supposed to deliver.

Amish Mafia found a new way of doing just that—by faking it. On the one hand, it showed what appeared to be spontaneous behavior in stressful situations, using the familiar follow-along techniques of *The Real World*. On the other hand, it appeared to have such complete access to its subjects that it could deliver its apparent revelations of reality in the form of nice coherent story beats, like *The Osbournes*. Because the production was both highly contrived *and* designed to look rough and spontaneous, it could be produced quickly and cheaply at the same time. And because it purported to show a secret subgroup within the already secretive Amish society, it could plausibly deny charges of fakery. Doubts could be met with the retort, "How do you *know* it is not true?"

Just the same, because its story scenes seem to be too well planned and executed to be genuinely spontaneous, viewers were bound to have doubts. Plus, the show dropped broad hints that all is not what it seems, like the disclaimer about reenactments of "the legend of the Amish Mafia." On *The Real World*, suspiciously over-the-top behavior comes off as part of the show's contrived "reality," just like the artificial living situation and deliberately planned outings. In *Amish Mafia*, in contrast, we see characters in their natural setting, going about business that supposedly has nothing to do with the show. In *The Osbournes*, the characters' outrageous behavior comes off as playful fun: Ozzy is a performer, Sharon is in charge, and the dog is okay in the end. The representations of *Amish Mafia*, in contrast, seem serious. They feature an actual religious group that does not like to be photographed. Moreover, much of the behavior in the show is antisocial, even criminal. If that behavior is real, it is appalling; if invented, it is scurrilous. Because of these distinctive qualities, *Amish Mafia* did not look quite like any other show on TV. It was a puzzle. That puzzle may have been part of the show's appeal.

Amish Mafia is fairly entertaining even if you assume it is mostly made up: it serves up sensational and mostly plausible stories about a little-known people. It also dishes up plenty to gossip about, particularly if you assume that some of what it shows is actual. But on top of these stories, at the meta level the show continually involves viewers in a kind of game of trying to figure out what is what. Much of the show seems authentic and spontaneous. Cast members assiduously deny in the show that what it depicts is made up, as did Discovery executives on the show's website when it was broadcast. At the same time, many things in the show, and scuttlebutt about it on the internet, invite skepticism and incredulity. So the design of the show and its publicity seemed to *deliberately* sow confusion about the show's reality status; they seemed to *intentionally* court questions and controversy about possible fakery. In this regard, *Amish Mafia* was quite different from *The Real World* or *Survivor* or any of the other reality TV shows discussed. Rather, it harkens back to Barnum's humbugs and the Feejee mermaid.

Discovery Network and the New Humbug

There is now solid scientific support for the existence of mermaids, based on physical evidence you can see with your own eyes. That is the claim Barnum made when he displayed his Feejee mermaid in 1842. That is also the claim made by the Discovery network's Animal Planet documentary *Mermaids: The Body Found* in 2012.[23]

Mermaids tells the story of three whale researchers who discovered startling and dumbfounding evidence for the existence of a previously unidentified sea mammal that they first took to be something like a manatee. When they examined the physical remains they had recovered from the stomach of a great white shark, it turned out to have webbed human-like hands. They also found pieces of what looked like a primitive harpoon, tipped with a stingray barb, in the shark's jaw and stomach.

The principal narrator of the story is Dr. Paul Robertson, an oceanographer with the National Oceanic and Atmospheric Administration. In 2004 he was working for esteemed marine biologist Brian McCormick looking into mass whale beachings, which McCormick suspected had been caused by secret testing of a sonar weapon by the U.S. Navy. Robertson and other scientists describe their research and findings in talking-head interviews. To illustrate and enliven these interviews, *Mermaids* employs actors who resemble the scientists to recreate the research—the beach, on boats, in the lab, and so on—in scenes labeled "Dramatic Reenactment."

As part of their research, McCormick and his team made an underwater recording of a Navy sonar blast. The blast on the recording was followed by an unearthly shrieking. Baffled, McCormick sent it to an animal communication expert at the University of South Florida for analysis. What the expert discovered was an incredibly complex sound signature, made up of "literally thousands of different signifiers . . . at least a half-dozen individual voice-prints. So what you see here is language. They are talking to one another." What "they" were nobody knew, since the shrieks did not sound like familiar whale and dolphin vocalizations.

Pursuing this puzzle, the scientists managed to track down a couple of boys who claimed to have found a strange monster on the beach among the carcasses of beached whales. In a startling revelation, *Mermaids* reveals a shaky cell phone video that the boys made of the creature, before it suddenly reached out for them and they ran away in terror. For a brief moment, the cell phone footage shows us a humanoid creature, with large eyes, a ridged head, and webbed hands (fig. 3.1).

The existence of a humanoid tool-using sea mammal is consistent with the so-called aquatic ape theory. This theory holds that, in the same way that whales and dolphins evolved from the return to the sea of semiaquatic land mammals tens of millions of years ago, a branch of our ape ancestors returned to the sea just a few million years ago, after they had developed language and primitive tools. Using computer animation and other kinds of illustration, *Mermaids* weaves the aquatic ape theory throughout the story of the research and discoveries of McCormick and his colleagues (fig. 3.2). For

Figure 3.1 A "mermaid" captured on a cell phone video, shown on Animal Planet's *Mermaids: The Body Found* (2012).

Figure 3.2 Illustration of the aquatic ape theory on *Mermaids: The Body Found.*

example, in one scene, designed to illustrate the intelligence, language, and social impulses that sustained the aquatic ape species, we see a merman father sacrifice his own life to save his family from a giant prehistoric shark.

The burning question is how the existence of such a creature could have remained unknown and out of the news until Animal Planet unveiled it. *Mermaids* offers two answers. First, the creature is clever and extremely elusive, having been hunted by humans for millennia, as cave paintings show. It was only the Navy's undiscriminating deep-water sonic blast that finally caught one off guard and brought it to light. Second, the U.S. Navy, supposing that the revelation of this new species would jeopardize its secret underwater weapons program, mounted a deliberate conspiracy to hide and deny it, impounding and destroying physical evidence that the scientists had found, even bullying the family of the two boys to make them recant their story of finding the creature on the beach (although fortuitously overlooking their cell-phone recording).

Mermaids is, of course, an elaborate hoax, propped up by fake evidence, a plausible but totally unfounded scientific hypothesis, professional actors hired to portray scientists (but uncredited, to perpetuate the ruse), and a colorful story that includes an astonishing and incredible find, plus a controversy and a cover-up. All of these tricks come straight out of P. T. Barnum's Feejee mermaid playbook. The only major difference is an "editor's note" on the program's website: "This two-hour special is science fiction based on some real events and scientific theory."[24] Apart from that little wink, Animal Planet presented *Mermaids* with a straight face as an actual documentary.

The reaction to this twenty-first-century humbug was surprisingly similar to what Barnum encountered 170 years earlier. Many viewers gushed and gossiped, apparently at least somewhat deceived, like those who tweeted "this is so crazy but makes so much sense!!" and "Yes! Im still tripping out but always knew it was trueRT."[25] Some were skeptical but curious, like a lad who wrote, "in this documentary they showed a video that was taken from a boys phone. . . . Now my father and i would like to know if this video is real i don't like to say we are suckers to everything we hear but i am open to new ideas."[26] The real National Oceanic and Atmospheric Administration received so many telephone queries about mermaids following the broadcast that it put up a special page on its website: "No evidence of aquatic humanoids has ever been found."[27] When they discovered the hoax, some viewers were angered or annoyed by what they perceived as a bait and switch, like those who tweeted "I feel so dumb" and "Thanks a lot history channel I think I just learned stuff but *animal planet*? Shame on you [expletives deleted]."[28] Scientists and scholars responded with particular irritation, partly at having real knowledge belittled, like one who blogged "way to denigrate scientists and the life we've dedicated ourselves to. I guess that big fancy Ph.D I have . . . was f'n pointless. I can just take an acting class online and make shit up."[29]

But the response that really mattered for the Discovery network, as for

Barnum, was audience draw. In that respect, the show "slayed," as an industry blog put it: more than 3.4 million viewers, who launched the Animal Planet channel to its most-watched week ever.[30] Propelled by this success, Animal Planet broadcast a sequel in 2013, *Mermaids: The New Evidence*, which once again smashed network records, drawing 3.6 million viewers.[31] A few months after that, Discovery Channel, the Discovery network's flagship channel, broadcast another fake documentary about the discovery of living specimens of an extinct prehistoric shark, *Megalodon: The Monster Shark That Lives*. Once again, the fake doc sent ratings through the roof: 4.8 million viewers. Many of these millions—71 percent, according to a post-broadcast poll by Discovery Channel—believed after watching the show that living megalodons still swim the seas.[32] Once again, critics slammed the nonfiction network for betraying the trust of its audience.

Critics' anger at Discovery is understandable but arguably misplaced. It is like blaming Kellogg's for putting too much sugar in its cereal. Discovery's foray into fakery was a response to market demand. This rationale may be perceived as a cynical excuse, particularly for a network whose mission is supposedly to inform and educate, but Discovery was clearly caught up in a trend. Over on the History Channel, for example, viewers were tuning in in large numbers to sensational pseudo-documentary series like *Ancient Aliens*, of which one science writer complained, "Fiction is presented as fact, and real scientific research is so grossly misrepresented that I can only conclude the producers are actively lying to viewers."[33] At Discovery, even top executives were uncomfortable with this trend. When asked in 2012 to reflect on the most negative development she had seen in the previous fifteen years, Discovery Channel president Eileen O'Neill replied, "Most concerning are producers who seem to be putting more of a premium on 'fiction' in the word 'non-fiction' and thus propelling unrealistic expectations on the programs."[34]

It is useful to step back here to consider the history of reality TV on the Discovery network. In 1999, before pitching *Survivor* to CBS, producer Mark Burnett brought it to Discovery. Discovery passed. Why? "The short answer," according to John Hendricks, the founder of Discovery and then CEO, is that "the series just seemed a bit too contrived for the real-world brand we'd cultivated for Discovery."[35] But it was clear that audiences loved reality TV and were flocking to other channels to see it, so Discovery introduced its own shows to keep pace—always, initially at least, with a deliberately wholesome twist. The standouts included *Monster Garage* (2002–2007), in which mechanics built monster machines that could transform from a car into a wood chipper, from a school bus into a pontoon boat, and so on. In *Mythbusters* (since 2003), two genial hosts use the scientific method to test popular beliefs and internet rumors, like whether using a cell phone near a gas pump can cause an explosion. *Dirty Jobs* (2005–2012) and *Deadliest Catch* (since 2005) both feature the hardships and pleasures of ordinary workers in unusual jobs. *Jon & Kate Plus 8* (2007–2017, just *Kate Plus 8* since Kate's divorce from Jon in 2009) follows the adventures and challenges of a family with both sextuplets and twins.

All of these shows are entertaining and at times actually informative. But with hundreds of reality shows playing on other channels, it was becoming increasingly hard to catch viewers' attention. Discovery turned to more sensationalism and exhibitionism, with shows like *Here Comes Honey Boo Boo* (2012–2014), about a poor Georgia family raising a child beauty pageant winner, and *Naked and Afraid* (since 2013), which strips the survival show to its bare essentials, so to speak. Discovery also dialed up the fakery, particularly with *Moonshiners* (since 2011), which uses Appalachian people to portray the lives and travails of illegal moonshiners.

From the perspective of Hendricks, Discovery's founder, these developments were not just sensible business choices, they "were in fact continuing the quest that has always been at the heart of our network—bringing knowledge TV to everyone. Even if the subject was, most controversially, a little six-year-old Atlanta beauty pageant phenomenon named Honey Boo Boo."[36] Hendricks conspicuously avoids any mention of how the outright fakery in *Mermaids* and *Megalodon* is supposed to contribute to "knowledge TV," but critic Adam Epstein states his situation sympathetically and succinctly:

> Striking the right balance between entertainment and education isn't easy. When you devolve into ridiculous cryptozoology, people will watch, but they surely won't be learning anything, and others will call you out hard for your lunacy. . . . At the same time, you can't just show hours and hours of sharks swimming in the ocean, with no dramatic tension or heightened stakes for the viewer. As cool as sharks are, that kind of footage is unlikely to captivate a broad base of viewers—and then you've got bigger problems than a few scientists on the internet complaining about the Megalodon.[37]

So it is hard to blame Discovery for its drift toward sensationalist storytelling. You can still blame the network for passing off fictional stories as factual ones. That is not storytelling, you may say; it is fraud. Still, like Barnum's Feejee mermaid, it proved to be a *popular* fraud. Even if audiences felt deceived, they watched it. More to the point, they did not watch once and walk away in disgust; they tuned in again for the sequels of both *Mermaids* and *Megalodon*. Both sequels got even higher ratings than the originals, even though by the time they aired most viewers had probably caught wind of the fakery. It seems that something about the fakery itself appealed to viewers.

It was into this context that *Amish Mafia* came into the world on Discovery Channel in December 2012: sandwiched between mermaids and megalodons. This larger context helps explain the kind of show it is. *Amish Mafia* looks a lot like *Here Comes Honey Boo Boo* in terms of how it is made, but it is in fact far closer to *Mermaids*: it is a fake reality TV show in much the same way that *Mermaids* is a fake documentary. To be sure, there are formal differences, given that it was faking a reality show instead of a documentary. For example, *Amish Mafia* hired ex-Amish as actors instead of using professional actors and called them by their actual names instead of made-up names. But in its deliberate use of familiar generic conventions to advance fictions as facts, *Amish Mafia* works just like *Mermaids*. It was, in a word, a hoax. All reality TV shows manipulate situations and fudge facts, but deliberate hoaxes are rare, and a hoax on the scale of *Amish Mafia* was unprecedented.

What *Amish Mafia* does, like the fake sea-creature documentaries, is invite viewers to test the boundaries of the believable. Again, as in the crafting of illusion described in a previous chapter, two levels are involved. First is the incredible story: mermaids, monster sharks, and gun-toting Amish. These do not just strain credulity; they also carry a hint of danger and secrecy that make them exciting. Plus, they violate conventional wisdom, which makes them more interesting still. So the response they invite is fascination, along with incredulity. This response tends to sweep viewers into the fiction, whether or not they are inclined to take it as fact.

The second level involves the believability of the discourse itself: Is the filmmaker telling the truth? Can the evidence be believed? Answering these questions requires scrutinizing the show for clues that what it presents is not what it seems. That takes a lot of effort—and distracts from the story—so viewers are not likely to do it unless they find the story totally implausible or something extremely fishy jumps out at them.

Viewers test the first level—the believability of the story—against things they know or think they know about the world. For example, only Amish and Mennonites drive buggies anymore, and it takes some skill to drive a buggy. So if you see somebody driving a buggy in *Amish Mafia*, there is a good chance it is really an Amish or Mennonite person. Viewers test the second level—the believability of the discourse—against things they know or think they know about similar discourses. For example, fictional television does not use interviews to tell a story because it can just *show* the story, so if you see a "talking head" in a TV show, the show is most likely nonfiction.

It is easy to see how a child would be taken in by a show like *Megalodon* or *Amish Mafia*. Children have less experience of the world to draw on, as well as less ability to think abstractly, than adults. Still, the fact that 71 percent of polled viewers of *Megalodon* believed after watching the show that members of the long-extinct species are still alive is surprising. It demonstrates that even ordinary adult viewers are lousy at testing the boundaries of the believable.

It is difficult to blame people for being deceived by *Megalodon*. For one thing, it is impossible to disprove the existence of something that does not exist. So if the existence of a megalodon is plausible (and it is common knowledge that giant sharks did swim the seas in prehistoric times) and if there is good reason to suppose that it might have escaped detection (indeed, most of the ocean is unexplored and new species continue to be discovered), then it is impossible to discredit claims to have seen one—unless one can discredit the claimant. And in this case that is difficult because *Megalodon* so effectively mimics a real documentary. It gives us little reason, on its face, to disbelieve it. It is a very good fake.

The same is true of *Amish Mafia*. It looks almost exactly like many other reality TV shows. The main difference is that it is a bit too good—cameras and mics are too conveniently placed, for example—but these features escape notice because they help advance the story, as chapter 1 explains. The fake is also appealing, since the idea of an Amish mafia is intriguing and makes for sensational stories. Finally, because the Amish mafia is supposed to be a secret group, the fakery is especially hard to prove. When I interviewed producer Eric Evangelista, he repeatedly asked me, "How do you *know* there is no Amish mafia?" The fact that the producer of *Megalodon* gave a similar reply to critics ("With 95% of the ocean unexplored, who really knows?") suggests that this response was preplanned.[38]

In January 2015 Rich Ross was named the new president of Discovery Channel and Animal Planet. He came off of a three-year stint as CEO of Shine America, the producer of *Big Brother*, *MasterChef*, and many other reality TV shows, plus several popular scripted series including *The Office*. Before that, he was the chairman of Disney Studios.

Ross's first public appearance in his new job was at the Television Critics

Association's semiannual press tour. The first question to Ross was about *Megalodon*. Would he be making more shows like that? "I don't think it's actually right for Discovery Channel," he replied. "And it's [a type of programming] that I think in some ways has run its course. I don't think you'll be sitting with me here next year asking me a question about something I put on—whether a series or a special—where that's the dilemma. They've done very well, many of them, but it's not something that's right for us."[39] I posed the question, previously, whether *Amish Mafia* was the leading edge of a new generation of reality TV or an outside boundary that reality TV approaches at its peril. This looks like a clue.

Meanwhile, on Discovery's sister channel TLC (The Learning Channel), Amish young adults (and one older woman—Mary Schmucker, the mother of one of the younger cast members, shunned by her community for agreeing to take part in the show) continued to tell made-for-TV stories about their lives on the reality TV show *Return to Amish*, written and produced by Evangelista and company. This raises another puzzle that this historical chapter needs to address: How is it that members of ordinarily media-averse and anti-celebrity Amish communities wound up being drawn into reality TV in the first place?

Celebrity Amish

The celebrity that comes from appearing in a show like *The Real World* or *Survivor* is typically modest and short-lived. It is the kind of fame that results in being recognized at airports and toasted at high school reunions until a year or two after a show ends. At best, for a select few, it leads to appearing on another reality TV show. For this reason, the term "reality TV star" usually carries at least a shade of irony. The heading "Celebrity Amish" is intended to carry that same irony, plus a more profound and trenchant irony.

Celebrity is antithetical to the Amish way of life. The reason the Amish dress alike is not just to telegraph their difference from the world, but to avoid the sin of pride, or *Hochmut*. Amish children are taught from a young age to avoid showing off or standing out, since these actions are counter to the spirit of modesty and community-mindedness that is central to Amish customs and beliefs. Singing among the Amish is not for show, as on *American Idol*; it is a way of bringing the community together. Higher education is forbidden not only because it promotes independence but also because it seems uppity. The green window shades in Amish homes are not just practical and simple; they are a way of avoiding decoration, which can easily become ostentatious.

The ban on photography is not mainly because of the biblical injunction against "graven images" but for the practical reason that having and looking at pictures of oneself or even just posing for pictures is narcissistic. In these and countless other ways, the ideal of humility and self-surrender, called *Gelassenheit*, lies at the center of Amish life and beliefs. The ideal of celebrity extolled by reality television is almost exactly the opposite. It revolves around self-presentation and self-advancement. Nothing could be further from *Gelassenheit*.

To be sure, self-interest is inevitable, even among the Amish. Amish young adults on rumspringa sometimes watch TV, including popular reality TV shows so, like most other Americans, they are vulnerable to the lure of celebrity. And *Gelassenheit* can chafe, particularly when it is imposed from outside by a stern patriarch or gossipy neighbors. Youth and young adults are particularly prone to feel this chafing. Many want to escape the confines of their community and experience the world. Some act out by buying fast cars, drinking excessively, and using drugs, and sometimes they get into trouble with the law as a result. Some, a small minority, leave their Amish communities and never return. Some members of that group harbor lingering anger and resentment because they were abused as children, or not given sufficient freedom as teenagers, or chastised for being gay, or for another such reason. It is from these three groups of young adults—the adventurous, the rebellious, and the disaffected—that almost all of the Amish participants of reality TV shows have been drawn.

The first Amish celebrity was a young man named Faron Yoder. He achieved TV celebrity inadvertently, by backing into it, as a result of appearing in the documentary *Devil's Playground* in 2002. Yoder was 18 at the time. He was smart, charming, outgoing, charismatic, talkative, and troubled—a serious methamphetamine addict. He likely had little idea of what he was getting into. *Amish Mafia* cast member Merlin Miller recalls bumping into the filmmaker, Lucy Walker, at an Amish party in Indiana. She was there with a friend, shooting with what looked like a home video camera. He says the two young filmmakers claimed to be filming a college project.[40]

In fact, Walker was shooting for HBO. At that point, in 1999, nobody was sure that a filmmaker could find any Amish willing to appear on camera. The producer who had pitched *Devil's Playground* to HBO, Steven Cantor, had tried to do that in Lancaster County for months without success, so he hired Walker to try her hand in the Amish community of LaGrange County, Indiana.[41] Walker found that the Amish young people there, as in Lancaster

County, had been "trained to keep their heads down, humble and invisible. . . . Of the few kids who would talk to us, very few wanted to be filmed, and fewer still could discuss themselves or their religion."[42] But she persisted. Eventually, at a hoedown, she bumped into Yoder. Yoder was by no means a typical Amish young man. In Walker's words:

> He stood out from the crowd with his Tupac swagger and twang. The next day we met again and he was mesmerizing. I didn't immediately catch on that he was high. Other kids were hesitant to describe what they ate for breakfast whereas Faron not only divvied up drugs on camera but shamelessly skimmed his dealer's cut too. He had an 'english' girlfriend and an escalating habit. But his ambition was to follow in his father's footsteps and become a minister. He could explain aspects of the religion that completely stumped everyone else. . . . That night I emailed Steven that I had found our star.[43]

Walker filmed among the Amish for two years. She studied the Bible; she talked to countless Amish people; some 100-hour weeks, she says, she scarcely took the camera out of the trunk. With her incredible perseverance, she pried the lid off the community of Amish young people. She proved that it was possible to find Amish and ex-Amish young adults who were willing to appear on camera. Cantor and his partner Daniel Laikind immediately proposed a new project: *Amish in the City*—a reality TV series along the lines of *The Real World*, in which five Amish and six mainstream American young adults would live together for a season in a house in Los Angeles, with outings for makeovers, adventures, competitions, and explorations of various religions.

To find Amish people willing to appear in *Amish in the City*, the producers hired five teams of two to live in Amish communities around the country. They put all of these scouts through an "Amish boot camp" to teach them how to approach Amish people without causing undue attention or suspicion. After two months of asking around, the teams managed to find a handful of people willing to take part in the show.[44] All of them had already left their Amish communities, so they were willing to appear on camera. For example, cast member Randy Stoll explained that he had moved from Montgomery, Indiana, to Sarasota, Florida—a major destination town for Amish youth seeking adventure. He initially lived there with his aunt but had been on his own for about two years, supporting himself doing construction work. When one of Laikind's talent scouts visited a local Amish restaurant, asking around to see who might be interested in taking part in a reality TV show, one of the staff members suggested Randy. Randy agreed to take part: "It sounded like a good time. Anybody would go for an opportunity to spend some time in L.A., wouldn't they?"[45] The problem was, none of the handful of ex-Amish youth the scouts had managed to turn up was particularly charismatic. They were not especially articulate about their thoughts and beliefs and not in the least given to the sort of navel gazing required by the "confessional" technique. As Laikind put it, "We just didn't have enough. We were still missing one character, someone who really could be the anchor of the show. We were missing our star."[46]

Mose Gingerich, a twenty-five-year-old former Amish schoolteacher from Wisconsin, then living in Columbia, Missouri, turned out to be that star. Gingerich, like Faron Yoder, was well suited to TV specifically because he was *not* typically Amish. In Laikind's words:

> Mose Gingerich was and is unlike any other Amish or ex-Amish person that I have ever met. . . . Mose asked questions. He wanted to know more. . . . The subject didn't matter; whether it was how something worked or why God chose his path, Mose didn't accept anything for what it was. . . . Mose was also able to articulate [his] feelings and excitement in ways that other Amish often struggle with. The Amish are taught to be humble, and they don't speak about themselves, so Mose's ability and desire to talk about his feelings was unique.[47]

It is because of these peculiar *non*-Amish qualities that Gingerich struck a chord with audiences, Laikind says. "Instantly, the public latched onto him. Mose was named one of *Entertainment Weekly's* 'Breakout Stars of the Year.' He appeared on *Good Morning America* and was interviewed by Diane Sawyer. He went on *Regis and Kelly*, *Jimmy Kimmel Live* and countless radio shows. Everyone wanted to talk to the Amish guy."[48]

Many Amish young folks watched *Amish in the City* enthusiastically. To some, like Merlin Miller, *Amish in the City* presented the possibility of television as a new avenue to break out, act out, make a little money, and, possibly, acquire a little fame—all while doing the service of educating a curious world about Amish customs and beliefs.[49]

Because of Gingerich's breakout success on *Amish in the City*, Laikind brought him back as the centerpiece of two subsequent reality TV shows produced for the National Geographic Channel: *Amish at the Altar* (2010) and *Amish: Out of Order* (2012). *Amish at the Altar* reenacted a traditional Amish wedding, with a married Amish couple from Lancaster County that had left the church. *Amish: Out of Order* followed Gingerich in the role of a self-appointed patron and guide for Amish young people who were leaving the church in and around Columbia, Missouri. Both of these shows cast Gingerich in a pivotal new reality TV role, in addition to being a star: that of uncredited producer or "fixer," charged with wrangling acquaintances and relatives to serve as cast members and extras. It was *Amish at the Altar* that also gave *Amish Mafia* star Alan Beiler his big break into reality TV as a fixer.

Since *Amish in the City*, just about every Amish reality TV star has in addition played the official or unofficial role of fixer on the side. *Amish Mafia* star Merlin Miller became a fixer, along with Beiler, for both *Amish Mafia* and *Breaking Amish*. *Amish Mafia* star Esther Schmucker introduced her cousin Abe to Evangelista. Abe was cast as one of the stars of *Breaking Amish*. He subsequently brought into the picture his mother Mary, who brought her daughters, and so on. All of the casting of Amish and ex-Amish in reality TV shows has relied to a large extent upon the luxuriant and tangled Amish grapevine, which includes family ties, far-flung rumspringa adventures to places like Sarasota, Florida, and in recent years, Facebook.

Breaking Amish

Before 2012 every Amish-themed reality show was pretty much what it seemed. *Devil's Playground* was a real documentary, and a good one. It revealed an aspect of actual Amish society that had never before been seen.[50] *Amish in the City* was a conventional reality TV show—a straight-up knock-off of *The Real World*. Critics both praised and criticized the show for the similarity.[51] *Amish: Out of Order* followed Mose Gingerich around as he talked to other ex-Amish people. *Amish at the Altar* revolved around the re-creation of an Amish wedding, with non-Amish extras playing the part of Amish people (including ex-Mennonite Sabrina High, who went on to become one of the stars of *Breaking Amish*), but the show did not pretend to be anything other than a re-creation. In 2012 that changed, largely courtesy of the Discovery network. That year brought *Mermaids* and *Amish Mafia*. It also brought Evangelista's *Breaking Amish*.

Breaking Amish is a reality TV show in the tradition of *The Real World*. In its first season, the show follows five ex-Amish young adults to New York City, where they experience new things like tattoos, makeovers, and the Manhattan Museum of Sex; squabble and deal with demons from their past; and lie to and fall in love with each other. The second season follows the same group to Sarasota, Florida. The third and fourth seasons, subtitled "Return to Amish," take the group to rural Punxsutawney, Pennsylvania, where Abe Schmucker's family lives, with side trips to New York where another cast member is pursuing a modeling career. Single-season *Breaking Amish* spinoffs take other groups of ex-Amish young people to Los Angeles (in 2013) and Brooklyn, New York (in 2014). Like *The Real World*, *Breaking Amish* is reality soap opera. Unlike *The Real World*, the main show follows the same cast over several seasons, going deeper and deeper into their lives.

Shortly after the start of the series, the gossip blog *Jezebel* published an exposé that begins as follows:

> When *Breaking Amish* premiered on TLC last month, it was described by the network as an unscripted series about a group of Amish people "leaving their communities for the first time"; the cameras purportedly followed their first experiences with electricity, cell phones, indoor plumbing, and cars. But recent court documents, arrest records and Facebook profiles prove that not only had the cast members left the religion for the secular world years ago. Two of them—who claim on the show to have just met—actually have a child together. Furthermore, family members of the cast who are speaking out about how the show is fake claim that TLC is trying to buy their silence.[52]

I will not address the question of what part of *Breaking Amish* is made up. Suffice it to say that plenty is. The pretense that ex-Amish young people are discovering cell phones and indoor plumbing for the first time is absurd. Much of what is supposed to be Punxsutawney was actually shot in and around a rented farmhouse in Lancaster County. *Breaking Amish* is clearly planned out in dramatic beats, just like *Amish Mafia*. In terms of the mechanics of production, it is also much the same. But in one respect it is crucially different: in *Breaking Amish*, the cast members are playing themselves; in *Amish Mafia*, they are pretending to be gangsters and their associates—people *like* themselves in some respects, with the same names and biographical details, but fictional characters nonetheless.

When cast members of *Breaking Amish* do things just for the show, like wander around Manhattan in Amish garb, they are for the most part being themselves in an artificial situation; in *Amish Mafia*, when cast members do things such as staking out a fake philandering Amishman, they are pretending to be someone they are not. Viewers may not pick up on this distinction, at least not consciously, but it makes an important difference, as best illustrated by the significance of shunning in the two shows. In *Amish Mafia*, all of the discussion of shunning is "just pretend." There is no way Lebanon Levi will actually be shunned because he never joined the Amish church. The same is true for all of the other cast members. In *Breaking Amish*, however, when the older Amish woman Mary Schmucker is shunned by her community for agreeing to take part in the show, the shunning and its consequences are real. They did not stop when the cameras stopped rolling. Mary Schmucker is the only Amish person with a significant role in any of the reality shows discussed here who is not one of those groups of young adults described earlier: the adventurous, the rebellious, and the disaffected. She is a real, traditional, ordinary, established Amish housewife, with an Amish husband and family. Because of that, her shunning continued to make her life difficult, even when the show ended.

As actors well know, there is a continuum between being yourself in an imaginary situation and pretending to be someone else. It is impossible to put a finger precisely on where the divide between the two occurs. Because of this, it would be pointless to engage in a debate about whether or not *Breaking Amish* is categorically like or unlike *Amish Mafia*. I would say that there is a difference between fakery that is a means to an end (a way of telling a better story, for example) and fakery that is an end in itself (a deliberate part of the entertainment) and that *Breaking Amish* and *Amish Mafia* clearly tend to fall on different sides of this divide. Again, however, the point at which the divide occurs is impossible to specify. One reason is that it involves the intentions of the producers, and, as I pointed out at the start of this chapter, Evangelista's intentions are not mainly rhetorical or aesthetic; they are commercial. His purpose is not to make either a fake reality TV show or a real one; it is to attract and hold audiences' attention and to abide by the requirements of distributors. The only clear and definitive difference about *Amish Mafia*, therefore, is the boldness and bravura of its fakery. It is for this reason that I have singled it out for scrutiny.

Lessons from the Past

As a discourse—that is, as a form of mediated social interaction—reality television has countless moving parts: story, sensation, celebrity, intimacy, ideology, fantasy, illusion, reality, artifice, and on and on. The purpose of this chapter and the previous one has been to try to pin down just one of these, fake reality as entertainment, by looking at where it came from. Several answers have emerged.

First, fakery exercises its own appeal, different from the appeal of what is faked. This was Barnum's discovery. A real mermaid would be a marvel. An obviously artificial mermaid might be interesting as a curiosity or fantasy but is otherwise no big deal. But if you make an artificial mermaid look real, provide convincing testimony to its reality, and come up with a plausible backstory for it, you can get people to really sit up and take notice, even if—*especially* if—they do not entirely believe you. You have created a fascinating puzzle.

The puzzle has two levels. One is the puzzle of the *existence* of the thing. Might mermaids truly exist? Might this be one? Note that for this puzzle to succeed, what is presented must be marvelous or peculiar. Nobody would be puzzled by a stuffed opossum—unless it had two heads. The sensational aspects of *Amish Mafia*—the guns and extortion, the witchcraft, the school for sex, and so on—all serve to magnify the marvelous and peculiar, mostly by making things up. The second puzzle, a social puzzle, concerns the *presentation* of the thing. Might the presenter be lying? If so, how and why? Note that for this puzzle to work, the audience must be suspicious. A viewer who totally believes the made-up story of the mermaid without suspicion will miss out on this level of the pleasure of the show.

Again and again, we have encountered these two distinct levels. I will call them the pleasure of the *story* (the narrative about the Amish mafia) and the pleasure of the *show* (the narrative—often implicit—about filming members of the group and their activities). An example of the first is the story of catching an Amish leader visiting a prostitute. Examples of the second are the jiggly camerawork and the blurred-out faces in that scene. Fakery in *Amish Mafia*, when it is perceived or discussed, is entirely bound up with the second pleasure—the pleasure of the *show*. That is another important takeaway of this chapter. To put it in concrete terms, some viewers may enjoy *Amish Mafia* while assuming it to be true from top to bottom. They may enjoy the show without ever questioning its authenticity. They are marks. Such naive and innocent souls (if they actually exist) entirely miss out on the pleasure of being a "smart fan"—the pleasure of seeing through the artifice, looking for sleights of hand, wondering about the extent to which marvelous scenes are made up, and gossiping about whether Lebanon Levi really is Amish. These viewers comprehend the *story* without getting the *show*. *Amish Mafia* tells an unusual *story*, to be sure, about the exploits and trials of a group of Amish gangsters, but it is the nature of the *show* more than the topic of the story—specifically, the deliberately deceptive presentation of fabulous stories as factual—that distinguishes *Amish Mafia* from other reality TV shows, as well as from documentary films and TV news.

Historically, this kind of show may be linked to particular periods when producers need more than a fabulous story to stand out from the crowd of fabulous stories (especially if they are on a budget) and when popular audiences are especially inclined to question received wisdom—periods like Barnum's and our own.

This brings us back to the *business* of reality TV. We have seen how economic concerns drive producers' formal and aesthetic choices in top-down fashion. Looking at the business of TV from the bottom up, from the consumer's point of view, it may be helpful to think of watching TV as a commercial transaction: the viewer's time and attention is exchanged for the "goods" delivered by a show. The particular goods of television vary: epic fantasy in the case of *Game of Thrones*, melodrama and intrigue in the case of *Days of Our Lives*, information about current events in the case of the evening news, and so on. In reality TV one of the main "goods" is seeing people in situations where they are (or appear to be) at risk: genuinely vulnerable and exposed to the vicissitudes of life and the vagaries of producers.

With most TV shows, including most reality TV shows, the nature of the exchange is transparent and the transaction fairly straightforward. The experience for viewers is a lot like picking a box of cereal off the grocery shelf. The ingredients are on the box. Producers compete with each other, but their goal is to give particular audiences more of the ingredients they want and expect. Their relationship with viewers is cooperative. But with *Amish Mafia* (along with Barnum's humbugs, Discovery's documentary hoaxes, and possibly a handful of other reality TV shows), the producer and the viewer appear to be engaged in a different kind of transaction: a somewhat adversarial one involving deception and distrust. The ingredients on the box are deliberately misleading. Indeed, a bizarre feature of *Mermaids* and *Megalodon*—part of the hoax—is that the professional actors who play the role of scientists do not receive acting credits, while those who play their doubles in scenes labeled "dramatic re-creations" do. In *Amish Mafia*, nobody receives an acting credit. None of the ex-Amish fixers receives a production credit either. The upshot of the misleading labeling of ingredients, not just in the credits but throughout the show, is that, for viewers, engaging in the transaction is more akin to buying a used car than buying a box of cereal.

A used-car salesperson has information that a prospective buyer does not have. He may reveal this information opportunistically, or he may hide it and make up false information in order to represent the car as better than it actually is (presuming that the seller is both a "he" and stereotypically sleazy). The wise buyer, suspecting deception, will kick the tires and check under the hood to gather her own information. In the information game, she is always at a disadvantage. The only advantage she has is the power to walk away. But if she really wants the car, she will have to eventually arrive at a sufficient level of trust to make the purchase.

This is a far-from-perfect analogy, of course. For one thing, whereas it takes a peculiar sort of masochist to enjoy buying a used car, a lot of people enjoyed *Amish Mafia*. The analogy also does not take repeat sales into account. A used-car salesperson who deceives a customer is unlikely to enjoy repeat business from the same customer. But we know from the success of the sequels of *Mermaids* and *Megalodon* that people who have been tricked by one fake nonfiction TV show often do come back for another. So, to stretch the used-car analogy past its breaking point, it is as though the interior of the car is so plush and its sound system so great that the buyer does not care that the car has no transmission. It is this conundrum that the next chapter takes up.

One other "moral" of this chapter merits emphasis. The business of reality TV does not just involve producers and consumers; it involves subjects too. Reality-based television turns real people into commodities—people like the Loud family and Faron Yoder and Mose Gingerich and Mary Schmucker, as well as "Lebanon" Levi Stoltzfus. Granted, the participants in *Amish Mafia* all agreed to be on TV. They all signed releases. Most of them got paid for their trouble. And maybe Levi *deserves* a bit of trouble for consenting to play the part of an Amish gangster and helping to deceive audiences. Just the same, having grown up Amish, none of the ex-Amish cast members of *Amish Mafia,* including Levi, had a very clear idea of what they were getting into. Merlin and Mary told me that, though they learned things and had an interesting adventure, taking part in the show also brought them considerable unhappiness and pain.

It is easy to point an outraged finger at the producers, at Discovery Channel and Eric Evangelista. But remember, those producers are ultimately working for *you.* Their role in the system is to make shows that TV viewers want to watch. That is by no means an excuse for lying to or manipulating cast members. It does, however, implicate audiences in the business of turning real people into commodities. I will return to this topic in chapter 6. In the meantime, it is important to remember that Lebanon Levi and Mary Schmucker and the other "stars" of reality TV shows are not just characters on TV; they are real people whose on-camera roles have real and unpredictable consequences for their off-camera lives. They really *are* at risk.

CHAPTER FOUR

The Pleasure in Being Deceived
(and Its Limits)

Anything Is Possible

"Mackenzie" was a big fan of *Amish Mafia*. (The names of the *Amish Mafia* fans in this chapter are fictional; their circumstances and words are not.) Mackenzie describes reality TV as her hobby. She watches a lot of it, avidly and unashamedly, and says she prefers it to scripted programming. She enjoys reading about reality TV stars in popular magazines and talking about reality TV shows with her friends. She is what television scholars call an *ideal* reality TV viewer. In other words, she is the kind of viewer reality TV producers have in mind when they make reality TV shows. Their shows, when they hit their mark, hit her.

This is by no means to suggest that Mackenzie is an easy mark—a viewer who is easily duped. On the contrary, one of the things that makes her an ideal viewer is that she is quite knowledgeable about reality TV. She knows that much of it is contrived. Back when she started watching reality TV in the early days of *The Real World*, she says, "that was *real* TV." Nowadays, "there's so much that they are just creating. Like, yes, they record people in their natural surroundings, but then they say, 'Come on, we need a catfight here, so start pulling each other's hair.' "[1] Mackenzie believes that producers on many shows routinely "script things" because they have "worn out the fun" of just observing reality. The reason she watches and enjoys reality shows, she says, is not because she believes they are real but because she finds the characters interesting and the situations compelling.

Take *Amish Mafia*. Mackenzie remembers when she started watching the show. "It was comical to me because I could not imagine the Amish carrying around these automatic rifles. Could it happen? Maybe. But to me it was funny. It was kind of like a train wreck that I had to watch, just because it seemed so far-fetched." I asked, What if she were to learn that the stars were pretending to be people they are not? "I wouldn't care," she replied. "It's good TV. I'm interested in it and I enjoy it. So it doesn't matter to me whether they really are actors or who they are." Indeed, Mackenzie claims that she assumed from the start that Lebanon Levi was "just somebody that Discovery Channel went out and found and said, 'Let's put on a show.'"

When I showed Mackenzie particular scenes, however, she admitted to being confused about what is real and what is not, even after having watched all four seasons of the show. She was not at all sure about the scene, described in chapter 1, showing an Amish leader caught with a prostitute. "It's been a while, but now it is coming back to me and I'm remembering . . . I just didn't know whether it was something I could truly believe. I just didn't know if that was real or if it was made up. . . . This [scene] is funny to me because I feel like it is an exaggeration of what might really happen in the Amish community, but I just can't imagine this stuff happening." As for the particulars, like the Amish elder with the blurred-out face, "That could be anybody dressed up in an Amish outfit. Well, part of me thinks that and part of me doesn't. I'm kind of torn between whether it's real or fake." Furthermore, Mackenzie admits that curiosity about what is real is part of what compels her attention. "I want to know, is it real? Does it really exist? Are they doing this show and the elders don't know about it? That kind of stuff makes me want to keep watching."

If some aspects of the show are real, I ask Mackenzie, how does that help make the show entertaining? She has trouble answering. "I never really thought about why I enjoy these shows. When I go for reality TV, it's a way I can live in another . . . I'm not just a preschool teacher and mom . . . like I can go into the world of . . . whatever." How is that different from a scripted soap opera like *Days of Our Lives*? "Soap operas are kind of like, you know, a guy falls down an elevator shaft and is decapitated and is dead, and ten years later he comes back to life because he wasn't really dead. . . . In real life, if someone is decapitated, they're dead."

Lauren is another long-time reality TV fan. She had an eye-opening encounter with *Amish Mafia* that profoundly changed the way she thinks about reality TV, even though it had little impact on the way she watches it. Lauren is in her sixties. Like Mackenzie, she watches a lot of reality TV and has for decades. She retired to Lancaster County five years ago from Wyoming and brought with her a couple of horses, which she rides and tends to daily at a stable in the southern part of the county. Not long after Lauren started using the stable, *Amish Mafia* started using it too, to shoot parts of several episodes.[2]

Even before observing *Amish Mafia*'s production, Lauren entertained no illusions about the so-called reality of reality TV. She describes herself as "a pretty good expert on reality TV" and knows that a lot of it is made up. Still, she was astonished by the extent of the fakery she saw on the *Amish Mafia* set: "Amish" cast members rolling up in cars and then changing from their street clothes to Amish clothes; producers giving characters story scenes to act out and coaching them on how to make their dialog believable; stable hands and other bystanders dressed up and passed off as Amish; Lancaster County locations presented as being in Ohio; and more. She was taken aback. You don't have to do that, she thought. Mainly, though, she was amused: "There was a lot of misleading going on, but it doesn't really matter."

Ultimately, Lauren explains, reality TV viewers do not care whether a show's particulars are true or false: "If it keeps your interest, you just go with it." What matters is the *impression* of reality—a viewing experience that reminds you of your own reality, or maybe your fantasies of reality. "Everybody likes to think that something's real. Like on *The Bachelor* and *The Bachelorette*, you know you believe that because you *want* to believe that people find each other and end up getting married, and that *is* real. There are always parts that maybe aren't real, but that's life! It's all in your perception of what's real and what isn't real," Lauren says. "Certain things you just can't believe. Certain things you go, 'Hmmm, well, that's good.' If you decide, Well, none of this is real, then you don't give it a chance. Then you just don't watch it."

But, I ask, aren't there different levels of reality in reality TV? Isn't *Amish Mafia* different in its treatment of reality from, say, *Keeping Up with the Kardashians*? "You watch that show because you just go, 'Oh my God I can't *believe* these people!'" Lauren replies. But the "can't believe" has to do with characters' behavior, not with whether or not the show is scripted. "The show is just amusing because those people are so filthy rich you want to see if they actually have any value of what is good or important in life." Granted, she says, *Keeping Up with the Kardashians* has become "less believable, if you want to put it that way—some of the plots just got a little more incredible or outlandish or boring . . . just not interesting." The same thing happened with *Amish Mafia*. "There were a lot of explosions and fires and things that were over the top." But with respect to the so-called reality of any reality TV show,

"If you go in thinking 'This is all real,' then you find out it's not, I suppose you will get a little upset. It just depends how seriously you take it. I don't take things really seriously. I mean, why would you? You watch things just to be entertained." That is how most people watch reality TV, Lauren says: to kick back, to relax, to turn off the critical faculties, to be entertained.

What about TV news? I ask incredulously. Surely people don't watch TV news that way. "Are you kidding me?" Lauren replies, laughing. "I want to believe the news is real but I'm never 100 percent sure." Do you suppose, I ask, that such skepticism and indifference might be a symptom of too much reality TV? "I don't want to believe it," Lauren says, "but it's possible. You know, *anything* is possible." That, she suggests, is the basic appeal of reality TV: the *possibility* that what you see on the screen is real.

You Can't Believe Everything People Tell You

I have three reasons for relating these conversations with Mackenzie and Lauren. The first is simply to observe that every viewer (indeed, every viewing instance) is somewhat peculiar, shaped by specific circumstances and interests. Tastes differ, among other things. Mackenzie gravitates to the sort of reality TV show that airs on Bravo: "Bravo's my channel; it does a lot of glamorous real life, like the *Real Housewives* franchise and *Shahs of Sunset,* about rich Persians living in Los Angeles." Lauren's go-to channel is the home-and-garden channel HGTV: "I don't know why I'm hooked on it, but I'll always just go there if I can't find anything else to watch." According to a popular saying, there is no accounting for taste.

There must in fact be some accounting. Both Mackenzie and Lauren say they prefer reality TV to scripted programming. The so-called reality of the shows must have something to do with this preference, even though neither Mackenzie nor Lauren can quite pin down what that particular appeal is. Whatever it is, it is built into reality TV shows. It is part of the way they are made. That is why an ideal viewer is a useful analytical concept: it allows scholars to tease out the formal features of shows or genres that are *intended* to target different kinds of viewers. For instance, the tough-guy protagonists and action sequences of *Amish Mafia* are intended to appeal to male audiences. In contrast, the domestic dramas and romantic intrigues of *Breaking Amish* are intended to attract typical female viewers. The producer of both shows, Eric Evangelista, acknowledges this. Mackenzie recognizes it too. Indeed, one of the reasons she enjoyed *Amish Mafia* is that she could get her husband to watch it with her. Another peculiar reason she enjoyed the show is that, as a resident of Lancaster County, she thought she might catch glimpses of places she recognized. People watch reality TV for many different reasons. Thus, as a methodological matter, if you want to find out about the impact of "reality" in a show like *Amish Mafia*, it is not enough to look at its formal features or put it into historical context; you need to talk to actual viewers. There is no getting around that.

Unfortunately, talking to viewers does not necessarily yield reliable answers. This is the second purpose for relating my conversations with Mackenzie and Lauren. The reasons viewers give for responding to reality TV in particular ways are not the real reasons—not because viewers are not telling the truth but because they do not actually know what is going on in their heads when they watch reality TV. Consider Mackenzie's answer to my question about whether it mattered to her if the characters in *Amish Mafia* were just actors. Not at all, she said at first, quite decisively. Later, when I showed her a clip, she said, Yes, it does kind of matter. Why? Simple curiosity, she said: "I want to know, is it real? . . . Are they doing this show and the elders don't know about it?" But the truest answer is one Lauren gave at one point: "I don't really know why I watch these shows."

It has been well established that people do not actually know why they think and act the way they do, even when they think they know. The vast majority of what goes on in our heads is automatic, not susceptible to direct scrutiny—behind the scenes, as it were. When we think and do things it is generally just because, under the circumstances, those seem like the things to think and do. When asked to explain or justify our thoughts and behavior, we take a mental step back to reflect upon our actions and assess our emotional responses, and then we infer or invent some causal or verbal explanation that feels plausible and fitting. If I ask you why you love your sweetheart, you might say, "Because she (or he) is spunky and has a great smile." In truth, all sorts of factors are involved, including chemistry, that you cannot possibly know through introspection, much less verbally explain. The spunk and the smile are just rationalizations that feel right.[3] So too when Mackenzie tells me, of *Amish Mafia*, "It was kind of like a trainwreck that I had to watch, just because it seemed so far-fetched." It takes a lot of mental effort to come up with such explanations, so people do not typically offer them unless compelled, as when someone prods them with questions. And, as many reality TV fans told me, the main reason they watch reality TV in the first place is to kick back, to relax, to escape the travails of the workaday world, to "veg out"—precisely to *avoid* expending a lot of mental effort. So when viewers offer explanations of why they respond to reality TV in particular ways, their responses need to be taken with at least a grain of salt.

Even though viewers do not know what is going on in their heads when they watch reality TV, they *do* know what they enjoy, what puts them off, and how they feel when they watch particular things. They are in a better position than anybody else to observe their own behavior and assess their emotional responses. Though we cannot take their explanations at face value, we can credit their *descriptions* of their responses. Still, making sense of their descriptions requires careful analysis and reverse engineering. So when somebody says (as did both Mackenzie and Lauren), "I don't believe this," we need to figure out whether they mean "I don't believe it is factual," "I find it scandalous," "I don't find it engaging," or something else. We need to prod a bit, to poke around in their responses. Above all, we need to look for patterns, which are most revealing of systemic and causal connections. If a lot of people respond in the same way—laugh at a scene or find it unbelievable—that is a strong indication that something in the scene tends to prompt such a response.

This brings me to the third reason for relating my conversations with Mackenzie and Lauren. In the responses compiled from lengthy interviews with a number of *Amish Mafia* fans, including Mackenzie and Lauren, certain striking and revealing patterns do pop out. First, everybody assumes that the show includes a good deal of fakery. They assume that scenes are selected, shot, and edited to create sensation and drama. They assume that characters are coached. Furthermore, they are all quite confident of their ability to recognize fakery when they see it.

Their touchstone is plausibility. If something strikes viewers as implausible, they see it as false or contrived. Mackenzie found scenes of Jolin with a lot of guns "funny" and "far-fetched" for the simple reason that they did not square with her mental image of the Amish. In contrast, if viewers find something plausible, they tacitly treat it as true. This does not necessarily mean they *believe* it is true; they simply do not question whether it is true or not. Mackenzie found it quite plausible that an Amishman might visit a prostitute. From this, she extrapolated that such things do in fact happen and that the scene of an Amishman caught in the act was based upon, or possibly even captured, such an actual incident. She didn't question the scene at all. Indeed, she was oblivious to the incongruities in the scene until I called them to her attention.

This kind of obliviousness is typical. It is also remarkable, in light of viewers' knowledge of reality TV fakery and their confidence in their ability to spot it. The *Amish Mafia* fans I spoke to have no trouble finding holes in plotlines that point to fabrication, when they are asked to. They know enough about camera angles and editing to recognize inconsistencies that indicate fakery, when those are pointed out. They are oblivious to such things not because they are incapable of seeing them but simply because they do not pay attention to them.

This lack of attention does not indicate of lack of interest. In fact, all of the fans I spoke to took great delight in speculating about what was true and false in *Amish Mafia*. Is there actually a gang of Amish with guns? Who are Levi and Esther, really? Was the scene with the prostitute staged? This kind of question fascinated them. Mackenzie was eager to tell me what she knew about the Amish, Lauren took pleasure in dishing about her behind-the-scenes experience, and all of the fans were curious about what I could tell them about the show's fabrication.

This evidence suggests that there are two different ways of engaging with *Amish Mafia* (and, presumably, with other reality TV shows). One is to relax and enjoy and not worry about whether what you see is real—to just *watch* it. Plausibility helps, because it provides a point of engagement—you can think about how scenes relate to your own real-world knowledge and experience. But implausibility is okay too, so long as you find it fascinating or funny. As Lauren put it, "I don't take things really seriously. I mean, why would you? You watch things just to be entertained." The second way of engaging with *Amish Mafia* is as something to *talk about*. The operative frame of mind here seems to be, to quote Lauren again, "Oh my God, I can't *believe* these people!" This frame of mind involves skepticism and critical distance, on the one hand, but also a certain openness to the possible reality of the sensational, on the other. It appears to be more interested in speculation than in definitive answers.

These patterns of engagement—the assumption of fakery but general obliviousness to specific instances; the tacit treatment of plausible scenarios as true; the avoidance of effort and the elevation of entertainment; the two modes of enjoyment, watching and talking about—all of these suggest that "reality" does indeed factor into the appeal of reality TV (at least of *Amish Mafia*) but in subtle and complicated ways, ways that Mackenzie and Lauren point to but cannot quite put their finger on.

Industry Insights

The Discovery network has an extensive stable of audience researchers working in departments like Audience Insights, Consumer Behavior, and Strategic Research. These researchers know quite a lot about the viewers of *Amish Mafia* and Discovery's other reality shows. They won't tell you though. At least they wouldn't tell me. That information, I was informed, is "proprietary."

Fortunately, audience researcher Dan McDonald was willing to share his knowledge. At the time, Dan was executive director of programming and consumer research at National Geographic Channel and had been doing TV audience research for 22 years. An important part of his job at National Geographic was to keep an eye on audience trends in the entire "nonfiction space," which includes the Discovery network and reality TV shows on other channels. He went on to become vice president of research for the National Association of Broadcasters. So he knows the business well.

In 2010 and 2012 National Geographic Channel broadcast a couple of its own shows about the Amish: *Amish at the Altar*, which reenacted an Amish wedding, and *Amish: Out of Order*, in which former *Amish in the City* star Mose Gingerich mentors Amish young people in the process of leaving the church. McDonald resisted calling these shows reality TV. He said:

> Reality is a bit of a loaded word in our industry. Typically when you talk about quote-unquote reality programming, you are talking about female-skewing, character-led programming like *The Kardashians* on E! and the *Real Housewives* franchise on Bravo, where they are casting groups of people and setting them up in scripted scenarios to see how they react and mostly, you know, act poorly. That's certainly not what's done on National Geographic. I won't tell you that our programming is 100 percent as-you-see-it television, because there is no such thing, but it's probably 90 percent as-you-see-it television.[4]

"Nat Geo" is something of an outlier in the industry in another way, McDonald told me. When he talks to colleagues who work for scripted entertainment channels, they report that what drives viewer interest is mainly characters. People tune into shows mainly to see fascinating people. This is also true for most of what plays on nonfiction channels like Discovery and History. It is true even of Animal Planet's animal shows, like *River Monsters*, which focus on the hosts of the show. Viewers of National Geographic Channel, in contrast, are most interested in "process." For instance, *Amish at the Altar* demonstrated the process of an Amish wedding. It staged a wedding using non-Amish stand-ins and ex-Amish explainers, but it created no artificial drama and it never pretended to show an actual Amish wedding, since that kind of pretense would have violated what viewers want and expect from the National Geographic brand.

To understand McDonald's insights into reality TV audiences, it helps to understand what he and his staff do. "If I would give you the mission statement," he says, "it is that we speak for the viewer. It's our job to translate all of the data that makes up our industry currency into meaningful insights so that we can produce better programming to attract more viewers." In other words, his job is to figure out what viewers want and then to explain that to programmers and producers so they can make more of it. To be clear, this is not actually about advocating for viewers; it is about figuring out how to corral them in order to deliver them to advertisers.

The day-to-day work of McDonald and his staff consists largely of poring over data about who watches their shows and how those people spend their money, because that is the information that advertisers want. Nielsen ratings are the main source of the data—the "industry currency" to which McDonald refers. "This is gold-standard measurement. You're talking about a survey of 40,000 households, derived through area probability, using door-to-door in-person recruiting that generates daily response rates of fifty percent and higher. It is a very rich database that goes beyond age and gender to tell you all sorts of things about your viewers, in terms of who they are, where they live, education, income, ethnicity." This information is often combined with consumer purchasing data. National Geographic also subscribes to syndicated services such as Q Scores, which poll large numbers of people to track the familiarity and appeal of celebrities, brands, and shows.

The art of McDonald's job is turning all this data into guidance for program developers and producers. This is challenging because it is not just the qualities of a show that determine its success, but the competitive environment. "If we put you in a room, you'll like a show," McDonald says. "Our producers are very good. But when you air it with 189 other channels as well as people with DVRs, Hulu, and so on, you really don't know if a show's going to work." Plus, the landscape keeps shifting. "We do have an idea of what has worked on our channel in the past, but all it takes is one outsized hit to radically change expectations not just for your channel but for the entire television industry. So, from a research perspective, we are always looking for 'Huh, I never thought of it that way' or 'I've never seen something like that!'"

While the quantitative data provides lots of information about who watches a show, it says little about why. That is the information producers and marketers need to attract audiences. To help answer the why question, McDonald and his staff study social media responses to shows and use focus groups. For the focus groups, they will hire ten or twelve ordinary people, typically from a show's target audience, have them watch a pilot or episode as a group, then ask them questions to prompt responses and conversation. Usually these questions have to do with program content. Are you interested in the topic of this show? Do you like the characters? Are some parts less interesting than others? Why?

The questions at the heart of this book concern the appeal of "reality" in reality TV. What is it? Why does it matter to viewers? Can and do viewers see through fakery? McDonald and his researchers rarely explore these questions with viewers. Their main concern is why viewers *like* a show. That is what drives ratings. McDonald's perception, from interacting with many viewers over many years, is that it is the content of a show that determines whether viewers like it—such things as characters, story, and process. The methods by which that content is derived—staging, scripting, or whatever—have little to do with it.

The reason that National Geographic Channel shuns scripted and artificial reality TV is merely a matter of brand identity. Viewers expect authenticity and credibility from National Geographic. It is part of what gives their channel its special niche in the industry. It would be bad for business to disregard this niche appeal, even in the interest of higher ratings for one or two particular shows. McDonald believes the Discovery network drew the same conclusion after its *Mermaids* and *Megalodon* experiments. He thinks that is why *Amish Mafia* was canceled too, since the show still had strong ratings for a reality TV show, even in its last year.

McDonald does not think that the possibility of being taken in or deceived by the artifice of *Amish Mafia* is a significant issue, at least not for the typical viewer. "The show is *obviously* scripted. Our understanding of the viewership is that many many more people were in on the joke as opposed to believing that it is a true story." Even dwelling on a show's artifice in order to puzzle it out does not hold much interest for viewers, he supposes:

> Viewers are very smart, but they don't think about programming as hard as you and I are right now. They found *Amish Mafia* an enjoyable experience, with outrageous characters, and yeah, maybe they picked up some insight into Amish life, but our understanding is that for the most part viewers were just looking

for an enjoyable viewing experience. They did not believe the show was on the up and up. They just went along for the ride.

In chapter 1 I explained how the mind works to organize stories and impressions into a coherent whole and how selective attention tends to simply overlook details that do not fit. McDonald believes that a similar process is at work in terms of what viewers *like*. "Viewers are smart. They enjoy what they enjoy and are going to make excuses when they see obvious holes in an unscripted program that they enjoy. If they see elements that are staged, they'll either rationalize it by saying they don't care or they'll just go completely 'meta' and say, 'Well of course it's scripted and I still don't care.'" Viewers understand that reality TV shows are artificial, he says. They just do not dwell on the artifice because it is not what interests them. If it serves to enhance the things they enjoy—interesting characters, stories, and processes—they welcome it. All that matters is that a show *feels* true to them, that it follows people they can relate to in the kind of situations they can imagine encountering in their day-to-day lives.

Seeing Is Believing

Amish Mafia fans Mackenzie and Lauren claim they are well aware that reality TV is highly artificial and assert that they do not really care, so they feel immune to possible deception. If they do happen to be deceived by something in the show, they say, it does not really matter. It is all part of the fun. Industry analyst Dan McDonald claims that reality is not what reality TV viewers tune in to see anyway. They tune in to see characters, stories, and processes. Consequently, they will gladly accept any sort of contrivance so long as it plausible and enjoyable. The supposedly real people and situations in reality TV are useful from a programming perspective, he says, because they are relatable, not because they are real.

Reality in reality TV is just a veneer, all of these respondents are suggesting—a fiction that everybody embraces because it is entertaining. Eric Evangelista, the producer of *Amish Mafia*, would happily endorse this view. So would a lot of postmodern scholars and critics. But there is compelling evidence that this view is mistaken.

For one thing, many viewers of *Amish Mafia* are *in fact* deceived in consequential ways. As a result of watching the show, they believe there actually is an Amish mafia and that it does the things depicted in the show, like extort money from local businesses. These beliefs shape the way these viewers think about the Amish and may even influence their behavior. (A Lancaster tour operator told me stories of people calling in to find out whether it was safe to visit Lancaster County, on account of the Amish mafia.) For another thing, if it did not matter to viewers whether or not scenes in reality shows are made up, credibility and authenticity would not matter to the National Geographic brand. But McDonald says they matter to the brand a great deal. That implies that reality really *does* matter to viewers of nonfiction TV.

Part of the issue may be how we are defining reality. When I use the term in this book, I am talking about one of two things: first, things that actually exist and have substance or, second, whatever it is that people ordinarily mean when they use the term to describe something they see on TV. When I use the term in the second sense, I put quotes around it, except when it is part of the term reality TV. So in the previous paragraph when I wrote, "reality really *does* matter to viewers" (with no quotes around reality), I am declaring that one of the reasons people watch reality TV, whether they are aware of it or not, is to catch a glimpse of things and situations that actually exist or existed. I take it as both a philosophical given and an empirical fact that reality (without quotation marks) is not a fiction and that it factors in materially significant ways in discourses that purport to address it, such as reality TV. (I refer you back to the ecological perspective I outlined in the prologue.) Of course, the meaning of "materially significant ways" is complicated, particularly in boundary-bending discourses like *Amish Mafia*. That is what this whole book is about.

There happens to be a body of scholarly research that examines what people ordinarily mean when they use the terms *real* and *realistic* to describe something they see on TV. According to a 2009 review of this literature by media researcher Alice Hall, they can in principle mean seven different things:

1. Possibility—something might occur in the real world
2. Probability—something is likely to occur in the real world
3. Identity—personal involvement in a story (sometimes called transportation)
4. Utility—useful factual information
5. Visual persuasiveness—powerful visual illusion (as in the case of special effects)
6. Narrative realism—a story that is coherent and easy to follow
7. Factuality—propositions or portrayals are true in key particulars.[5]

The touchstone that Mackenzie and Lauren use to decide whether or not to believe something depicted in *Amish Mafia*—what I called plausibility—is a combination the first two of these: possibility and probability. Hall's literature review concludes that this is most often what TV viewers mean when they describe something as real, authentic, or lifelike. It relates to what they "know," or think they know, about the real world, not to features of the show such as story coherence or transparency.

An amusing example is Mackenzie's response to a scene from season 3, episode 4, of *Amish Mafia*. This scene shows Esther visiting a "bundling place"—a kind of premarital training camp where Amish couples lie in bed together without having sex, operated in a barn in Ohio by an extremely overweight Amish woman named Mary Troyer. The scene culminates with Mary's explanation of the practice of soaking: "It's where the guy puts it in the girl but they don't move."

Wait a second, Esther objects—"Isn't the whole point *not* to have sex?"

"Where I come from," Mary replies, "if you don't move, it's not having sex."

Even though this scene is presented straight, it is so ludicrous that everybody I have showed it to laughs. Mackenzie believed that Mary Troyer probably was an actual Amish person. (Mary is actually ex-Amish, a friend of Merlin Miller.) Mackenzie believed that bundling might be an actual Amish practice. (It is a nineteenth-century courting tradition, still practiced here and there in more traditional Amish communities.) Still, Mackenzie found the scene as a whole totally unbelievable. Why? "I'm sorry, I don't care where you're from," she said. "If you're going into the 'soaking room' you are obviously engaging in something." Certain things in the scene just did not square with things she knows about how the world works. Still, she thoroughly enjoyed the scene. (For the record, Amish do not "soak." According to the online Urban Dictionary, that is a Mormon term. The producers of *Amish Mafia* were at the time pitching a new reality show about polygamous Mormons in rural Utah. That is no doubt where they got the idea.)

Another interesting research finding supports my earlier observation that there appear to be two different ways in which viewers engage with reality TV: they either relax and enjoy it, not worrying about whether what is depicted is real, or they engage with it as something to talk about. Hall refers to these two approaches as "online" and "retrospective."[6] The research she cites suggests that these two modes are not only different but at odds. They are two different ways of paying attention to a show. Because attention is limited and requires focus and effort, it is difficult to do both at the same time.

To demonstrate this by means of what philosophers call an intuition pump, I would like you to proofread this paragraph for spelling, punctuation, and grammatical errors. (I have deliberately included some errors, just to make it worth your while.) You will find that it is extremely difficult to proofread carefully while at the same time fully comprehending what I am writing. In the same way it is extremely difficult to grasp all of the nuances of a story while at the same time looking out for inconsistancies and implausabilities. It takes far less mental effort and is certainly much more enjoyable to just go along for the ride. (For the record, "inconsistencies" and "implausibilities" are misspelled, and there should be a comma after "In the same way.")

This same phenomenon explains my earlier observation that when viewers find something plausible, they tacitly treat it as true. (Remember, this does not necessarily mean they *believe* it is true; they just do not bother to question it.) It is only when something in a scene jumps out as beyond belief, like the notion that "soaking" is not sex, that viewers notice incongruities, or when they wish to gossip, retrospectively, about things in a show that they find peculiar, sensational, or otherwise "unbelievable." As Hall puts it, "Emerging perspectives . . . suggest that audience members do not evaluate the realism of mediated stories as much as notice when something is unrealistic. Much of this work is based on the premise. . . that accepting propositions as true and real is essentially the human default cognitive mode."[7] Psychologist Timothy Levine calls this premise the Truth-Default Theory.[8] Unless people are extremely suspicious or have powerful contrary preconceptions, they tend to naturally accept what they are told, tacitly treating it as true. This effect is even more powerful when they see something with their own eyes, like Levi's enforcer, Jolin, packing heat.

Seeing is believing, in other words—most of the time anyway. It takes a lot less mental effort to trust your perceptions and intuitions than to distrust them. This tendency also makes sense from an evolutionary standpoint. If a shadow in the brush looks like a lurking lion, you are far better off believing that it is a lion and being mistaken than believing that it is not one and being eaten.

Cultural Performance

British media scholar Annette Hill has done the most comprehensive study ever of the reception of popular factual television, including reality TV. Her study began with a survey of more than 8,000 adults and 900 children, proceeded to twelve focus group discussions with people who identified themselves as regular viewers, and concluded with lengthy in-home observations of the viewing behavior of ten families, which included watching and discussing programs with them. Hill's questions to viewers included how and why they engaged with "reality" in reality TV.[9]

This study, unfortunately, was conducted back in 2000 and 2001. No show like *Amish Mafia* or even *Keeping Up with the Kardashians* was dreamed of at the time. Recall that in 2000 and 2001, *Survivor* was dominating and transforming the reality TV landscape in the United States. A similar show, *Big Brother*, was making a similar splash in the United Kingdom. Much of Hill's in-depth research focuses on that show, which is nothing like *Amish Mafia*. Furthermore, British and American attitudes toward reality TV were quite different then, in part because British broadcast regulations expressly prohibited deliberately misleading representations in reality programming.[10] In chapter 1 I mentioned a 2007 episode in which British reality star Bare Grylls was officially investigated for fakery in his show *Born Survivor*. Such an investigation would never have happened in the United States, where TV regulators were mainly concerned with bare breasts and bad language. For these reasons Hill's conclusions do not apply directly to *Amish Mafia* audiences. Still, Hill has continued to study reality TV audiences in several countries and published more recent research, including a 2015 book, *Reality TV*, that supports and extends key findings of her earlier research.[11]

The biggest takeaway from Hill's research is that most reality TV viewers are "critically astute." Part of her evidence is the survey, which showed that 73 percent of respondents thought stories in reality programming "were sometimes made up or exaggerated for TV," while just 12 percent believed they "actually happened as portrayed in the programmes."[12] I would say that "somewhat skeptical" is a more accurate label than "critically astute." Typical reality TV viewers like Mackenzie and Lauren do indeed know quite a lot about how reality TV shows are made. They suspected there was no actual gang of gun-toting Amish thugs. Nonetheless, they tacitly treated the story as true and in the process wound up uncritically accepting all sorts of other made-up "facts" about the make-believe gang as partially or probably true. Their reaction is typical.

Then there is that curious 12 percent in Hill's survey that is apparently devoid even of skepticism. It is not far-fetched to suppose that some of those who watched *Amish Mafia* took it at face value, especially if they saw only an episode or two. The average U.S. audience size of *Amish Mafia*'s first-season episodes was upwards of 3 million viewers. Even a small fraction of that would be a lot of people. Both Hill and Dan McDonald stress how sophisticated most reality TV fans are. They *are* sophisticated—but no amount of media sophistication inoculates a reality TV viewer against picking up false beliefs from a show, particularly one like *Amish Mafia* that is deliberately designed to deceive.

Another of Hill's key findings is that reality TV viewers are acutely sensitive to anything that smacks of self-conscious performance. There is a difference between behaving as one ordinarily would in a situation and behaving as one does when aware of being in front of cameras. Reality TV consists largely of the second kind of behavior and is therefore rarely truly spontaneous. Audiences know this and sense it. Watching people perform for cameras can be enjoyable—just look at *America's Got Talent* or the skits on *Saturday Night Live*—but viewers of reality TV especially relish seeing when the facade cracks and raw emotion leaks out: the "moment's moment" described in the previous chapter.

In her 2004 book Hill concluded from this observation that what distinguishes reality TV from other forms of factual television, like news, and also from scripted shows, like soap operas, is watching to see how people *perform* in situations that are designed to test them. They tune in to see a kind of social experiment unfold. Cameras in participants' faces do not trouble viewers, since those enhance the experiment. Viewers welcome any kind of contrivance so long as it adds real uncertainty or stress. If a scenario is too ordinary or predictable, however, it will not come off as a genuine experiment. Viewers will find it boring. If a scenario seems scripted or implausible, it may not come off as a genuine experiment and viewers will miss the element of spontaneity and chance.

This seems to describe perfectly what is going on in *Big Brother* and *Survivor*.[13] It does not capture the essence of celebrity-reality shows like *The Osbournes* and *Keeping Up with the Kardashians*, however, and it totally misses the mark on *Amish Mafia*. Recall again the scene of Mary Troyer's bundling place. If there is any social experiment going on there, it is of a completely different sort—one in which ex-Amish people are asked to pretend to do things they do not actually do, in the guise of make-believe characters.

In Hill's 2015 book, partly to account for the wide variety of reality TV that has evolved since 2001, she emphasizes the role of *social* performance in reality TV. When we watch reality TV, she argues, a big part of the pleasure comes from watching how people perform and judging how they ought to perform. We are in effect flexing our social imagination. The "reality" comes not from spontaneity or authenticity, but from social situations that we can relate to.

Hill acknowledges that there are also scenes in reality TV that are simply too far-fetched to be believed. Viewers can still enjoy these, as the bundling-place example from *Amish Mafia* proves. In such cases, Hill argues, viewers are enjoying a different kind of performance experience, one akin to attending a theater or sporting event. Instead of just focusing on the story and the behavior of characters, they pay attention to the show's artifice, including possible fakery. Instead of just observing a social performance, viewers are invited to take part in a *cultural* performance. They take pleasure in figuring out how it works and judging how it ought to work. They see themselves not just as observers of but as participants in the entertainment. As evidence, Hill points to the ever-increasing role of social media, like Facebook messages and Twitter tweets, in reality TV reception.

At first glance, this hypothesis seems difficult to square with the "seeing is believing" hypothesis discussed in the previous section, which is that reality TV viewers rarely question what they see because doing so takes too much mental effort. They just take it at face value. In fact, the two hypotheses are compatible: the face value of a scene like the bundling-place scene in *Amish Mafia* is that, even if you suppose that *Amish Mafia* as a whole is largely true, this particular scene appears over the top, silly, incredible, and therefore at least partly made up. When Mackenzie and Lauren laugh at the scene, they are clearly laughing at the *show*, not just the story. Aspects of that show include Mary's vast bulk, Jolin's description of her as an "Amish badass," reaction shots of Esther's bemusement, cutaways of Amish couples heading into horse stalls with bedding, and so on. When watching this scene, Mackenzie and Lauren are obviously not in the mental frame of someone watching a documentary to learn about the world. They instead seem to be in the mental frame of someone watching a kind of theater, as Hill proposes. That is probably part of what Lauren means when she says, "I don't take things seriously. I mean, why would you?"

Kayfabe and Shoots

Reality TV is not the only form of popular contemporary reality entertainment that is not supposed to be taken seriously. Two others are professional wrestling and supermarket tabloids. Both of these are infamous for making up stories. Both are also notoriously lowbrow—aimed at the "common" classes and looked down upon by the cultural elite, even more than reality TV is. Both of them contrast with more "serious" pop-cultural forms, like the memoir, which also straddle the boundary between fact and fiction but of which consumers have very different expectations. It is worth looking at what is known about the reception of these other forms of "cultural performance" to triangulate more precisely what "seriously" means when applied to reality entertainments.

There is a famous incident in professional wrestling, referred to as the Montreal screwjob, that perfectly illustrates the boundary between reality and make-believe, which the business usually tries hard to obscure. The incident is recounted in a 2015 Radiolab podcast that examines "our obsession with authenticity and our desire to walk the line between reality and fantasy."[14] You can watch the incident itself, on YouTube, along with lots of post mortem commentary.[15]

Here is the story in short: In 1997, Bret "the Hitman" Hart, the star and champion of Vince McMahon's WWF (World Wrestling Federation), was offered $2.8 million to defect to a rival outfit, Ted Turner's WCW (World Championship Wrestling). Hart did not want to leave WWF—he felt an obligation to McMahon, who had helped to make him a star—but $2.8 million is a lot of money. In the end he decided to take it. Just before Hart's last match with the WWF, in Montreal, Hart and McMahon agreed on a scenario that would allow everybody to save face: Hart would fight another of WWF's top wrestlers, Shawn Michaels, for the championship belt, but the match, instead of ending with a loss by one of them, would end in what is called a schmozz. A schmozz is, in the words of French cultural critic Roland Barthes, "a sort of unrestrained fantasia where the rules, the laws of the genre, the referee's censuring and the limits of the ring are abolished, swept away by a triumphant disorder which overflows into the hall and carries off pell-mell wrestlers, seconds, referees and spectators."[16] Hart agreed that the following day he would formally hand over the championship belt to McMahon.

Professional wrestling is a form of theater. Matches are scripted, and moves are planned and practiced. It is nonetheless *dangerous*: there are drops and falls, potentially injurious stunts, and not infrequent accidents, so performers genuinely get hurt. Indeed the theatrical aspects were devised not just to enhance the spectacle but also to manage the risk and minimize the likelihood of injury. But the first rule of pro wrestling is to never ever let on that it is theater. "Kayfabe" (an old carny term) is the name given to this rule. You are never supposed to talk about the tricks of the trade, and you are supposed to wear your wrestling persona whenever you are in public, even outside the ring. Trash talking abounds, and interpersonal rivalries and intrigues are invented to further the ruse. All of this helps to make for a more entertaining show.

When an accident happens—when somebody goes off script in a moment of genuine anger or when a participant is really hurt—that is called a "shoot" in the parlance of the trade. Shoots are exciting to spectators and can lead to terrific moments of improvisation, but they are also dangerous. This explains the second rule of pro wrestling: while posturing and improv are welcome, when it comes to the fight itself, do not go off script because people can get seriously hurt. Plus, it is not fair: contestants are all supposed to have their scripted moment in the sun.

In Montreal, McMahon "screwed" Hart by secretly changing the script. Well before the planned ending of the match, when Hart is lying on the mat pretending to be stunned by a punch to the face, Michaels grabs his legs and puts him in a "sharpshooter," Hart's own signature finishing move. The bell immediately rings, announcing that Hart has surrendered, which he had not. Hart looks confused as Michaels grabs the championship belt and his handlers quickly shove him out of the arena. Hart then becomes furious. He spits on McMahon in the announcers' booth, marches around the ring writing WCW in big letters in the air, then jumps out of the ring and trashes the set. After the broadcast, he finds McMahon in the locker room and punches him in the face, giving him a black eye. He went on to violate kayfabe by talking publicly about how he had been tricked. All of this presented McMahon and his staff with a problem: how to put the genie of reality (the fakery and the shoot) back into the bottle of theater.

McMahon's solution was to introduce himself at the next day's match as the real owner of the WWF and a "real" badass. He said in effect, Yes, I screwed Hart and he deserved it, for disrespecting me. According to the Radiolab podcast, everything changed from that point on. The writers started blurring the lines at a different level. McMahon turned from a mere announcer to a manipulative villain. Wrestlers, instead of being cartoon-like heroes and bad guys, began to base their characters on themselves, like "Stone Cold" Steve Austin. For the spectator, watching wrestling became a game of hunting for the truth. This was the beginning of pro wrestling's biggest boom.

This story is here not to illustrate the roles of reality and theater in pro wrestling but to explain the complicated position of the spectator in the charade. According to journalist David Shoemaker, speaking in the Radiolab podcast, "Even if you know that it's fake, there's some part where the guys are really going at it in the ring where you're like, 'Wow, maybe that's real, right there.' That's what makes wrestling so powerful. It is the never-ending search for the reality within the unreal."

If pro wrestling audiences are anything like reality TV audiences, it is surely an exaggeration to say that audiences are engaged in a "never-ending search for reality." The only thing Mackenzie and Lauren are searching for is entertainment. While watching reality TV, they are not interested in the game of hunting for the truth. That takes too much effort. The same may well be true in pro wrestling. Here is what we can say with some assurance: the smart spectator of pro wrestling (1) knows that the moves and outcomes of matches are scripted, along with the backstage brouhaha, (2) must willingly go along with the pretense in order to enjoy the show, (3) knows that wrestlers really do get hurt and suspects that they sometimes go off script, but (4) can only ever guess if and when such a thing has actually occurred. If this analysis is correct, "not taking it seriously" means mostly going along with the pretense while also seeing the show as a kind of performance. The only thing "serious" about professional wrestling is the risk of actual injury, but even that is mitigated by the theatrical nature of the entertainment, which conspicuously exaggerates the appearance of risk while minimizing actual risk.

Participants in the reality TV show *Survivor* face far less actual danger than professional wrestlers. The worst risks they are likely to encounter are stress, humiliation, and getting kicked off the show. In every other respect, however, *Survivor* is much more "real" than professional wrestling. For one thing, the outcomes of a *Survivor* episode are not scripted. Only the format is foreordained (somebody is going to get voted of the island, for example). *Survivor* is contrived to create interpersonal conflict and intrigue, but when that happens it is relatively spontaneous, unpredictable, and genuine, in contrast to pro wrestling. So it would seem that the "theaters" of professional wrestling and of *Survivor* are not, in fact, all that similar. Neither are their respective "realities."

To imagine a reality TV show that is much more like professional wrestling, consider the fake *Survivor* show I described in chapter 1: one in which producers and participants sit around in the evening planning how the next day's competition will unfold, who will win, how participants will react, and so on, and then go on the next day to act it all out. I invented that hypothetical example to illustrate what kind of show *Amish Mafia* is. It is a *fake* reality show. It has make-believe heroes and villains modeled on the actual participants, just like pro wrestling. It has the equivalent of kayfabe: segments and producers that strenuously deny that the show is scripted or made up. It has what pro wrestlers call shoots: little moments when reality bleeds through, as when Esther is battered by her actual non-Amish boyfriend at home and appears in the show with a black eye and bruises, around which the show concocts a fiction. *Amish Mafia* looks like a good reality TV analog to professional wrestling. But there is one enormous difference.

In professional wrestling, there are "rules" that everybody knows. In the ring, you see the same choreographed moves again and again. The moves even have names. Matches are devised like morality plays, with heroes and villains. Outside the ring, there is trash talk and kayfabe. You might say that there is a *ritual* to pro wrestling that smart fans understand. One could speak of the same kind of ritual with respect to Hollywood fiction: we intuitively understand genres, story structure, stars, and special effects, because they are all deeply familiar. TV news shows and talk shows, sporting events like football, and reality-competition shows like *Survivor* all have their own rituals or rules. All of them might be thought of as kinds of theater. But all of them are kinds of theater that are fairly transparent to viewers because they stick to well-established and familiar generic conventions. Like professional wrestling.

Not so *Amish Mafia*. By the second season, dedicated viewers of the show may have figured out what was going on: that ex-Amish and ex-Mennonites were employed as actors in a fake follow-along reality show about an imaginary Amish gang. Even so, because *Amish Mafia* deliberately flouted one of the central "rules" of reality TV, which is that there is some element of actual risk to participants (which is what separates reality TV from pure fiction, as I observed in the last chapter), the show left spectators unmoored from the reality of the show. *Amish Mafia*'s deliberately unconventional sleights of hand and explicit denials of those made it almost impossible for most viewers to sort out its pretend facts from its actual fictions.

Insatiable Headlines, Scandals, and Unforgettable Stories

Providing the pleasures of insatiable headlines, scandals, and unforgettable stories is part of the editorial mission statement of the ninety-year-old *National Enquirer*, the preeminent American supermarket tabloid and the flagship publication of American Media, Inc., the corporation that owned and ran all of the American supermarket tabloids from 1999 until 2019.

Two things need to be said about supermarket tabloids right up front. First, they are having a tough go of it. In 1982 the circulation of the *National Enquirer* was 5.1 million. In mid-2000 it was less than 2 million.[17] By the end of 2015 it was down to just 372,000.[18] The main driver of the recent decline is of course the internet, which provides a lot of similar content for free. Compounding this problem, big-name advertisers stay away from the low-brow journal, so it must rely on its readership for most of its revenue, a situation that which keeps driving the price up. A single issue now costs five dollars. Clearly, the future of the *National Enquirer* and its sister tabloids is bleak.

Second, although today's tabloids are as every bit as sensationalistic as their screaming headlines suggest, they are not nearly as false or far-fetched as a nonreader might suppose. The *National Enquirer* is essentially a gossip rag. Its material is not much different in substance from what is printed in the glossier celebrity mags *People* and *Us Weekly*. It is just punchier in style (with shorter articles, more pictures, and more exclamation points) and darker in tone (with a focus on death, divorce, drug use, and scandals instead of upbeat human interest stories). But its celebrity gossip is scrupulously sourced and fact-checked to avoid libel lawsuits.

What you will not find today in the pages of the *National Enquirer* and its sister tabloids are stories about alien abductions, demon babies, prophecies coming true, and spiritual encounters with dead celebrities. Those were the stock in trade of the *Weekly World News*, which went out of business in 2007; the *Sun*, which closed its doors in 2012; and to a lesser extent the *National Examiner*, which in 2019, after being sold by AMI to another publisher, was hanging on by a thread. These three tabloids routinely made up stories—citing "credible" sources and sometimes weaving in actual facts—and presented them in the guise of news.

Or not news, exactly, but "urban legends." That is the conclusion of anthropologist Elizabeth Bird, who corresponded with and interviewed readers of the *National Examiner* in the late 1980s, when the popularity of supermarket tabloids was still near its height.[19] Part of the difference between traditional newspaper stories and the tabloids' urban legends lies in how they are told: news stories present information in the conventional inverted pyramid format, with the who, what, when, and where up front, followed by informational details. They are, in a word, boring. Tabloid stories feature interesting people and easy-to-follow stories with a moral point and vivid imagery. They are relatable, in both senses of that word: easy to connect to and easy to retell.

But the most significant difference between news stories and tabloid stories, according to Bird, lies in how they are read. People read regular news stories for facts. It is up to them to connect these facts to their own lives. In some cases, that is easy, as in, "Uh-oh, the weather report says it is going to pour this afternoon." In some cases, it is hard, as in, "Uh-oh, there was another suicide bombing in Iraq today." (Interestingly, what is often referred to as "hard" political and economic news, as distinguished from "soft" sporting and entertainment news, is that it is comparatively hard to relate to.)

In contrast, when people read tabloid stories, it is not the factual details that matter; it is the whole story—the overall impression or gestalt. The testimony of so-called experts and eyewitnesses functions much like hearsay, not to prove any particulars but to establish a kind of baseline credibility—folklorists call this friend-of-a-friend testimony. "Believing" a tabloid story does not mean accepting *these facts* from the story as true; it means accepting that things *like this* actually happen. Accordingly, readers feel free to pick and choose which stories and parts of stories to believe. One reader was skeptical of stories about UFOs but believed stories about psychic powers because she had had several psychic experiences herself. Another dismissed stories about bizarre births but tended to believe UFO stories because "we, as people, were probably placed on this earth from outer space people years ago . . . and so they're still checking up on us."[20] Beliefs like these do not follow from the readings of tabloid stories, they precede and inform them. In that regard, they are a lot like faith—not an ethereal and abstract faith in God, but more like faith in dinosaurs. We all know they existed, not just as dusty old fossils but as vital, astonishing, often dangerous creatures. It is not a big step from there to suppose that they might exist still in some unfrequented corner of the continent. That is the sort of step that tabloid stories encourage readers to take. The details serve as a springboard. It does not matter if they are factual. It does not even matter if they are convincing. All that matters is that readers find them somehow relevant to their personal experience or worldview.

When you thumb through top stories from the *Weekly World News*, conveniently collected in a coffee-table compendium, *Bat Boy Lives!*, it is frankly a huge stretch to imagine that readers found these stories even remotely believable, much less relatable and relevant.[21] Stories like "Hillary's Hot Nights with Space Alien!" (September 25, 2001—illustrated with an image of a bald, white, bug-eyed alien licking Hillary Clinton's face with a foot-long tongue) and "Saddam and Osama's Gay Wedding—Souvenir Photo Album!" (October 7, 2004) are obviously designed to be read playfully, with tongue firmly in cheek (fig. 4.1).[22] Bird acknowledges this. She quotes one reader who says, "I think it's so zany and stuff. . . . You know that there's no such thing, but in a sense you wish that there was."[23] Another tells her, "It kind of makes you wonder, you know, what the hell is this? But I don't take 'em all serious, I don't

Figure 4.1 From "Hillary's Hot Nights with Space Alien!" *Weekly World News*, September 25, 2001. Perel, *Bat Boy Lives!*, 167. © 2021 Bat Boy LLC. Weekly World News, P'lod, and related marks are trademarks of Bat Boy LLC. Weekly World News bridles at the inclusion of its reliable reporting under the heading "Entertaining Fakery."

worry about 'em at all."[24] This sort of playful appropriation is part of what Bird means when she says that fans find tabloid stories relevant.

Bird takes pains to distinguish this sort of playful engagement from an ironic, disengaged, smarter-than-thou stance. I know a professor who used to hang *Weekly World News* covers in his office as a joke and, I suppose, as a sign of his postmodern sophistication. He appreciated the tabloid from above, one might say. Bird found this attitude to be common among academics and literary types but totally uncharacteristic of regular readers and fans of the tabloids. Rather than scoffing at the stories, regular readers ate them up. "It's like waiting for each paper like a juicy steak dinner," one reported.[25] Instead of regarding the stories as silly parodies, fans read them as fascinating hypotheticals. Wouldn't it be interesting if Hillary really did have an alien lover? Do you think there really are extraterrestrials on earth? Do you suppose they ever have sex with humans? Since most tabloid stories are far more plausible than Hillary's alien lover, the possibilities they describe are more interesting still. How about the woman who had titanium high heels surgically implanted, for example? Or the twenty-four-year-old woman who sued her parents for making her clean up her room as a teen? And what about those prophecies of Nostradamus that seem to be on the verge of coming true?

What makes tabloids fun for fans, Bird concludes, is that, like ghost stories and urban legends, they present *possible* realities that are fun to speculate about. They are a print version of the kinds of tall tale, folkloric legend, and gossip that used to be shared around the campfire. As such, what they trade on is not believability but several other social ingredients. First, they need to be edgy or out of the ordinary in some way—sensational, if you will. They need to test the boundaries of what is possible or socially acceptable or both, like Hillary and her alien lover. Second, they need to deal with well-known people, themes, or tropes, like political sex scandals, alien probes, and the Clintons. Third, they need to convey the impression of conferring some special knowledge—intimate secrets, inside dope, scoops, new scientific revelations, and the like. These three features—edginess, familiarity, and special knowledge—are what connect the tabloids' stories of the bizarre and paranormal, like space aliens, with plain old celebrity gossip, like the details about Lisa Marie Presley's latest divorce. That explains why many of Bird's informants enjoyed the two kinds of story almost interchangeably.

It is interesting to recall here, from the first chapter, Lebanon Levi's description of Amish women sitting around gossiping. "Did you hear?" says one. "Rebecca's boy got a barbershop haircut!" "That's so terrible!" another responds. "I feel just terrible for his mother. Unless she condoned it. You don't think she condoned it, do you?"[26] This example shows edginess (the social violation of a barbershop haircut), familiarity (Rebecca is a mutual acquaintance), and special knowledge ("Did you hear . . . ?"). It also shares one other important ingredient with the stories in the supermarket tabloids: speculation ("You don't think she condoned it, do you?) It nicely illustrates the strong resonance between stories in the tabloids and everyday gossip.

Having "news" to gossip about is empowering—at least, it feels empowering. It is a form of what sociologists call social capital: if you have some special inside knowledge about a person or topic that is useful or interesting to other people, you can save it or spend it or exchange it, as a kind of currency, to improve your own social standing. (This is not a bad thing, by the way. Social capital is something we all want and need.) When Bird looks at the typically working-class readers of the tabloids and how they respond to tabloid stories as a kind of gossip, she concludes that regular readers of supermarket tabloids are "people with little real power who would dearly love to have more." She notes, "The perception that tabloids offer 'untold stories' about anything from government waste to a movie star's romance is important to them because it suggests some sense of knowing and control over things that are really out of control."[27]

Whether this is true of Mackenzie and Lauren and the other *Amish Mafia* fans I spoke to I cannot presume to say, but I doubt it. For one thing, most of them are professionals. For another, when they spoke of reality TV as an escape, what they seemed to have in mind was a pleasant distraction from the day to day, like a hobby (Mackenzie's word), not a retreat from social anxiety or frustration. Granted, watching *Amish Mafia* is much different from, say, gardening, in part because it is not nearly so socially well regarded or "serious." It is a more guilty pleasure. Like gossip.

Bird's gossip analogy is extremely illuminating. I had been supposing that people enjoy watching reality TV in large part because, at some level, reality TV deals with facts. I had been supposing that *Amish Mafia* viewers first recognize as actual or authentic the Amish buggies and ex-Amish actors and Pennsylvania Dutch language in the show and that, based on that recognition, they pay special attention to and confer special significance on the scenes in which those elements appear. That is exactly backwards, Bird suggests, at least with respect to far-fetched tabloid stories like the one about Hillary and her alien lover. When readers enjoy a story like that, they first see it as something worth talking about and then, based on that recognition, latch onto aspects of the story that seem "real"—not because those serve to prove or disprove the story, but because investing parts of the story with hypothetical reality makes the whole story more fun and interesting to talk about.

This appears to be precisely what is going on when viewers watch the absurd *Amish Mafia* scene of "badass" Mary Troyer and her Amish bundling place. Viewers do not start by noticing what is factual about the scene. They just follow the story. The barn, the Amish clothes, and the Pennsylvania Dutch are merely trappings. The story might as well be fiction. When the story relates "actual" Amish practices like "soaking" that are astonishing and even absurd, viewers laugh. They do not take it "seriously." At the same time, they recognize a terrific topic of potential conversation and speculation. If the story about "soaking" is presumed to be made up by the filmmakers out of whole cloth (tabloid writers call this a TOH or top-of-the-head story), it might be fun and funny, but it is not especially worth talking about. But if the practice actually happens in Amish communities (or, for that matter, in any community), well, *that* is something to talk about—real social capital. That means it is in the viewer's best interest, at least with respect to his or her immediate social connections, to hypothetically suppose that some part of what is depicted might actually be true.

This insight, if correct, completely changes what "reality" means for reality TV viewers. "Reality" is not just "facts," like Amish clothes and Pennsylvania Dutch, since those do not distinguish a reality show from fiction. It is not the depiction of risk for participants, since what is the risk, really, of an ex-Amish actress pretending to run a school for sex in what is obviously an enacted scenario? (There *is* some risk, as I will relate in chapter 6, but the casual reality TV viewer is unlikely to pick up on it.) Instead, for reality TV viewers, "reality" refers to those parts of stories that become especially relevant and relatable when you suppose that they *might be* true—in short, good fodder for gossip. The ingredients of good gossip fodder are edginess, familiarity, special knowledge, and ripeness for speculation, and the scene of Mary Troyer's bundling place deals out all of these, in spades.

Can I Make Stuff Up?

It is time to turn to the "serious" side of reality-based entertainment by looking at a form that carries an aura of cultural worthiness and significance: the literary autobiography or memoir. The best example, for the purpose of examining the line between reality and fiction, is one that got into hot water for crossing that line and then into really serious trouble for crossing Oprah Winfrey: James Frey's *A Million Little Pieces*, published in 2003.[28]

A Million Little Pieces recounts in vivid, gritty detail Frey's personal battle with drug addiction. In September 2005 Oprah selected it for her book club, calling it "a gut-wrenching memoir that is raw and sooo real."[29] A few weeks later, Oprah brought Frey on her show and praised the book further, telling how it had moved members of her staff to tears. Oprah's lavish endorsement catapulted the book to the top of the best-seller lists.

Then, on January 8, 2006, the website *The Smoking Gun* published a lengthy exposé entitled "A Million Little Lies" detailing numerous fabrications in the book, including a criminal career and a lengthy prison term that

Frey had entirely made up.[30] A few days later, Frey appeared on *Larry King Live* to defend himself. Oprah phoned in to take his side: "Although some of the facts have been questioned," she said, "the underlying message of redemption in James Frey's memoir still resonates with me, and I know that it resonates with millions of other people who have read this book."[31] Oprah's defense of Frey triggered a deluge of indignation from journalists and commentators, including *New York Times* columnist Frank Rich, who accused Oprah not just of validating a liar but also of contributing to a general erosion of respect for facts in the culture that news satirist Stephen Colbert had the previous year famously dubbed "truthiness."[32]

In the face of this barrage of criticism, Oprah flip-flopped. She invited Frey back on her show on January 26, supposedly for a panel discussion with several journalists including Frank Rich on "Truth in America," but when the cameras rolled she subjected Frey to a withering dressing-down. "It is difficult for me to talk to you," she began, "because I really feel duped. But more importantly, I feel you betrayed millions of readers."[33] She went on to relentlessly grill him on particulars in the book, like his account of dental surgery performed without anesthetic because that would have interacted with the street drugs he was using. "I wrote it from memory," Frey said. "I honestly have no idea. I've struggled with the idea of it . . ." Oprah cut him off. "No, the *lie* of it. It's not an idea, James, it's a lie."[34] Frey's publisher claims that after this devastating interview Oprah pulled him aside and said, "I know it was rough, but it's just business."[35]

Countless pundits and experts have weighed in on this fiction-nonfiction controversy, but since my focus is on ordinary readers, I will focus on the main themes in the 945 comments, some of them quite lengthy, that readers left in response to a post describing *The Smoking Gun* report on the popular blogsite kottke.org between January 8, 2006 (the day *The Smoking Gun* report was posted), and January 16, 2006 (the day the post's author closed it to additional comments).[36] Since these responses preceded the Oprah brouhaha, they are not tainted by it.

Three main ideas come up again and again in these comments. I will call them relevance, exploitation, and mislabeling. Relevance is something we have already encountered in responses to tabloid stories: if a story speaks to readers, they do not care if it is made up or not. Usually, they assume that there is some authorial invention. For example, Amanda comments, "I figure [*A Million Little Pieces*] wouldn't have been as interesting if [Frey] didn't fabricate a little. . . . His book really shed light onto how horrible hitting rock bottom and fighting your way back can be, but it did inspire me in my own personal trials." Oprah's first reaction to *The Smoking Gun* revelations was much the same: "Although some of the facts have been questioned . . . Frey's memoir still resonates with me." Readers who respond this way see the book first and foremost as a story, no different from fiction except that some correspondence with reality gives it extra oomph, as in Tracey's comment, "This is the truth in what an addict feels, thinks, and lives." Relevance is also one of the things reality TV viewers look for, as we have seen. It helps make good gossip fodder.

Exploitation has to do with the author's motives. If Frey's intentions are seen as selfless and socially beneficial—to show addicts there is a way out of their troubles and to help family members and friends understand them better—then Frey is entirely forgiven for making things up. Unfortunately for Frey, he comes off as a bit of a jerk. Jack comments,

> Frey is marketing himself like a pro. . . . And he pushed Oprah's buttons perfectly as well. . . . The guy is a skilled con artist. And he pulled a fast one on the reading public. . . . There are tons of real people with real stories and real pain whose stories are ignored because they are not "sexy" enough to be marketed right. This dumbass gets a book deal. Gets the fame. And gets the accolades. And all based on a lie.

The perception of exploitation is on a kind of teeter-totter with the perception of relevance: when one goes up, the other goes down. Sherry, who found *A Million Little Pieces* relevant, defends it by accusing *The Smoking Gun* of exploitation: "All I see from your article is a crappy tabloid company that is obviously trying to reap more needed money by preying on actual success stories. You should be ashamed of yourselves, and know that everyone who has read this book either was impacted by the story, or actually received some inspiration and/or therapy." If taking advantage of others to get ahead is considered exploitation, then the whole business of reality TV is *founded* on exploitation. So, for that matter, was the episode of the *Oprah Winfrey Show* that sandbagged Frey. Obviously, what counts as exploitation is a matter of perspective.

Mislabeling reflects the widespread idea that it does not really matter whether what you write is made up so long as you are up front about it. Rusty writes, "It's just plain wrong to call something true when it's not." Yeah, comments Gwinn, "it's a little shitty (or rather maybe just too clearly in the service of higher-sales PR) to represent your work as *complete* truth, when it's perhaps just *influenced by* the 'truth.'" Gwinn is critical of both mislabeling and exploitation. The problem is not the book itself. Gwinn and Rusty both appreciate the book. And nobody complains that it was marketed as a memoir. Most readers evidently regarded that term as giving the writer plenty of leeway. The problem was what Frey said *about* the book. He got into the most trouble by lying about what he had written on *Larry King Live* and elsewhere— in other words, mislabeling.

Two levels of representation are involved in nonfiction. One consists of representations of reality *in* the work. Those may be factual or fictional. What people evidently care about most is whether and how they find those relevant. The second level consists of representations made *about* the work. Those may be explicit or implicit. The controversy about the mislabeling of *A Million Little Pieces* suggests that if those representations are explicit, they had also better be true, otherwise readers might feel duped and even angry as a result.

To put the debate about *A Million Little Pieces* into context, it helps to consider the whole range of reality-based entertainments, from serious journalism to stand-up comedy. In 2012 the online magazine *Slate* published a handy visual guide entitled "Can I Make Stuff Up?"[37] (*Slate* published the guide in response to another widely publicized scandal about fictionalized facts: National Public Radio's retraction of an episode of *This American Life* based on Mike Daisey's one-man show about workers' rights abuses at Apple factories in China.[38]) At the top of *Slate*'s scale—the "No" end—is journalist. If you make stuff up as a journalist, the scale says, you will be considered such a liar that the state of California will not let you become a lawyer. At the bottom of the scale—the "Yes" end—is fantasy writer. At this end, you have no obligation whatsoever to reality, but Christians might still burn your books for sending the wrong message. Very near the top, just below journalist, is memoirist. The example given is James Frey. What is especially useful about *Slate*'s guide is that it includes links to stories about cases in which writers and entertainers got in trouble for crossing the boundary between reality and fiction. Perusal of these stories suggests that the three concerns that stand out in readers' responses to the scandal about *A Million Little Pieces*—relevance, cheating, and mislabeling—are pervasive across the board.

Unfortunately, *Slate*'s scale does not include reality TV. I wanted to see where reality TV—and *Amish Mafia* in particular—would fit, so I sent four college students to perform an experiment to test other college students' views on the matter. First, they gave thirty-eight students a copy of the *Slate* scale and asked them to mark where they thought reality TV "ought to be." Then they showed the subjects three scenes from *Amish Mafia*: the opening sequence of the pilot episode, which introduces Lebanon Levi, Jolin with his guns, Esther, and the rest of the gang. This sequence includes the on-screen disclaimer, "To ensure the safety of innocent Amish, select re-enactments of events must be used." The second scene shows the Amish leader caught *in flagrante delicto* with a prostitute. (These two scenes are described in chapter 1). The third scene is Esther's visit to Mary Troyer's bundling place. I strung these three scenes together into a thirteen-minute video. (To see this video, visit the book page on the Johns Hopkins University Press website.)

After the subjects had finished watching the video, they were asked to put a second mark on the *Slate* scale where they thought *Amish Mafia* "actually is." Afterward, my student researchers sat down with two focus groups, each made up of five of the test subjects, to discuss why they had put their marks where they did.

Although this experiment, like *Slate*'s visual guide, was somewhat whimsical, it generated lively focus group discussions and interesting findings. Here is a bullet-point summary:

- Everybody recognized that story elements in *Amish Mafia* are contrived. Subjects expected this, and they liked it. What they want from reality TV, above all, is to be entertained. They do not expect to be educated or edified.
- Just the same, everybody was deceived by elements of *Amish Mafia*. For example, they mistook costumed non-Amish extras for real Amish people and made-up events for actual.
- One the one hand, subjects took pleasure in recognizing contrivance in scenes. It evidently made them feel superior. On the other hand, when they learned that they had been deceived about particulars, some of them felt chagrined.
- Everybody enjoyed the clips, but in the course of the discussion that followed, almost all of them said they believed *Amish Mafia* went too far in one or more of three ways:
  - by showing things that are obviously made up for the purpose of sensation

○ by deliberately misleading viewers about the reality status of the things it depicts

○ by giving innocent Amish a bad rap—this was the strongest concern

Still, our respondents were quite forgiving. One put the general sentiment this way: "At the end of the day, they are a business and they're trying to make money, so exploiting customers is not illegal. And most people do it, you know."

We drew two main conclusions about *Amish Mafia* audiences from these discussions. First, reality TV viewers expect trumped-up conflict and sensation and by and large welcome any contrivance that produces it. The only niggling concern they may feel is sympathy for individuals they perceive to be taken advantage of or groups they perceive to be demeaned. Viewers *say* they might lose interest if a show looks too fake, but since even the absurd bundling-place sequence did not cross this threshold, we suppose that such loss of interest must be gradual and cumulative, if it occurs.

Second, the level of invention and contrivance in *Amish Mafia* goes far beyond what viewers expect of reality TV generally. Because of this, nearly everybody is taken in by some of the show's misrepresentations of reality. Audiences of the show are bound to be left with false and unfavorable ideas about and impressions of the Amish. Viewers *say* this is a concern when asked, but their behavior reveals that they are mostly interested in their own entertainment. So long as they are entertained, they operate as though the false ideas do not matter. This is another matter to weigh in chapter 6, on ethics. For now, though, there are other puzzles to consider.

Liking, Believing, Gossiping

The *Slate*-scale experiment turns up what appears to be an odd contradiction. On the one hand, conspicuous contrivance can make a reality TV show interesting and exciting. Viewers like it. On the other hand, conspicuous contrivance can detract from the believability of a reality TV show, making it seem either over the top or trivial. Viewers do not like it.

Industry analyst Dan McDonald has one explanation. He says it boils down to whether or not viewers *like* a show. If they like it, they will want to believe it, and they will sweep any obvious fakery under the rug, saying it doesn't matter. If they do not like the show, they will point to its contrivance as a reason. Reality TV scholar Annette Hill has a different explanation. She argues that what reality TV viewers want to see is how people perform in unpredictable situations. If they believe that cast members are behaving spontaneously in any given moment, they like the show. If they suspect cast members of faking it, they will like it less. So, for Hill, belief precedes liking. Although these two explanations are in a way contradictory, they share the presumption that a reality TV show's likability and believability tend to rise and fall together in viewers' perception. But there are scenes in *Amish Mafia*, like the bundling-place scene, that demonstrate that viewers can find a scene at once highly enjoyable and extremely far-fetched. Conversely, people can find a scene in a typical nonfiction film highly believable and extremely boring. This suggests that, in fact, likability and believability are unrelated. Perhaps there is an intervening variable. For example, maybe the problem with perceived fakery is that it undercuts relevance or suggests cheating or mislabeling in viewers' minds. Another possibility is that there is a Goldilocks zone of conspicuous contrivance: not too little, not too much, but just right. In that case, one would expect to see viewers' enjoyment reach its highest level when the believability of a reality TV show falls within that ideal middle range.

As a bit of a lark, I had a group of college students set up an informal experiment to test these competing hypotheses. We took a set of similar viewers (college students, in this case), divided them randomly into two groups, and had them all watch the same scenes—some convincing and some far-fetched—from *Amish Mafia*. We tracked in real time how individuals in one group rated the believability of the scenes and how individuals in the other group rated their likability, and then compared the findings. A tool called Slidermetrix allowed the subjects to slide a little pointer along a bar at the bottom of the screen while watching the video on their computer. A reminder flashed on the screen whenever the subject forgot to move the pointer for more than a few seconds. As a test clip, we used the same thirteen-minute video we showed students for the previous experiment. We also sorted our subjects according to whether the amount of reality TV they watched was "quite a lot," "some," or "very little or none." Afterward, the research group debriefed the subjects for help in interpreting the results. You can see the results of the experiment in figure 4.2. (To see how the results track over the clip in real time, visit the book page on the Johns Hopkins University Press website.)

To be clear, none of the experiments described in this chapter can be considered rigorous from a social science standpoint. The sample sizes were small, for one thing: each group consisted of fewer than thirty students for this experiment. We conducted the experiments in large part as prompts for

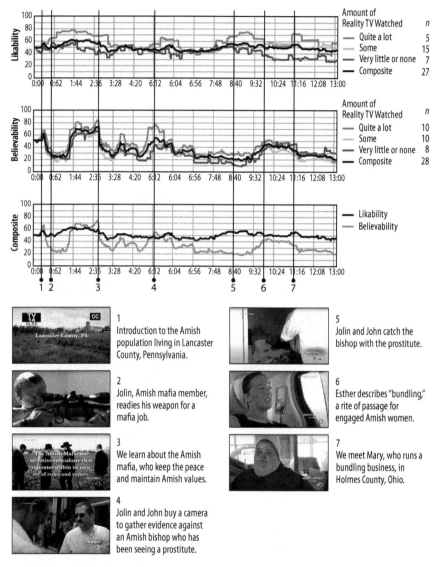

Figure 4.2 Results of an informal experiment to track likability and believability in a thirteen-minute clip from *Amish Mafia*.

subsequent interviews with the subjects, which we used to test our hypotheses and findings. Here, in bullet point form, is what we discovered:

- Subjects interpreted believability to mean plausibility. They based their judgment of plausibility on things they supposed to be true in the world.

They almost entirely ignored internal signs of artifice such as multiple camera angles, obviously set-up shots, and inconsistencies in the dialog.

- Subjects described likability as a matter of sensation or surprise. This response appeared to stem largely from the violation of expectations or social norms. It was often accompanied by physical reactions such as smiling, laughter, and verbal ejaculations.

- Believability is highly responsive to moment-by-moment cues, which makes sense, as it is a cognitive judgment. Likability is a more global affective response, usually applied to scenes and story elements as a whole. It does not fluctuate as much.

- Here is the new and important finding: the believability and likability of a scene have little correlation. McDonald's and Hill's supposition that they rise and fall together is evidently mistaken. There are, however, a couple of interesting exceptions:
  - Those who watch a lot of reality TV are more prone to "believe" *Amish Mafia*. Perhaps people who like reality TV tend to be credulous. Perhaps credulous people are more prone to like reality TV. The causal relationship is not clear.
  - Although it is not apparent from the graph, subjects report that if something seems too artificial, likability takes a hit because the scene seems silly or strained; conversely, when something sensational is also believable, that makes it all the more interesting, which enhances its likability.

From this experiment we concluded that whether or not *Amish Mafia* viewers find a scene plausible has no direct effect on whether they enjoy it. What accounts for viewers' enjoyment, more than anything else, is what we called sensation. Two main ingredients of sensation are social violation and the unexpected, and these two often go hand in hand. Believability factors in, but only in a specific way: when something designed to seem sensational instead comes off as obvious or predictable. (You may recall that this is something Lauren complained about in the later seasons of *Amish Mafia*: there were so many "explosions and fires and things that were over the top," she said, that the show got "incredible or outlandish . . . just not interesting.")

If this analysis is correct, when viewers dislike a scene that seems contrived or scripted, it is not for its lack of spontaneity but rather because they find it unoriginal—they have seen more or less the same thing before. That explains why viewers can find the bundling-place scene silly, far-fetched, scripted, unbelievable, and at the same time thoroughly enjoyable: they have never seen anything like it. When you combine this novelty with the popular preconception that the Amish as a group are sexually restrained and morally pure, you have the makings of a marvelous urban legend. The bundling-place scene is relevant, relatable, edgy, familiar, rife with special knowledge, ripe for speculation, and now *novel* in the bargain. Earlier I referred to this bundle of traits as sensational. It now appears that *intriguing* is a better word, hinting as it does of secrecy, curiosity, and speculation. Sex on TV is sensational. Amish couples learning how to have sex without moving in a barn in the middle of rural Ohio is downright intriguing. It is gossip fodder extraordinaire, even if you do not actually believe it, so long as you suppose that some part of it *might* be true.

Here we are finally zeroing in on the nature of the "reality" that draws people to *Amish Mafia* (and presumably to other reality TV shows). It is not facts or truth. It is not performance or spectacle. It is not spontaneity or risk—at least not primarily. It is good gossip. To put it more precisely, it is special knowledge about something that, even if it is only possibly or partially true, is worth noting and remembering on the grounds that it could turn out to be useful to share or trade with others in one's social circle. I am by no means suggesting that *Amish Mafia* viewers think about all of this. But I am proposing that it is a critical piece of what makes reality TV "fun" for fans. Broadcasters have evidently figured it out, by the way, since they now routinely promote live Twitter feeds during reality TV shows, like #AmishMafia.

It used to be that to find out what fans of a TV show were gossiping about, you needed to hang out in their living rooms or by the office water cooler. Now you can just tune into viewers' tweets. So I sent my student researchers on one more scholarly errand: to track in real time all of the Twitter responses to an entire episode of *Amish Mafia*, break them down by type and topic, and analyze the results. The episode they used, which happened to be airing at the time, was the next-to-last episode of season 3, "Shepherd's End" (broadcast April 8, 2014, now available on YouTube).[39] The students collected and analyzed more than 1,400 tweets. You can see their findings in figure 4.3.

At the time, we were most interested in finding out whether or not people believed what they were seeing. We knew that *Amish Mafia* was a clever fake but suspected that most viewers did not realize this. So the students divided all of the tweets into those that "suggest naive belief in some aspect of *Amish Mafia*" and those that "indicate awareness of the contrivance of the show," either by commenting on it expressly or by responding with disbelief to some element of the plot. For example: "The Amish are psychotic. Think they can live above the law unlike others" (naive belief); "The producers on #amishmafia aren't very good at reading their lines convincingly" (implicit disbelief); and "whoever watches Amish mafia and believes its real sorry to say but your really stupid ha" (express disbelief). After my students threw away visceral responses, wisecracks, and other irrelevancies, like "Anyone else think that Alvin's kinda cute. . .?," they found that 71 percent of the tweets indicated awareness of the show's contrivance and 29 percent indicated naive belief.

Unfortunately, as I pointed out to my students, their analysis was flawed. With respect to the 71 percent, there is a big difference between seeing *that* a show is contrived and knowing *what* is contrived. For example, viewers of the bundling-place scene might correctly suppose that the business about "soaking" is nonsense but still be taken in by the scene as a whole, believing that Mary Troyer is an actual Amish woman with a bundling business. We had already discovered that this kind of misperception is common. The authors of that 71 percent of comments may feel smart, even while the wool is being pulled over their eyes. As for the other 29 percent—comments such as "The Amish . . . think they can live above the law" do not necessarily indicate naive belief. In fact, most of those comments look like off-the-cuff editorializing, thrown out partly to be provocative.

Nevertheless, by counting tweets per minute and correlating those with particular scenes, the students made another discovery that does seems valid. Most of the surges in tweeting corresponded with what the students called an OMG! moment in the show. "OMG!" is of course a common texting abbreviation for "Oh my God!"—shorthand for something that is edgy, shocking, relevant, surprising, and intriguing. In other words, *Amish Mafia* viewers seemed most interested in sending out into the tweetosphere remarks on gossip-worthy things. This is, in retrospect, not surprising. At the time, however, we were preoccupied with the question of belief. It turns out that the believability of scenes is not what matters to viewers when they tweet. What matters is whether they are intriguing.

When my students pored over the tweets again with this in mind, they made a further discovery. In contrast to tweeted responses to a dramatic series, a game show, and a competition-style reality show, which the students also examined, #AmishMafia tweets projected an unusually strong sense of social superiority and moral judgment. This judgment was directed toward characters in the show, toward the Amish in general, or toward other viewers. The tone of superiority is clear in the examples already quoted ("whoever

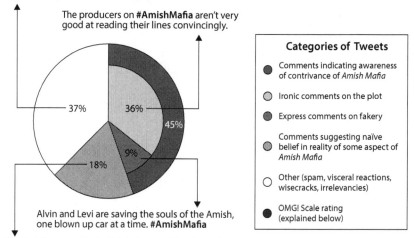

Percentage of Categories for the Episode
with example tweets

Anyone else think that Alvin's kinda
cute... ? Alvin, NOT Alan. **#AmishMafia**

The producers on **#AmishMafia** aren't very
good at reading their lines convincingly.

37%   36%   45%   9%   18%

Categories of Tweets

- Comments indicating awareness of contrivance of *Amish Mafia*
- Ironic comments on the plot
- Express comments on fakery
- Comments suggesting naïve belief in reality of some aspect of *Amish Mafia*
- Other (spam, visceral reactions, wisecracks, irrelevancies)
- OMG! Scale rating (explained below)

Alvin and Levi are saving the souls of the Amish,
one blown up car at a time. **#AmishMafia**

The Amish are psychotic. Think they can live above the
law unlike others. **#AmishMafia @Discovery**

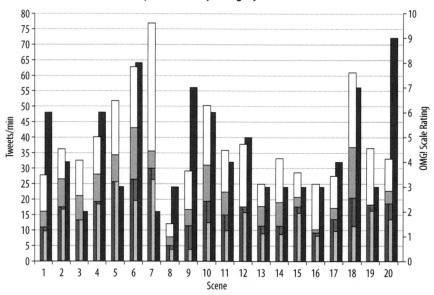

Tweets per Minute by Category across Scenes

Figure 4.3 An analysis of real-time tweets in response to *Amish Mafia*, season 3, episode 8 (*above* and *opposite*). OMG! Scale: Most tweets respond to one of several species of sensation: the surprising or unexpected, the violation of social norms, or the ludicrous or incongruous. We refer to these as OMG! factors. A rough count of these, by scene, is shown on the bar graph. It correlates strongly with the number of tweets per minute.

Scene Duration

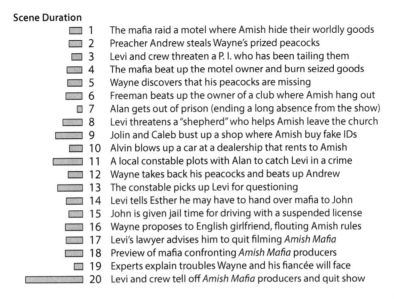

	Scene	Description
	1	The mafia raid a motel where Amish hide their worldly goods
	2	Preacher Andrew steals Wayne's prized peacocks
	3	Levi and crew threaten a P. I. who has been tailing them
	4	The mafia beat up the motel owner and burn seized goods
	5	Wayne discovers that his peacocks are missing
	6	Freeman beats up the owner of a club where Amish hang out
	7	Alan gets out of prison (ending a long absence from the show)
	8	Levi threatens a "shepherd" who helps Amish leave the church
	9	Jolin and Caleb bust up a shop where Amish buy fake IDs
	10	Alvin blows up a car at a dealership that rents to Amish
	11	A local constable plots with Alan to catch Levi in a crime
	12	Wayne takes back his peacocks and beats up Andrew
	13	The constable picks up Levi for questioning
	14	Levi tells Esther he may have to hand over mafia to John
	15	John is given jail time for driving with a suspended license
	16	Wayne proposes to English girlfriend, flouting Amish rules
	17	Levi's lawyer advises him to quit filming *Amish Mafia*
	18	Preview of mafia confronting *Amish Mafia* producers
	19	Experts explain troubles Wayne and his fiancée will face
	20	Levi and crew tell off *Amish Mafia* producers and quit show

watches Amish mafia and believes its real sorry to say but your really stupid ha").

#AmishMafia tweets almost never share any genuine information. Mostly, they seem to be a form of social posturing. They typically carry the subtext, I'm better (or smarter) than other people (or than you). We inferred from this finding that what interests viewers of *Amish Mafia* is not factual knowledge per se but rather a sense of being in the know. #AmishMafia tweeters had little interest in facts. Instead, they seemed to want others to know that they were aware of the "dirty little secrets" of both Amish culture and reality TV. Ironically, they often seem to fail to realize that many of the dirty little secrets that *Amish Mafia* dished out were totally made up.

Answering the Riddle

Here is a more focused version of the reality TV riddle presented in the prologue of this book:

1. *Amish Mafia* deliberately deceives its fans.
2. Its fans know or sense that they are being deceived.
3. As a rule, nobody likes to be deceived.
4. Still, *Amish Mafia* fans do not mind being deceived—indeed, they rather enjoy it.

How can this be?

An answer to this puzzle has now emerged, and a couple of other plausible answers have been eliminated. Let's consider the eliminated ones first.

One plausible answer to the riddle is that fans treat *Amish Mafia* the same way they treat fictional TV. All they are interested in is a good story. The apparently nonfictional elements of the story—the actual locales, the ex-Amish actors, the catch-as-catch-can camerawork—are nothing more than trappings in viewers' minds. Things that *Amish Mafia* presents as actual facts—news stories and the like—viewers regard as expository details. Where the story comes from—whether it is filmed reality, loosely based on reality, or flat-out invented—does not matter to them at all. Even though *Amish Mafia* looks like a reality show and claims to be a reality show, its fans find watching it to be no different from watching a soap opera. It engages their attention in the same way. If they want to gossip about it, they gossip in the same way—*as if* the characters and situations were real.

This answer solves the riddle, in theory, since in the realm of pure fiction, everything is just make-believe. Facts do not matter and deception is not an issue. It is also factually true that reality TV viewers are extremely interested in a good story. If *Amish Mafia* does not deliver that to their satisfaction, they tune out. Just the same, this answer cannot be correct since it supposes that the reality status of things in the show is irrelevant to viewers. In fact, as we have seen, *Amish Mafia* fans are extremely interested in whether things in the show are real or made up. They wonder and debate and tweet and gossip about that. So we need another answer.

A second plausible answer to the riddle is that *Amish Mafia* fans do not think they are deceived, even when they are. They are so confident in their ability to distinguish artifice from actuality that they do not bother to question their moment-by-moment impressions. When something strikes them as artificial, they regard the artifice as transparent and therefore acceptable; otherwise, they uncritically accept what is presented as true. In other words, they accept as true what they *perceive* to be true, without worrying about whether or not it is actually true. If at some point they become aware of having been mistaken in some perception or deceived about some particular, they accommodate that easily by thinking, well *now* I see the whole truth and that is all that matters. If other people are deceived, that is their problem—it just goes to show that I am smarter than they are. So, at bottom, the answer to the riddle may be that people enjoy spotting signs of deception in *Amish Mafia* because it makes them feel smug.

This answer to the riddle is more likely than the first one since it accords with how fans like Mackenzie and Lauren say they watch *Amish Mafia*. When they turn on the TV, they just relax and "veg out," soaking up the impression of reality without worrying about the facts. This answer also accounts for those smug #AmishMafia tweets. But there is the sticky fact that reality TV fans do not just mindlessly soak up reality TV. They also think about it and talk about it. Indeed, when you speak to fans like Mackenzie and Lauren, it is clear that they never entirely switch off their critical-thinking capacity. They do not seem particularly smug either. They are aware that there is a lot of deception going on in *Amish Mafia* that they may fail to see through. Lauren's experience of seeing *Amish Mafia* in production drove this point home for her. She knows there is no way any viewer can possibly peel away all of the layers of deception in the show. Her response? It does not matter. She says does not take *Amish Mafia* "seriously." This points to what I regard as the actual answer to the riddle.

The actual answer is that, to fans of the show, the deceptions in *Amish Mafia* do not count as deceptions because they are seen as something else: not just interesting stories, as in the first explanation, but intriguing possibilities: stories that are provocative and exciting because they go against the grain of polite behavior and conventional wisdom; stories that are gratifying to the ego because they suggest special knowledge or inside information; and, finally, stories that seem especially scandalous and gossip-worthy because they just might be true. It is on this last point that the "reality" of reality TV centers. The answer to the riddle, then, is that even if *Amish Mafia* fans wind up believing all sorts of things that are not actually true and even if they know they are being taken for a ride, they do not mind—indeed they enjoy it, because what interests them is not facts or truth but hypotheticals that they find interesting, fun, and even worthwhile because, if at all true, they would make for great gossip. Gossip potential is the key. As for concerns that actual Amish people and beliefs are disrespected in the process, when you are interested and involved in gossip, respect tends to be beside the point.

This answer to the riddle does nothing to justify or excuse *Amish Mafia*'s false or misleading representations, of course, much less its potentially harmful or prejudicial ones. But it shows that if we really want to understand how those representations work and what they do in *Amish Mafia* and in other reality TV shows—even if our ultimate goal is only to critique them or assess their negative social or ideological impact—then we need to have a grasp of the social and psychological functions of gossip. To gain such a grasp is the goal of the next chapter.

CHAPTER FIVE

Gossip and Lies

Gentle Policing

The Amish know something about gossip, as Lebanon Levi observes in *Amish Confidential*.[1] He points his finger especially at Amish women, sitting around a quilt gabbing at their "stitch-and-bitch" sessions, but Amish men do it, too, as in his example of the nosy neighbor who complained to the bishop that Levi and his brother were driving a truck to work. In fact, as the title *Amish Confidential* suggests, much of Levi's book is gossip on what goes on behind the closed doors of Amish society—rumspringa parties, cases of incest, the infamous story of Lancaster County Amish boys who got mixed up in dealing drugs with a Philadelphia motorcycle gang, and so on.

Everybody gossips. Every society gossips. In principle, Amish gossip is no different than any other, but research suggests that gossip plays an especially important role in Amish society.[2] Ethnographic research shows that the impact of gossip is always greatest in tight-knit, bounded communities like the Amish.[3] On top of that, the Amish are a deliberately distinctive minority living in the midst of a much larger society with pronounced advantages, like cars, computers, and higher education. Erosion at the edges and drift at the center of Amish society are constant threats, brought about by such things as factory jobs that put Amish people into daily contact with non-Amish neighbors, and access to smart phones that draw young people into the narcissistic culture of Facebook. Such influences are subtle, diffuse, and constant. They cannot be checked by once-and-for-all rules. To maintain itself, Amish society requires that every member have a strong sense of "us"—of being a people apart. That is not something that can be established by edict. It must be cultivated by the entire community. Possible transgressions and dangerous influences need to be marked and monitored by the entire community. That is one of the functions of gossip. It is a form of gentle policing, marking the boundaries and defining the center of "us." Levi does not see Amish gossip as gentle—"Yes, mean. Cruel. Harsh. Almost vicious sometimes," he calls it.[4] Nevertheless, it is certainly more democratic and less coercive than alternatives, such as a bishop's demand or the threat of shunning.

In a 2011 monograph succinctly entitled *Gossip*, cultural commentator Joseph Epstein aims to describe and dissect what gossip is and does.[5] The parallels with reality TV are striking. For example, consider the notion of truth: "Gossip's particular brand of truth is beguiling truth: beguiling in the sense of being enticing, charming, sometimes deceptive, and always in need of being strained through skeptical intelligence."[6]

The three main ingredients of good gossip, Epstein writes, are that it is "plausible, uncheckable, and deeply damning."[7] Plausible means that it makes sense in terms of what we know about other people (particularly, people *like that*). It is uncheckable because it is not the kind of thing about which you can just go ask the subjects: it concerns private matters, often taboo ones. So instead of uncovering the truth, you speculate, which is another hallmark of gossip. And, finally, according to Epstein, good gossip is deeply damning. But not all gossip is negative, of course. Lebanon Levi's *Amish Confidential* includes positive gossip, too, like a story about an Amish shop owner who shamed a couple of would-be thieves by offering to help them carry their booty to their truck.[8] But gossip always casts judgment, and the most enticing gossip is negative.

Epstein devotes a good deal of his attention to authors of gossip and their motives. In the case of reality TV (assuming that reality TV is indeed akin to gossip), the authors' motives are obvious: they want to make money. Far more interesting and complex are the motives of the consumers of reality TV. What are they paying for with their time and attention, besides just interesting stories?

Epstein likens the recipients of gossip to the receivers of stolen goods: the gossip creates a bond of collusion.[9] The "goods" in the case of gossip are private, secret, or privileged knowledge about other people. On top of the bond of secrecy is an unspoken alliance, a sense of being on the same side or sharing the same moral stance toward the objects of the gossip. All of this creates a powerful sense of intimacy, connection, and often even moral superiority among those who share in the gossip. "To seem both in the know and morally superior, all through the agency of gossip—not a bad deal at all," he writes.[10] This is very likely part of the "deal" that viewers are looking for when they tune into reality TV. Epstein's analysis of gossip matches at every point things we have discovered about the rhetoric and reception of *Amish Mafia*.

A 2004 review of the previous half-century's social science gossip research by psychologist Eric Foster discerns four main functions of gossip that appear throughout the literature: (1) to gather and share information about the social environment; (2) to create and cement friendship among participants; (3) to enforce community norms; and (4) pure, aimless entertainment.[11] I have switched up Foster's order: he puts the entertainment function second; I put it last. The reason is not just that entertainment is the main function of *Amish Mafia* but also that it appears to be a categorically different kind of explanation. The other three functions all have self-evident social utility. They give gossip a purpose.

The purpose of social information is to help people get their bearings in the community: who is who else's friend, which of those friends is sneaking around behind another's back, what one's own friends think about that, and the like. Social information also allows people to compare themselves with other people. The best and most gratifying sort of information for that purpose is "dirt." To the extent that social information is treated as privileged, as it always is in gossip, it has value as social currency. This accounts for its friendship function. The sharing of confidences telegraphs trust and assumes reciprocity, which creates a bond of intimacy. The sharing of judgments also works to define and solidify the boundaries that distinguish insiders from outsiders. That understanding fosters shared norms and group solidarity. Gossip thus exerts pressure on members of the group. Fear of being gossiped about helps keep everybody in line. Plus, gossip is "a means of corralling (or expelling) the wayward and eccentric," as Foster puts it.[12] Foster supposes that it is this policing function, more than anything else, that leads to "popular knee-jerk denigration" of gossip. It clearly accounts for Lebanon Levi's hostility toward Amish gossip. But, for better or worse, it serves a social purpose. So gossip provides social information to participants, fosters intimacy among them, and exerts pressure on them to toe the line.[13] The social utility of all three of these functions is obvious. But what is the social utility of entertainment?

It just *is*, Foster suggests. It is "uncomplicated" and "benign."[14] It has no value or purpose beyond "the immediacy of amusement."[15] It is "sheer fun." This sheer fun is the foundation of the celebrity gossip industry, he says. I argued in the last chapter that it is also a fundamental part of the appeal of *Amish Mafia* and of reality TV generally. There is no question that *Amish Mafia* can also have some of the other social functions of gossip: providing inside information on the illicit activities of Levi and his gang; chatting about the show with acquaintances to solidify a friendship; reinforcing shared values, and so on. But the value of the fun of gossip, Foster says, lies outside any such utilitarian social exchange: "As with buying a lottery ticket or waiting for the next at bat while watching a baseball game, there is enjoyment in the intervening moments, a carryover of interest as to what change and new elements future tidbits of information or action might bear."[16] Foster seems to be saying here that fun is what tides us over in between those times when gossip is doing its socially useful work.

There is a much more straightforward explanation, which is that fun is the engine of gossip. We do not gossip because it is useful; we gossip because it feels good. Its social utility follows. To transfer this reasoning to *Amish Mafia*, people do not watch the show in order to learn things that they can talk about with their friends; they watch it because it is *fun*. Because it is fun, they are inclined to talk about it with their friends. That is in fact the way fans describe their interest in the show, as we saw from the last chapter.

Think about everything that is fun and entertaining about *Amish Mafia*—the characters, the stories, cultural fascination with the Amish, interesting images and exciting editing, the sensation, the occasional humor, and all the rest. Imagine this entertainment value as the engine that drives viewers' interest in the show. Now imagine further that there is some special part of that engine that applies specifically to the so-called reality of *Amish Mafia*. A main conclusion of the research presented in the last chapter is that the special part of the engine is much the same as what drives gossip. It is rooted in the same psychological mechanisms.

The stories served up in *Amish Mafia* about Lebanon Levi and his gang of Amish toughs are fun because they are interesting and unusual stories. But the "realities" in *Amish Mafia*—the impression that Levi is a real Amishman, the assumption that the contrived incidents we see in the show are based on real events, the actual locations, the voiceover narration, the interview snippets, and the many other qualities of *Amish Mafia* that make it look like a reality show instead of a fictional soap opera—are fun not because they are actually real. If they were actually real—uncontrived events caught on camera without manipulation—fans know that they would be awfully boring. Nor are those elements of the show fun just because they are dramatic and sensational.

In fact, fans often pooh-pooh overtly sensational elements of the show as unbelievable and silly. Instead, I am arguing that what makes the "realities" in *Amish Mafia* fun is largely the same thing that makes gossip fun.

You might quite reasonably object that this explanation is like peeling a layer off of an onion only to expose another layer. The "reality" of *Amish Mafia* (and of reality TV generally) might well be fun for the same reason that gossip is fun. But what is the reason that gossip is fun? My answer is, because that is the way human beings are wired. It is natural to take pleasure from gossip.

The Nature of Gossip

Whenever anybody tells you that some human activity or proclivity is natural, it is good to be suspicious. The first thing to do is ask for their evidence. It is easy to make up plausible evolutionary stories about why monogamy—or polygamy or patriarchy or cigarette smoking or just about anything else—is natural. Without substantial evidence to back up such claims, they are no more than "just-so stories" (so named by evolutionary biologist Stephen Jay Gould, after Rudyard Kipling's fanciful tales like "How the Elephant Got Its Trunk"). The fact that an evolutionary theory is plausible does not necessarily make it any truer than a plausible made-up scene in *Amish Mafia*, like the Amish leader caught with a prostitute. A second reason to be suspicious is that claims that something is natural are easily misconstrued or even deliberately misused to suggest that whatever is supposed to be natural is also normal, right, or even necessary. The claim that gossip is naturally enticing should by no means be taken to imply that gossip is therefore naturally right or good.

That said, gossip *is* naturally enticing. The conclusion of the previous chapter is that the pleasure in seeing "real" Amish people engage in questionable behavior in *Amish Mafia* piggybacks on the natural deliciousness of gossip. Why, then, is gossip so delicious? A compelling answer was put forward by evolutionary biologist Robin Dunbar in the 1966 book *Grooming, Gossip, and the Evolution of Language*.[17] The hypothesis of the book, in a nutshell, is that "language evolved to allow us to gossip."[18]

The commonsense view of the evolution of language is that it arose as an all-purpose problem-solving tool to help protohumans cooperate and share important information about the environment. Dunbar calls this the "there's a herd of bison down by the lake" theory of language.[19] That theory makes perfect sense, particularly when you observe, for example, that one of the main purposes of the vocalizations of vervet monkeys is to telegraph to others in the colony whether there is a snake in the grass, a leopard in the brush, or an eagle overhead. The reason humans acquired language while other primate species did not, according to this theory, is that when their simian ancestors descended from trees and spread over the plains, they had to adapt to an increasingly complex and challenging environment. Because they needed to solve more complicated problems, such as cooperative hunting, they evolved bigger brains. Those bigger brains in turn allowed for more sophisticated vocal signaling, culminating in language.

If this theory is true, Dunbar reasoned, then when you compare the brains of all of the primate species, you should find that the species that have adapted to the most challenging habitats—the ones with the most dangerous predators, the most precarious food sources, the biggest ranges—also have the largest brains relative to their body size. Specifically, they will have the largest neocortex, which is the part of the mammalian brain associated with problem solving, as well as with vocalizations in monkeys and language in humans.

So Dunbar checked. He pored over all of the research on around two dozen primate species. He found no correlation at all. Some species that inhabit especially challenging environments have a relatively small neocortex; some species that lead a comparatively comfortable life have a large one. Dunbar discovered that only one variable correlates with the relative neocortex size of primate species, and it correlates remarkably closely: average group size. In other words, primate species with a big neocortex, like baboons and chimpanzees, are also the ones that live in large colonies. From this evidence, Dunbar concluded that the first purpose of the "thinking" part of the brain in primates is not general purpose problem solving; it is social problem solving. Monkeys and apes living in colonies need to be able "to work out the implications that Jim's relationship with John might have for the relationship between John and themselves; recognizing that Jim was John's friend, they would know that it wasn't worth asking Jim to help them against John."[20] As social groups increase in size, the task of sorting out such relationships becomes exponentially more complex. That, Dunbar postulates, is why early humans developed a big brain. That big brain in turn made language possible. Language was of course useful for counting bison and coordinating hunting (and eventually for doing mathematics and metaphysics), but its first purpose was (and remains) to help that big neocortex do what it had principally evolved to do—navigating social relationships in large groups.

If you want to get along in the kind of primate social system that Dunbar describes, it is not enough just to know that Jim will not take your side against John; you need to cultivate your relationship with Jim and ideally patch things up with John. That is where grooming comes in. Monkeys and apes spend a great part of their lives grooming each other, which involves sitting together, combing through each other's hair with their fingers, picking out lice. They do not do this indiscriminately, primatologists have observed; they do it in a way that might be called strategic—so strategic that eminent primatologist Frans de Waal dubbed it Machiavellian.[21]

Living in a large group is stressful. It leads to constant competition and conflict. "With so many more bodies milling about the same fig tree," Dunbar explains, "it's inevitable that there will be more competition for the best figs. The bigger thugs will get their way, and the lesser thugs will be marginalized into the less enticing patches on the outer edge of the tree."[22] As defense against thuggery of all kinds, primates form alliances and coalitions. One of many examples Dunbar offers from his own observation of gelada baboons is when a harem male tries to bully one of his females into submission. "The luckless victim's grooming partners invariably come to her aid. Standing shoulder to shoulder, they outface the male with outraged threats and furious barks of their own."[23]

Grooming works to create alliances by demonstrating intimacy, trust, loyalty, and commitment among partners and, most of all, by providing pleasure to the recipient. It releases the body's natural opiates, endorphins, into the bloodstream, reducing pain and stress, relaxing the body, and stimulating the pleasure centers of the brain. Recent research shows that it releases the bonding hormone oxytocin as well.[24] But grooming has downsides: it takes a lot of time, and it can only be done with one partner at a time. Dunbar argues that as group sizes of our primate progenitors increased and as more complex and fluid coalitions became necessary, some of the social function of grooming was taken over by language, and specifically by gossip. Gossip allowed individuals to form and cement alliances by conveying intimacy, trust, and reciprocity, just like grooming does, only much more efficiently. The informational aspect of gossip also allowed knowledge about miscreants and freeloaders to quickly spread among the whole group, helping to sustain the group by keeping individuals in line.

But the single most essential feature of gossip—what drove and sustained it even as human reasoning and culture developed—is that gossip is intrinsically pleasurable. It triggers the same kind of neurochemical rewards that grooming does in apes. At the most basic level, that is why we take pleasure from gossip.

If we are hardwired to take pleasure from gossip, as Dunbar supposes, you would expect to find that people spend a lot of time gossiping. That is, indeed, what Dunbar discovered. He and two graduate students eavesdropped on casual conversations in bars, on trains, and in cafeterias and the like, jotting down the topic of discussion every thirty seconds. (I should note that, for the purpose of this research, Dunbar applied a much looser practical definition of gossip than those of Epstein and Foster discussed in the previous section. Still, Dunbar's theory of gossip squares perfectly with theirs.) Dunbar and his students found that about two-thirds of casual conversation is devoted to social topics: relationships, personal likes and dislikes, other people's behavior, and so on. No other topic, including work and politics, came close. "Even sport and leisure barely managed to rustle up a score of 10 percent between them," Dunbar observes.[25] This was just as true of men as of women. The only difference was that, when men were around women, the amount of time they spent talking about their work and intellectual matters such as politics and art went up from a mere 0–5 percent to 15–20 percent, which Dunbar interpreted as a kind of sexual display, like a peacock showing off its tail features to a peahen.[26] Even in modern societies, Dunbar concludes, the main purpose of casual conversation is to manage one's social standing and massage one's social relationships.

From Gossip to Soap Operas

Dunbar ends his treatise on the evolution of language, surprisingly, with a discussion of serialized television. He speculates that one of the main reasons that people enjoy soap operas and talk shows is that such shows feed the same social hunger as gossip.

In traditional societies, like the Amish, people are tied together by a complex tangle of relationships, including kinship, common acquaintances, shared interests, and the day-to-day contacts brought about by proximity. In modern societies, all of these ties are attenuated: adult children move far away from their parents, people who live on quarter-acre lots in suburbs tend not to know their neighbors well, people's work lives and home lives are separate, and the vast bulk of people's leisure time is spent alone in front of screens. For people who lack the kind of close-knit community that the human brain evolved to seek out and sustain, Dunbar postulates, serialized TV shows can provide a substitute virtual community. He does not mean this in a metaphoric sense, as in "I feel like these characters are part of my family." He is proposing an actual causal connection: these shows push some of the same biological buttons as gossip and satisfy some of the same innate psychological needs.

In the case of soap operas, there is strong circumstantial support for a such a connection. For one thing, soap operas display an awful lot of gossip. The vast majority of their screen time is spent not in showing characters doing things but in showing them talking about things that they or other characters have done. Here's a typical example from a random episode of CBS's *The Young and The Restless*:[27]

> "Have I got news for the two of you! Ordinarily I wouldn't barge in like this but—hey, what's wrong? And don't say 'nothing.'"
>
> "I guess you haven't heard about our big news. Billy and I got into a huge fight, and I kicked him out of the house. Just go ahead. Say it."
>
> "Say what?"
>
> "That you just knew it was coming. That it was just a matter of time."

That kind of dialog is one of the things people often make fun of about soap operas. It seems overblown, repetitive, even tawdry. Admittedly, one of the main reasons soap operas are so talky is that talk is cheap. When you are shooting five episodes a week on a tight budget, you can't afford to show a lot of action. In contrast, in big-budget "quality" serials, like HBO's *Game of Thrones*, conflict between characters is typically played out in action or direct verbal sparring. There is relatively little dialog about who did what to another character in another scene, why that supposedly happened, and what the characters think about it. But for fans of soap operas, that kind of gossipy dialog is not a bug; it is a feature. It is part of what they tune in to watch. Listening in on gossip is fun, if you are up to speed on who and what the gossip is about.

A second striking feature of soap operas is the kind of community they represent. All of the gossip in soap operas arises in and from closed communities in which social relationships are as deeply and thoroughly entangled as those in the most traditional societies. Soap opera scholar Laura Stempel Mumford observes:

> Soap opera characters are diegetically entangled by their past, present, and potential future ties of kinship and romance, blood, marriage, and friendship. They are narratively entangled by the fact that their economic, political, and

thus other "public" relationships are subordinated to these personal ties. Thus, the intimate connections among soap opera characters mean that events in one storyline inevitably have consequences in others.[28]

A practical purpose of such entanglements is to permit the juggling of multiple simultaneous storylines, which soap operas need to do to sustain themselves day after day. But a deeper reason is likely that they feed an innate human need to tease out the relationships between people in social groups.

A third characteristic of soap operas is their focus on intimate, personal, privileged, often secret information about characters' lives and affairs. In the world of soap operas, Mumford observes, everything is everybody's business. Nothing is truly private because there is no privacy. Characters "rent rooms in boardinghouses with common living rooms and kitchens or dwell in multigenerational family groups, work in buildings with open lounges, eat and drink in busy bars and restaurants, and socialize at large public gatherings. Because they spend nearly all of their time in such spaces, they must conduct their most private business essentially in public." Mumford explains, "This in turn works to construct a fictional community whose members have an unrestricted right of access to each other's most personal experiences and feelings."[29] Compare this to the way Dunbar describes traditional communities: "In traditional peasant communities the world over, everyone lives in everyone else's pocket. They have to, of course, because houses are crammed together and walls are like paper. But more than that, people want to: the community is a genuine community, a co-operative whose members share the same problems of day-to-day survival. They are also bound by ties of kinship."[30]

Gossip is part of the glue that holds communities like these together. Being privy to other people's business is not just a matter of being in the know. It is essential for getting along and getting ahead in the group. Evolution has thus given gossip several intrinsic appeals, one of which is that it creates a sense of intimacy and connection among those who share in it. The hypothesis that some of this appeal would transfer to the gossip in soap operas makes perfect sense.

There is another demonstrable causal connection between soap operas and real-world gossip. Even though, nowadays, most people watch soap operas alone and probably don't talk about them much, there are occasions when fans do "gossip" with each other about the shows. In an essay discussing her own experience as a soap opera fan, journalist Julie Porter describes how she developed a taste for soap operas as a child by watching and talking about them with her mother.[31] Those conversations often revolved around values, since soap opera crises tend to be presented as moral predicaments. When Porter became an adult, she turned for conversation about soap operas to online social networking sites. On those sites, she experienced a real sense of community. She writes that the Web is an apt term "for the tangle of relationships and emotions, the lines that become woven together and the connections we make—and break—online." Sometimes, "online friendships can lead to phone meetings or 'IRL' (in real life) meetings (honest-to-gosh, face-to-face get-togethers)."[32] It is clear from many accounts like this that the intense fictional gossip on display in soap operas sometimes spills over into real-world gossip.

Human beings need gossip, Dunbar argues. Soap operas seem perfectly designed to satisfy that need. They serve up lots of fictional gossip. They depict communities that revolve around gossip. They trade in intimacies and inside information. They provide occasions and topics for gossip with friends. You would think, therefore, that the future of soap operas is assured.

Ironically, in today's media marketplace, soap operas are in trouble. CBS's *As the World Turns*—the top-rated daytime soap of the 1960s and 1970s—averaged 13.6 million viewers in 1970, according to the Nielsen ratings. In 1980, it averaged 7.9; in 1990, 5.8; and in 2000, 3.8. By 2009 its viewership had fallen to fewer than 2 million, and CBS canceled the show. Within three years, two other decades-old soap operas were canceled. In 2020 just four daytime soaps remained on the air. The top-ranked of these, CBS's *The Young and the Restless*, averaged about 2.2 million viewers. Year after year, its ratings continue to decline.[33]

The long-term decline in daytime soap opera audiences likely has two main causes. One is demographic: there are simply fewer people at home during the day to watch TV. The other is the proliferation of alternative entertainment on cable television, the internet, gaming stations, and social media. This abundance of alternatives has led to a decline in audiences for all kinds of network programming. These two trends have been exacerbated by other factors: the relatively high cost of even inexpensive scripted shows, like soap operas, compared with talk shows and reality TV; the rise of "quality" TV shows like *Game of Thrones*, which attract larger and broader audiences and generate more buzz than the housewife-oriented soaps; and new viewing habits like binge viewing, made possible by the online distribution of TV programming.[34] Note that none of these factors indicates a decline in audiences' appetite for gossip. To the contrary, the big challenge that soap operas face today is not a reduction in media audiences' itch for gossip; it is that there are now so many more ways to scratch that itch. Reality TV is one of them.

From Soap Operas to Reality TV

I have pointed out four ways in which soap operas are designed to satisfy the itch for gossip: they display a lot of it; they portray closed communities in which characters' lives are thoroughly entangled; they trade in intimacies, secrets, and "private" matters; and they prompt gossip from viewers. Reality TV does all of these same things, often even better than soap operas do.

Take *Amish Mafia*. Characters in *Amish Mafia* don't just gossip with each other; they also gossip directly to viewers through on-camera "confessionals" (a reality TV staple). The reality show *Survivor* foments gossip among its cast members by isolating them from the outside world and requiring them to compete for social advancement within and between "tribes." *Amish Mafia* does one better by purporting to find the same sort of closed, dog-eat-dog community in the real world. The gossip in *Amish Mafia* is triply "private": it deals with such intimate matters as family and romance; it concerns a closed and secretive society; and, within that society, it focuses on a group of gangsters engaged in shady and often illegal business. Finally, *Amish Mafia* explicitly encourages viewers to gossip by expressly inviting them to tweet reactions to the show and displaying some of these tweets on screen during the broadcast. In terms of its plot twists and dialog, *Amish Mafia* is strikingly similar to soap operas. In fact, one could say that *Amish Mafia* is just another soap opera, except for one crucial difference: it purports to be real.

Soap opera fans routinely connect the shows they watch to "real life." Laura Stempel Mumford describes the experience this way:

> As viewers, we . . . make constant, albeit not always direct or conscious, comparisons between the fictional world of the soaps we watch and the nonfictional world in which we live. This means in turn that we both understand and evaluate the sexual politics and other ideological aspects of the soap opera narrative in terms of the "real" world and come to understand the "real" world to some extent in terms of the programs we watch.[35]

Soap operas invite this kind of comparison by portraying worlds that are supposed to be much like the real world, at least in terms of people's social relationships. Reality TV does the same thing, so reality TV fans make the same kinds of comparisons between shows' characters and events and their own lives and experience. But reality TV goes a huge step further. It presents social interactions not just as *like* those in the real world but as *part of* the real world. Even when the situations shown are obviously highly contrived, as in *Survivor* and *The Bachelorette*, the interactions between cast members are assumed to be somewhat spontaneous and actual. This has enormous implications for the stance that viewers adopt when watching reality TV. Essentially, they treat it as nonfiction.

Nonfiction has three special emotional appeals that are different from the appeals of fiction. All three are closely related to the appeals of gossip.[36] The first of these is an appeal to the viewer as a social actor. If you see an actor on stage pretend to have a heart attack, you can sit back and admire the performance. If you see an actor have an actual heart attack, you feel a powerful urge to act. Even if you are in the balcony and can do nothing to help, you feel that somebody needs to act, and so you sit on the edge of your seat, waiting for somebody to provide help. It is possible for fiction to prompt this same kind of response—particularly fiction that is based on actual events, like *Hotel Rwanda* or *12 Years a Slave*—but nonfiction does it routinely. That is part of its distinctive appeal.

Admittedly, this effect is tenuous in the many parts of *Amish Mafia* that are far-fetched, fabulous, or just plain silly—like the scene about the bundling place. Even there, though, it works indirectly, as in the case of gossip. If a friend gossips to you, "Did you see Henry got a new BMW?" that statement has more to do with your relationship with your friend and with Henry than it does with the car. It implicitly invites you to make some sort of judgment about Henry, which in turn creates a kind of alliance between you and your friend. *Amish Mafia* works similarly. By invoking reality, it prompts special attention and concern. It implicitly invites viewers to take a stance on what they see and hear in order to be part of a community that is supposedly also watching and judging. It feels good to belong to such a community.

A second special emotional appeal shared by nonfiction and gossip is an appeal to our egos. This is most obvious in the case of "serious" nonfiction, like social-issues documentaries. Like gossip, those can make us feel good about ourselves by implying that we are part of a special group that is in the know. We may imagine ourselves to be especially smart and sophisticated, morally superior, privy to special knowledge or inside information, or part of a community that shares particularly worthwhile values, beliefs, or concerns. It is harder for a reality TV show to pull this emotional lever for the simple reason that reality TV is widely regarded as manipulative, minimally informative, and not terribly worthwhile. Even so, one satisfaction that people get from watching *Amish Mafia* is a sense of learning interesting facts that are not widely known about Amish people and Amish society. There is always some pride in this kind of "learning."

Third, nonfiction and gossip share the emotional appeal of an implied social alliance. Whenever a discourse presents some remote state of affairs as actual, like "Henry got a new BMW," we have no alternative but to take it on faith. This applies to *Amish Mafia* too. In order to accept the "reality" it invokes as legitimate and worthwhile, we must take on faith that it is what it appears to be—that a person who looks Amish is Amish, that an apparently spontaneous conversation is unscripted, and so on. This implicit appeal for trust implies reciprocity and good faith and so creates the feeling of an alliance between author and audience.

To be clear, taking something on faith does not mean regarding it as factual. Viewers of even serious nonfiction films welcome setup situations, reenactments, continuity editing, melodramatic music, and all sorts of other artificial elements. "Trust me" has little to do with facts per se. It is an implied social pact. Consider how Donald Trump used the phrase. It obviously did not mean, "You may rely on the specific facts I'm relating here." What it meant is, "You can trust my *intent*; I've got your back." Whether true or false, that is the seductive appeal that he was making to his followers. Nonfiction relies on the same kind of implied social pact with viewers.

Facts do matter, of course. When Trump got them wrong, it undermined the idea that he is worthy of our trust. It is the same with nonfiction. Again, the analogy to gossip is illuminating. If your friend speculates about how Henry was able to pay for such an expensive car, that's "just gossip." The facts are not a central concern. But what if your friend tells you, as a matter of fact, that Henry's car was a gift from his boyfriend and you later discover that the car was a rental because Henry's regular car was in the shop? If you suppose that your friend was merely passing on hearsay, you will likely forgive the falsehood as an honest mistake. But if you suppose that your friend deliberately made up the story to manipulate your feelings about Henry, you are bound to be incensed. It's not the falsehood that matters; it's the intent. Similarly, with *Amish Mafia*, if the pretense that non-Amish actors are actual Amish people is seen as a way to make a story loosely based on reality more interesting to viewers, it's no big deal. If, however, it is perceived as cynical or self-serving—an attempt to take unfair advantage of viewers' credulity or to drum up sensation for profit—then it's seen as a violation of the viewer's trust: the moral equivalent of false gossip.

Amish Mafia routinely and purposefully presents situations—like a small-time roofing contractor as the head of a gang of Amish enforcers—as other than they are. On top of that, its cast members routinely make voiceover statements that are intentionally misleading or flat-out false. It is hard to see these kinds of deliberate deception as anything other than taking advantage of viewers' trust, so one would expect them to alienate viewers. Yet, remarkably, when fans of *Amish Mafia* suspect this kind of deception, even when they get wise to it, that rarely diminishes their enjoyment of the show. To the contrary, they seem to relish the deception, or at least to relish gossiping about it in tweets and conversations. It is worth looking at the psychological and sociological literature on lying and deception to see if that casts any light on this phenomenon. First, though, I would like to address one other peculiar puzzle about gossip: Why is it that gossip in all of its cultural forms, from Amish quilting bees to the *National Enquirer* to reality TV, is so closely associated with women?

Gossip, Gangsters, and Gender

In *Grooming, Gossip, and the Evolution of Language*, Dunbar has remarkably little to say about gender differences. Basically, he argues that gossip is something we *all* do, because our social well-being depends upon it. He does mention, however, that in all primate species males are on average much bigger than females and tend to try to get what they want by throwing their weight around. Because of that, and also because young primate males typically roam in search of mates while young females stay with their groups, female primates of all species tend to become more reliant on social alliances, more attentive to group dynamics, and more sensitive to social cues.

One might reasonably suppose that, through evolution, some of this gender difference has become heritable and innate, which would help explain why women are more likely to watch soap operas than men. Interestingly, Dunbar does not say that. He says the reason that women are more likely to watch soap operas is that, in our society, they are more likely to be trapped in the house taking care of children and doing laundry and therefore more in need of the sense of social connectedness that soap operas provide.[37] This does not imply that innate gender differences play no role at all, only that they are minor compared with situational factors.

Primatologist Frans de Waal has drawn the same conclusion about differences in the way male and female chimpanzees behave. He writes:

> In the course of time, I have changed my opinion about sex differences in chimpanzees from explaining them as inborn behavioral tendencies to viewing them as reflecting different social objectives in males and females. If the sexes are trying to get something different out of life we obviously expect different behavior: the road to goal X requires another behavioral strategy than the road to goal Y. These strategies need not be genetically specified; they may develop through experience and learning.[38]

How does this relate to grooming, which Dunbar sees as a precursor to human gossip?

Male chimpanzees tend to be far more aggressive than females. In one chimpanzee group observed in the wild, a male would fight with another male every five hours and with a female every thirteen hours on average. Fights among females, in contrast, would occur only once every hundred hours.[39] It is possible that testosterone is responsible for this difference. But by closely observing when and with whom individuals fought, de Waal came to a different conclusion. The oldest and biggest males fought strategically, for dominance, to keep or gain control of mating privileges. These males groomed strategically as well, to create alliances and heal rifts with other physically powerful males, in order to cement their dominance. When weaker or lower-ranking individuals fought, regardless of their sex, it was mainly to come to the aid of relatives or close friends. These less powerful individuals tended to use grooming to create a broad, stable network of alliances, as a means of staying safe by maintaining stability in the group and keeping the power of bullies in check. In other words, grooming in chimpanzee groups, like fighting, depends mainly upon the circumstances of the individual.

If human gossip is also a form of social grooming, as Dunbar supposes, this leads to an interesting hypothesis. Perhaps gossip is a natural self-preservation strategy for people who lack social power and privilege, a majority of whom, in our society, happen to be women. Perhaps, for those people, gossip can be empowering. Perhaps it can help them give voice to their wishes and concerns. Perhaps it can provide them with group solidarity and support. Perhaps it can help them withstand pressures to conform to the status quo or to knuckle under to bullies. Perhaps in these ways it can bring some healing to damaged or damaging social situations. Feminist literary scholar Patricia Meyer Spacks makes an argument along these lines in a 1982 essay entitled "In

Praise of Gossip."[40] (Spacks acknowledges that gossip can also be malicious, self-aggrandizing, or idly destructive. That is not the kind of gossip she wishes to praise.)

It is easy to imagine how actual gossip can be empowering. Consider, once again, Lebanon Levi's illustration of Amish women gossiping:

> "Rebecca's boy got a haircut!" (Meaning a *barbershop* haircut—without a bowl.)
>
> "That's so terrible. . . . I feel just terrible for his mother. Unless she condoned it. You don't think she condoned it, do you?"
>
> "Well, I certainly hope not!"[41]

The women in this example are clearly engaged in a form of what I called gentle policing. At the same time, they are doing many of the things Spacks praises: articulating their concerns, discovering shared values, creating coalitions, providing each other with emotional support, and strengthening their social ties.

What about reality TV? Is it possible for *Amish Mafia* to serve as a form of what Spacks calls healing gossip? Can *Amish Mafia* empower its viewers? If people talk about the show face to face, then it certainly can. In that case, the show functions just like Rebecca's boy's haircut—as a juicy gossip item. But most TV viewing today, by far, is solitary. It is hard to imagine how anybody could be empowered by watching *Amish Mafia* alone. Picture a young mother at the end of an exhausting day, stuck at home with her small children while her husband works late. Picture her watching *Amish Mafia* all by herself. It is easy to see how a gathering of friends would empower her. But watching *Amish Mafia*? Not very likely.

Still, there are scholars who have argued that merely watching popular TV shows—particularly ones that are a little "trashy," like *Amish Mafia*—can be empowering for people who are relatively powerless or on the fringes of society, even for people who watch them alone.[42] *Amish Mafia* is edgy. It does not tell charming stories about happy and well-adjusted Amish people. To the contrary, it tells stories about a group of people who are outsiders to both the Amish community and mainstream society who go about deliberately challenging the authority of both the bishops and the law. (They claim to be protecting the Amish way of life, but in fact they go against it at every turn.) Furthermore, *Amish Mafia* takes what in the popular imagination is possibly the most respected and traditional community in America and dishes dirt about it. "Aha!" the show implies. "That so-called upstanding community, with all its piety and quaint customs, is really nothing like it is supposed to be."

You can see how this might appeal to viewers who feel disrespected or downtrodden in their own society. More important, you can see how it implicitly authorizes the viewer—encourages the viewer, in fact—to disbelieve commonly held beliefs and to challenge widely respected authorities. "Don't believe what you've been told," it says, in effect. "Believe your eyes and trust your gut."

This contrarian tendency in *Amish Mafia* is surely appealing to some people, particularly those with a strong independent streak or those who feel pushed around. But whether it is truly empowering is a matter of debate. Most feminists would argue that it is not. To be truly empowering, something needs to improve your ability to change your actual social circumstances. How likely is it that watching *Amish Mafia* by yourself will help you articulate what troubles you, provide you with emotional support, create and strengthen friendships, and do all those other truly empowering things that good gossip can do? Again, not very likely.

Nonetheless, watching *Amish Mafia* might well provide a kind of emotional validation. If you feel pushed around or pushed aside in society, identifying with gangsters and even just enjoying a show that is a bit disreputable can be ego affirming. Like gossip, it can in this way make you feel good about yourself. To argue that this will give you energy and courage to face troubles in the real world is something of a stretch. (How likely is it that watching *Amish Mafia* will help somebody confront an abusive boss, for example?) Even so, it must have some therapeutic value.

When I asked *Amish Mafia* fans why they enjoyed the show, a common answer was "for escape." People watch entertainment TV in order to put aside work, relax from stress, and forget about real-life troubles. People need to relax and de-stress from time to time. Whether they do that by reading, knitting, walking, or watching TV, done in moderation it is healthy and beneficial, even therapeutic. The only problem with using TV as therapy is that watching it alone, as people often do, is socially isolating. An authoritative study of the decline of community in America in the latter part of the twentieth century, Robert Putnam's *Bowling Alone*, suggests that television may be the single greatest cause.[43] Even though *Amish Mafia* is designed to satisfy some viewers' emotional need for gossip, it cannot fulfill viewers' actual social needs in the ways that actual gossip does. That said, the *Amish Mafia* fans

I spoke to seemed to be socially quite healthy. They had strong families, good friends, satisfying social activities, and real-world gossip buddies. For people like these, de-stressing by watching *Amish Mafia* is likely healthy and beneficial. Even if it does not empower them, it can reenergize them so that they can reengage with the challenges of the real world.

That's all well and good, you might say, but what about all the lying? What about the fact that *Amish Mafia* deliberately spreads false information? What about the fact that it knowingly deceives and misleads viewers? What about the fact that it invents stories that make the Amish look bad and presents those as factual?

What about the Lying?

About midway through *Amish Mafia*'s run, after many phone calls to Discovery's corporate headquarters in a suburb of Washington, DC, I finally managed to get a meeting with one of the senior executives in charge of *Amish Mafia*. I will use the name "Boss" and the pronoun "they" to mask the executive's identity, for reasons that will become clear. I was hoping to get an executive's perspective on the fabrication and deception in *Amish Mafia*, but I was afraid that if I admitted that up front, they would refuse to talk to me, so I told them, instead, that I wanted to learn more about an executive producer's job at Discovery.

When we met over lunch, I asked Boss about their background, their work, and a new fiction series they were developing. They were friendly and forthcoming. But when I started to ask about *Amish Mafia*, they immediately turned cagey and told me a couple of things that I knew to be false. First, they told me that the activities depicted in the show were "totally real." (Those were their words.) When I asked about particulars that I knew were made up—like the fact that Levi was a roofer, not a gangster—they told me that they were proscribed from discussing any details of the show because of a legal case in Lancaster involving one of the cast members. I'd read about that case in the local papers. It had nothing to do with the show or its producers. It was a domestic violence case. Boss was just using it as an excuse.

I'm not going to say that Boss lied to me. Even though their statements were untrue and they knew that, they must have supposed that I would also know they were untrue. So whatever Boss may have intended with those false statements, it is unlikely that they were trying to pull the wool over my eyes. I supposed at the time that they were just protecting their job, part of which was to maintain the show's masquerade. Even so, I felt a bit insulted and abused by the fact that Boss had deliberately fed me falsehoods. That is not surprising: such emotions are a natural response to being lied to. What is surprising and curious—and one of the points of this gossipy anecdote—is that I never experienced such emotions while watching *Amish Mafia*. I felt perplexed and bemused by the show's falsehoods, but never insulted or abused.

My first thought, in reflecting on this afterward, is that there must be a fundamental difference between a mediated lie on TV, like the claim that Lebanon Levi is an actual Amish gangster, and an interpersonal lie, like the same claim made by a producer to my face. After all, a lie to your face is aimed right at you. It is personal. For that reason, it is bound to feel like an insult or affront. A lie on TV, on the other hand, is broadcast: it is put out there for anybody and everybody and nobody in particular. Even if you happen to find it distasteful or unethical, you probably won't take it personally. And so, I thought, nobody is going to feel insulted or disrespected by *Amish Mafia*, with the possible exception of Amish people. But then I remembered talking to people—non-Amish people—who *did* feel deeply and personally insulted by the show. I'll say more about these people in the next chapter. For now, I'll just say that their anger made me rethink my initial intuitions.

Upon further reflection, I surmised that whether or not one feels insulted by a lie has nothing to do with the lie's form or how it is delivered; it has to do with its perceived intent. I have already discussed how this works with false gossip, using the hypothetical example of Henry's BMW: if you perceive an intentional falsehood in gossip to be cooperative—as being on your side in some way—you'll gladly overlook its falsity. If, however, you perceive it as adversarial—intended to manipulate or take advantage of you—you're bound to feel incensed. The same thing is true of the deceptions in *Amish Mafia*. If you see the show as "just entertainment," designed to amuse and satisfy you, its deceptions will seem harmless and possibly even amusing. If you are looking to it for true information, its deceptions will feel like an abuse of your trust and are likely to make you a little angry. I never took *Amish Mafia* seriously, except as an object of study. My interest in its falsehoods and deceptions was purely academic. That is why they didn't bother me. In contrast, I really wanted reliable information from the executive at Discovery, which is why their lies felt manipulative to me.

A viewer can choose whether to regard the deceptions in *Amish Mafia* as either adversarial or cooperative. But which are they really? Are they intended to take advantage of viewers' gullibility or just to show viewers a good time? In fact, they are designed to do both of these things, and more besides. Deception in discourse, like gossip, is complicated. If you happen to have a negative knee-jerk reaction to the gossip about Rebecca's boy's haircut in Lebanon Levi's anecdote, you are seeing only half the picture. In the same way, if you happen to have a negative knee-jerk reaction to the fakery in *Amish Mafia*, you are seeing only half the picture. To see the whole picture, you need to deliberately set aside questions of "ought" and "should," which almost inevitably prompt those knee-jerk reactions. With that in mind, it is worth revisiting the anecdote about the Discovery executive who did not tell me the truth.

The first thing to note is that I was not entirely honest with Boss when I arranged the interview. I wanted something from them: information about *Amish Mafia*. I supposed that part of their job was to maintain a shroud of secrecy around the show, and I figured they might not agree to talk to me if they knew my real agenda, so I gave a different reason for wanting to meet with them: to learn about Boss's job. Boss had no particular reason to help me. They didn't even have any reason to trust me. Since I was visiting from Lancaster, where *Amish Mafia* had received some heat in the press, Boss even had reason to be suspicious of me. Nonetheless, they generously agreed to meet with me.

Under these circumstances, when I started to question Boss about the fabrications and falsehoods in *Amish Mafia*, they might have felt perfectly justified in telling me to mind my own business and walking away from the interview. But they didn't, because that would have been unfriendly. Instead, they told me a couple of transparent and rather harmless lies, to put me off. So Boss was not trying to deceive and insult me. To the contrary, they were just trying to be tactful!

You will often find justification at work in that little word "just." "It was *just* an accident." "*Amish Mafia* is *just* entertainment." "They were *just* trying to be tactful." Just to be clear, explaining deception in this way does not make it right. Similarly, arguing that deceit is natural, as I am about to do, is by no means to say that it is either normal or necessary in any particular instance. Some lying can be utterly commonplace and still be antisocial, harmful, and morally repugnant. And lying is almost never necessary, even when it seems almost instinctual. To say that deceit is natural means only that it is an evolved tendency or trait, like human sociality and language. What is right and wrong is a different matter that I will take up in the next chapter. But what is crucial to recognize up front—what I have tried to demonstrate with this anecdote— is that in any discussion of the rights and wrongs of deception, one must take into account the nature of the social transaction and the interests of the participants.

The Nature of Deception

The fact is, people lie casually and routinely in everyday conversation. Cognitive psychologist Robert Feldman secretly videotaped ten-minute get-acquainted conversations between fifty pairs of strangers in his lab. Afterward, he and his associates sat down with each subject individually to watch that person's recorded conversation and asked them to report every "inaccuracy" in something they said. According to his subjects' own tallies, they told on average three lies in every ten minutes of conversation.[44] From self-aggrandizement to flattery, from friendly banter to sneaky manipulation, from exaggeration to excuses, from little white lies to outright prevarication, lying is something all people do when they are around other people, not just to get ahead, but to get along. Lying is part of human nature.

The reason is simple. In any environment in which there are creatures with competing interests, like predators and prey, deception and counterdeception naturally evolve. Antelopes evolved the ability to feint and dodge to avoid being caught by cheetahs. Cheetahs evolved speed and agility to counter the antelope's feints. As a result of the same evolutionary process, there are insects disguised as twigs, moths that emit clicks to jam bat radar, harmless snakes that mimic poisonous ones, squirrels that make fake food caches to trick onlookers, opossums that play dead when threatened, dogs with fur that stands up to make them look larger when aggressive, and a whole cosmetics industry for humans.

Sociality ups the ante for skillful subterfuge enormously. When animals live in groups that require cooperation for survival, like prairie dogs, wolves, and baboons, individuals can advance their own interests, like eating more than their fair share or working less for it, by being sneaky. Primatologists Richard Byrne and Andrew Whiten reported seeing a juvenile baboon watch an adult female laboriously dig up a tasty root. As soon as the root was out of the ground, the youngster sidled up to the adult and shrieked as though being attacked. The youngster's mother came charging out of the nearby brush and drove the other adult away, assuming that it had attacked her child. As soon as both adult baboons were out of sight, the juvenile picked up the root and ate it. Byrne and Whiten saw the young baboon use the same trick a couple of other times with other adults.[45]

Individuals living in social groups clearly benefit by having an aptitude for this sort of trickery and using it. Other individuals in the group need to be able to see through such subterfuge to subvert or punish it in order to protect their own interests. As a result, social creatures like baboons developed social intelligence, including not just the ability to be tricky and sneaky but also the ability to perceive whether their groupmates' intentions are cooperative and straightforward or self-serving and deceptive. Robin Dunbar demonstrated that the size of the neocortex of primate species was a strong predictor of the size of their typical social groupings. Richard Byrne and Nadia Corp went a step further and discovered that the size of the neocortex also predicts the frequency of different primate species' deceptive behavior.[46]

Once early humans had language, they naturally turned it to trickery. When a dog growls and bares its teeth, that indicates aggression. It may be a bluff to keep another dog from attacking. Still, there is a strong causal connection between the behavior and the intention it signals: a growl indicates an actual readiness to bite. Symbolic language breaks this link. For example, the statement "I'm about to bite you" need not mean what it says at all. That makes language ideal for deception. Semiotician Umberto Eco goes so far as to define symbolic language that way. A sign, he says, is "anything that can be used to lie."[47] *Self*-deception is a natural next step in the evolutionary process, according to biologist Robert Trivers.[48] We unconsciously rationalize our lying and cheating not just so we can feel good about ourselves, but because believing our own lies and rationalizing our own cheats makes us better liars and cheaters—better at deceiving others and therefore more likely to get away with our deceptions.

These theories of the origins of language and lying are speculative, but they do an excellent job of explaining the well-established fact that human beings are natural liars and cheats. That fact alone suggests we would do well to flip the analytical framework that critics often bring to the discussion of deception in reality TV. Instead of regarding deception as peculiar and aberrant, like a form of TV journalism gone awry, we need to recognize that what is actually peculiar and aberrant is any discourse in which scrupulous honesty or factuality is expected, like scientific research and news reportage. All such specialized discourses have one of two defining characteristics. They are cooperative transactions in which accurate information is vital. (It would not serve me well to give you a deceptive shopping list, for example.) Or they are highly ritualized or rule-governed interactions in which certain kinds of behavior are expressly proscribed. (It is unacceptable to partially deflate your own team's football in a professional match to make it easier to handle, for instance.) When NBC newscaster Brian Williams made up a story, in 2015, about flying in a helicopter that was forced down by enemy fire in Iraq, he tripped over both of these special circumstances: he fed viewers false information in a form of discourse that depends upon facts, and he violated well-established conventions of journalism.[49] Everyday conversation is not normally governed by either of these rules. Nor is gossip. Nor, obviously, is reality TV.

The point here is not that deception in reality TV is perfectly acceptable. The point is that, instead of regarding it as intrinsically immoral or wrong, it is more apt and accurate to regard it as part of a social transaction from which all participants are trying to get something they want—a transaction not that different, in principle, from buying a used car.

Deception as Transaction

In traditional economic theory, people lie and cheat to get things they want using minimal effort, like an A on an exam, easy money, or a sexual fling. According to this theory, people do a quick cost-benefit analysis in which they take three things into account: How much do I want it? How likely am I to get caught? And if I do get caught, how bad will the punishment be? In short, whether or not to lie is a deliberate decision.

This explanation of lying is partially mistaken. Lying *is* about trying to get what you want—that part is true. But lying is not deliberate. Scientific evidence suggests that people do not *choose* to lie or cheat. When you ask a child why he or she did something bad, the answer is often, "I don't know. I just did it." That response is literally true. The same thing happens to adults. When people offer explanations or justifications for something they did, they are looking back at their behavior and interpreting it, just as an observer would.

Reality TV producers behave the same way. They are not thinking, How much can I get away with? They are thinking, How can I get what I want? They may want a more dramatic scene, higher ratings, or a bit of controversy to attract more attention. Although they also want to stay out of trouble, they are not typically reflecting on honesty or ethics. They are simply trying to get a job done. If in the process they get called on the carpet for manipulation or deception, they come up with after-the-fact excuses or self-justifications, like "It's just entertainment."

The motivations for cheating (and also for *not* cheating when the opportunity is available) are largely unconscious. Although there is some cost-benefit analysis involved, that is also largely unconscious. Crows and blue jays look around while hiding food, and, if they see another bird looking, they'll dig the food back up and hide it elsewhere. Such behavior obviously involves a kind of calculation, but it is largely instinctual and automatic, not like logical reasoning. People are likewise instinctively attuned to whether or not they are being seen when they are involved in a deceptive act, and they automatically adjust their behavior accordingly.

In a clever experiment, psychologist Melissa Bateson and colleagues at Newcastle University put a sign above a beverage station asking people to put contributions for their drinks into an honesty box. For ten weeks, on alternating weeks, the sign was decorated either with different flowers or with different pairs of eyes. On the weeks in which the sign was decorated with eyes, the contribution box held roughly three times as much money as those weeks in which it was decorated with flowers,[50] revealing the extent to which nonconscious factors drive decision making in deception.

Behavioral economist Dan Ariely and associates performed clever experiments to try to identify these nonconscious factors.[51] Many of the experiments had subjects do a simple but time-consuming arithmetic task, after which they were paid for correct answers. But instead of turning in their actual answers, subjects were given the answer key and asked to tally and report their own scores in order to be paid. The researchers manipulated an array of variables, including how much money people got for correct answers, whether they turned in their answer sheets along with their report, whether they were monitored while taking the test, whether they signed an honor code before tallying their score, whether they exchanged papers with someone else, whether they pooled their earnings with other test takers, whether they collaborated on the test, and others. What Ariely discovered is that nearly everybody cheats a little bit whenever there is any chance they can get away with it, claiming to have correctly answered a couple more questions than they actually did for a bit more pay. Even more surprising, almost nobody cheats a lot, even when they have no chance of getting caught—even when they are allowed to help themselves to their own "earnings" from an unmonitored envelope of money.

It is obvious why people cheat: we cheat to get ahead. The more interesting question, Ariely says, is, Why don't we cheat more when we know we can get away with it? Ariely's answer is ego: people want to feel good about themselves. When we tell a little lie or cheat a little bit, we justify our behavior with a little act of self-deceit. Instead of thinking, Look how much I cheated, we in effect think, Look how much I *didn't* cheat. Ariely writes, "This is where our amazing cognitive flexibility comes into play. Thanks to this human skill, as long as we cheat by only a little bit, we can benefit from cheating and still view ourselves as marvelous human beings."[52] This is not a deliberate act; it is something we do automatically and unconsciously.

Ariely offers lots of circumstantial evidence to support this hypothesis. For example, when people were asked to remember as many of the Ten Commandments as they could before doing his test, they didn't cheat at all. This was true of even self-professed atheists. Asking subjects to remember ten books they had read recently had no such effect. Signing an honor code also briefly works to stop cheating because it is hard to justify even a little bit of cheating when you've just been reminded that honorable people don't cheat. In contrast, when people's cheating benefited somebody other than themselves, particularly a partner or an acquaintance, they cheated a lot more than usual. That is because it is much easier to justify cheating when it's not self-serving.

Incidentally, Ariel found that people who score high on a creativity test cheat more than others. The reason he offers is that creative people are especially adroit rationalizers. "Just as creativity enables us to develop original paths around rules," Ariely writes, "it can also enable us to develop original paths around rules, all the while allowing us to reinterpret information in a self-serving way."[53] Reality TV producers tend to be exceptionally creative people.

But the mystery I set out to explain is not why reality TV producers use trickery and deception. That is simple: they want to make maximally entertaining shows with minimal effort and expense. The real mystery is why audiences don't mind being tricked and deceived. A likely answer, suggested by Ariely's research, is that people are perfectly happy to overlook deceit whenever it gives them something that they find gratifying. Think of flattery in conversation. If a lie gives you something you want, you tend not even to see it as a lie. As Ariely puts it, we are blinded by our own motivations. He offers examples ranging from the behavior of Enron executives to decisions he made in his own scientific research. In the same way, if you really enjoy watching *Amish Mafia*, you'll naturally feel there is nothing wrong with it, however devious or exploitative the show may actually be.

The most significant takeaway of Ariely's research on cheating is that people justify lying and cheating by finding ways to feel good about themselves. Many critics have observed that one of the key appeals of reality TV is that it makes viewers feel good about themselves. Shows like *Hell's Kitchen* appeal to a sense of self-improvement; shows like *American Idol* suggest that there is really not much that separates each of us from celebrity; and shows like *Real Housewives of New Jersey* encourage us to feel that we are better or smarter than the folks we see depicted. *Amish Mafia* does all three of these things. The evident delight many *Amish Mafia* fans take in spotting and talking about the show's lies and fabrications is also explicable as a way for fans to feel good about themselves. It makes them feel smart when they spot a deception. It makes them feel like an insider when they gossip about it. It makes them feel righteous to be scandalized by it. In all of these ways, spotting subterfuge in *Amish Mafia* can give fans a subtle ego boost.

In transactional terms, the chicanery in *Amish Mafia* is a twofer. First, it delivers more dramatic and sensational stories than could possibly be found by just filming reality. Second, by insisting that these stories are real, it allows viewers to feel good about themselves in the same ways that gossip does—both in the know and morally superior. A straight-up documentary about actual ex-Amish roofer Lebanon Levi and his business might initially appeal to curiosity, but in the long run it would be boring. A straight-up fictional series about an imaginary group of Amish gangsters might be entertaining, but in the long run it would have no more impact than any other made-up story. By using fakery—by presenting made-up events in ways that make them appear to be largely actual and spontaneous—*Amish Mafia* is able to simultaneously deliver both the drama of fiction and the special emotional appeals of nonfiction. For viewers who are mainly interested in the emotional payoff of their leisure-time investment, this is a good deal. In view of Ariely's findings on the psychology of deceit, it is no wonder they forgive the fakery.

When Is a Lie Not a Lie?

"You haven't aged a day!" can hardly be called a lie. "There was an old woman who lived in a shoe" is by no means a lie. "Watch closely; I'm going to make this card disappear" is obviously not a lie either.

False flattery, fairy tales, and magic acts all have this in common: their purpose is cooperative. That is one thing that separates them from "real" lies. I briefly addressed the difference between cooperative and adversarial lying in the section on gossip. If you perceive a lie in gossip as being friendly or supportive, you'll gladly overlook its falsity. If you perceive it as an attempt to manipulate or take advantage of you, you are bound to feel incensed.

British social anthropologist Frederick Bailey expands on this difference in a 1991 book, *The Prevalence of Deceit*.[54] Bailey considers deceit to be any attempt to control or manipulate another person by subtle or covert means. Magic tricks are not a form of deceit by this definition. Most TV commercials are. The fakery in *Amish Mafia* may or may not be, depending upon what one supposes its purpose or social consequences to be. If it is just idle entertainment, it is not deceit. If it is designed to instill false beliefs about the Amish, then it is. It is not the show's "text" that determines whether or not it is deceitful; it is the social context.

Whenever the interests of people or groups of people are opposed, there is always the possibility of hostility, aggression, coercion, or out-and-out conflict. Deceit is a way of avoiding all that. It is a way of trying to get one's way and circumventing conflict at the same time. For example, if I want information from you that it is your job to protect, I can try to get the information by stealth, you can protect it by giving me false information, and we can still be very friendly. That is a perfect example of adversarial deceit. Those who are weak use adversarial deceit to protect their interests against the powerful without antagonizing them. They may keep secrets, or collude, or give false information. Those in power use adversarial deceit to get others to willingly comply with their interests. When a TV commercial suggests that buying an X-brand car will improve your leisure, your social status, and your love life, that is an example of a powerful social class (capitalists) using a form of subterfuge to get others (consumers) to literally buy into ideas that support the wealth, privilege, and power of the powerful. That is what ideology is, according to Bailey: the exercise of adversarial deceit by a powerful class.

That situation seems quite different from what happens with *Amish Mafia*. There are no opposing interests. The show—and even its fakery—is designed to give consumers what they want. The producers want nothing from viewers except for their time and attention. In exchange, they offer viewers something they like: the twofer deal I described previously—the appeal of sensational stories plus the appeal of what feels like nonfiction. Even though *Amish Mafia* fans indirectly help line the pockets of Discovery Inc. investors through their cable subscriptions, the contrarian tendencies of the show that I pointed out earlier, including its fairly overt fakery, seem to do more to validate those who feel disrespected and downtrodden in society than to support the interests of the powerful. So in terms of the way *Amish Mafia* typically works, as idle entertainment, its lies and deceptions do not seem to be adversarial. Compared with other forms of deceit, the fakery in *Amish Mafia* seems most akin to flattery: the producers are trying to win us over by delivering lies that we are happy to hear because they make us feel good about ourselves. I called this kind of deception collaborative. Bailey calls it collusive.

"Collusive lying occurs when two parties, knowing full well that what they are saying or doing is false, collude in ignoring the falsity," Bailey writes.[55] He explains with anthropological examples, most of which are quite complicated, like a traditional marriage ritual in northern India in which two families customarily enact a ritual conflict in order to pretend there is no actual conflict, when in fact marriages in that society take place only after a long, fraught, often acrimonious negotiation involving money, status, and family pride. But if you tease apart Bailey's examples, you will find that they all share several features. First, they have some narrow objective that benefits both sides and that can be achieved only through cooperation—like bringing about a marriage. Second, they take place in some moment or space that is set apart from ordinary social activities—like a wedding. Third, they involve mutually agreed-upon protocols, conventions, or rules that allow the two parties to collude in deliberately ignoring concerns—like opposing interests—that might otherwise interfere with the achievement of their immediate goal. That is where the pretense comes in. This kind of pretense is not lying exactly. It is a transaction: a deal to temporarily put aside the truth so that both parties can get something they want.

This seems to describe what is taking place with *Amish Mafia*. Viewers want to be entertained; producers want to profit from their time and attention. Together they enter into a special zone, called reality TV, in which both parties agree that the truth does not matter because that agreement allows both to get something they want. Viewers get the "deal" I described earlier: the drama of fiction plus the special emotional appeal of nonfiction. The fakery involved is not a lie. It's not even a price that viewers pay for what they want, because it costs them essentially nothing but time and attention. It's just part of the deal, not unlike the hocus pocus of a magic act, the suspension of disbelief during a fairy tale, and the ritualistic aspect of flattery. With magic acts, fairy tales, and well-meaning flattery, there is no harm and no foul. Everybody benefits; nobody suffers. That is why it would be absurd to regard them as lying, even though they deliberately trade in falsehoods. *Amish Mafia* appears to be the same sort of transaction, when you take only its producers and viewers into account. But *Amish Mafia* does not just involve those two parties; there are others with skin in the game.

Gossip, likewise, never involves just two parties. Besides the gossiper and gossipee, there is always also the party being gossiped about and the society that all three are part of. When people gossip, they are clearly cooperating. They are creating an implicit alliance from which they all stand to benefit. But they are also deliberately excluding others from their alliance. When somebody gets hurt by gossip, it is almost always those excluded. Gossip is fundamentally about maneuvering for social advantage. You might say that it is fundamentally about power. In that respect, gossip is fundamentally different from magic acts, fairy tales, and well-meaning flattery. That is why Bailey chooses the term "collusion" instead of "cooperation" to describe the pretense that occurs in such social transactions.

So far, in discussing *Amish Mafia*, I have focused mainly on producers and fans of the show. These two parties both benefit by treating the show's deliberate falsehoods as trivial and inconsequential. They collude in choosing to discount not just the show's misrepresentations of facts but also, importantly, the possibility that other people may pay some price for those misrepresentations. Others who may pay a price obviously include the ordinary people who appear in the show, many of whom are Amish and ex-Amish youth who, because they did not grow up with television, did not know exactly what they were getting into. Others include the Amish generally, whose society is demeaned by the show's falsehoods and whose reputation stands to suffer. Others include credulous viewers, including children, who may wind up believing nonsense and absorbing prejudicial attitudes, not just about the Amish but about society. And, if one effect of *Amish Mafia* and other shows like it is to make TV producers and audiences more tolerant of or less discerning about falsehoods presented in the form of facts, then those others who stand to pay a price for *Amish Mafia*'s collusive deceptions include all the rest of us too. It is to these others and the price they pay that the next chapter turns.

CHAPTER SIX

Rights and Wrongs

Respect Amish

On June 11, 2014, the online edition of the local newspaper in Lancaster, Pennsylvania, announced that a new TV show entitled *Amish Haunting* was going to be shot in the county. The show was to be produced by Hot Snakes Media, the same company that produced *Amish Mafia*, the third season of which had just aired. The new show would present dramatizations of Amish horror stories using actors as stand-ins for Amish people. *Amish Haunting* "might make *Amish Mafia* look like a documentary in comparison," the news writer quipped.[1]

Lancastrian Mary Haverstick stumbled across this announcement while eating her lunch and just about choked. From Amish gangsters to Amish horrors! What next? Haverstick was fed up with outsiders coming into Lancaster County to make so-called reality shows that depicted Amish people in demeaning ways. Somebody has to put a stop to this, she thought.[2] So, somewhat impulsively, she created a Facebook group, added a bunch of friends, and launched what she would call the Respect Amish movement, to end "Amish-sploitation" in the media.

Haverstick grew up and lives in Lancaster County, the home of the oldest and most famous community of Amish people. She lives in Lancaster city, miles from the rural parts of the county where the Amish live and farm (and where most of the reality TV was shot). Still, like most long-time locals, she has had a fair amount of contact with Amish people over the years. As a child she had an Amish nanny. She buys baked goods and produce from Amish vendors at Lancaster's Central Market. She passes Amish buggies and farms when she drives out of town. And, as with many long-time locals, the way she talks about the Amish evinces a subtle proprietary interest: these are *our* neighbors, *our* acquaintances, part of *our* community. Saying bad things about them reflects badly on *us*. "This is tarnishing our entire area!" Haverstick complained. "What are tourists coming in to see? What do they think Lancaster is like? When we go out and shop our goods and say we are from Lancaster County, how is this branding all of us?"[3]

Haverstick, who is herself a professional filmmaker, disliked the sensationalism of *Amish Mafia*—its focus on trumped-up violence and bad behavior, in particular. She found it obnoxious and tawdry: distasteful media bottom feeding, like much of contemporary reality TV. But she was perfectly happy to ignore that, to just tune it out. What stuck in her craw, what she could not just tune out, was her sense that Amish-themed reality TV shows were tarnishing the good reputation of the Amish as a group. She saw that as bigotry, plain and simple. "Let's be clear, distasteful reality programs are not what we are talking about. We're talking about targeting a religion, the Amish religion— a community that has very strong beliefs," she argued. "A show called Jewish Mafia or Catholic Mafia or Muslim Mafia would never get support. It would never get sponsorship. It would never get on the air because right in your face is the blatant fact that those shows are prejudiced! They're wrong!"

There have been reality TV shows called *All-American Muslim*; *Sister Wives* (about fundamentalist Mormons); *The Sisterhood: Becoming Nuns* (also produced by Hot Snakes Media); *God or the Girl* (about Catholic young men contemplating priesthood); and *Princesses: Long Island* (about Jewish women in their late twenties living at home with their parents). These shows demonstrate that religion is fair game and that negative stereotypes abound in reality TV. Still, all of them make some effort to be respectful of their subjects' religions. None comes anywhere close to *Amish Mafia*'s trick of depicting cast members as gangsters, involved in made-up criminal activities.

"Since these [Amish-themed reality] shows have come out in the last four years," Haverstick observed, "people seem more likely to dump on the Amish in bigoted ways, broadening our stereotypes about puppy mills and Amish misbehavior. This is one of the germs of bigotry and prejudice. . . . It's a responsibility we all have to step in and try to nip these things in the bud." Haverstick made these claims on a public radio call-in show.[4] As if to prove her point, a listener emailed in this response, which was read on the air: "I think the show *Amish Mafia* is completely real and exposes these people for the way they really are, what really happens behind the false front that the Amish project to the general public." Besides being uninformed, this listener's generalization about "these people" clearly telegraphs a negative bias, which *Amish Mafia* no doubt encouraged.

The problem of disrespect for the Amish, their religion, and their way of life was compounded by another injustice in Haverstick's mind: exploitation, with its potentially harmful fallout on Amish individuals. Exploitation of the Amish by the tourist industry has been a fact of life in Lancaster County for more than a half-century. There are "Amish" buggy rides, smorgasbords, farm museums, multimedia shows, "Amish Country" motels, bus tours, knick-knacks galore (many manufactured in China), and other faux Amish "experiences" all over the area. Arguably, shows like *Amish Mafia* merely capitalize on the same understandable curiosity about the quaint and self-secluding Amish that the local tourist industry has traded on for years. Plenty of local Amish people happily profit from this curiosity and from the tourist traffic that it brings by selling their quilts, crafts, baked goods, furniture, and garden sheds. And while many of the tourist activities and products may be tasteless, they at least portray a generally positive picture of Amish life.

But reality TV is different, Haverstick argued. The Amish "are a religion that does not believe in being photographed. All these youth on these programs are being filmed in their Amish garb. I think that takes it to another level." It is not just the violation of principles that is problematic; it is the economics as well. "This has created a marketplace for young people in the Amish church who are disaffected and gives them an opportunity to rebel against their religion on camera, in religious garb, sow their wild oats and get paid by Discovery Channel to do it! . . . There is no market for them to be filmed being pious, good Amish folks. These shows are not interested in that."[5] *Amish Mafia*'s deliberate focus on a supposed sick underbelly of Amish society can be hurtful. "I got a call from an Old Order Amishman," Haverstick said. "I was very surprised. It was only a few days into our group being announced. He said that the shows make us look, quote, like garbage. When he said that to me on the phone, I heard the pain in the gentleman's voice. Right then, it became clear to me how much injury, silent injury, there is on the other side of this."[6]

So Haverstick launched a campaign to put a stop to reality TV's insults to the Amish. She created a website and a Twitter feed. She called a community meeting that was attended by about seventy-five people. Her group printed "Respect Amish" t-shirts. She drafted a statement calling for the end of *Amish*

Mafia and sent it to all of Lancaster's elected officials, from the mayor of the city to the governor of Pennsylvania.[7] Within a few weeks, nineteen of them had signed. She wrote another statement that many local religious leaders signed:

> Each of us has a responsibility to consider how we, and members of our faith community, would feel if these shows attacked us as they are attacking the Amish. All religions observe some form of the Golden Rule—that we treat others as we would want to be treated. To stand by silently while these shows mistreat the Amish in our community would make us complicit in breaking that rule.[8]

Haverstick contacted the local chamber of commerce and tourism board to try to organize a boycott to deprive *Amish Mafia*'s producers of hospitality and services in Lancaster County. She sent letters to executives of Discovery Channel and Hot Snakes Media asking for a sit-down. Then she started sending out press releases. In early August the local public radio station did a program on the topic.[9] In mid-August the news agency Reuters had picked up the story.[10] In late August National Public Radio's *All Things Considered* broadcast the story nationally under the title "A Growing Backlash against 'Amish Exploitation' in Pennsylvania."[11]

No Such Thing as Bad Publicity

One of the peculiar things about reality TV is that it thrives on scandal. The Respect Amish controversy is a case in point. Mary Haverstick intended her campaign to cause trouble for the producers of *Amish Mafia* and *Amish Haunting*. It may have created a bit of discomfort for them on the local scene, and Haverstick claims it caused some sponsors to withdraw their support from the series.[12] Still, to the producers, it mostly represented opportunity. In the first place, it was free publicity for the series. The audience of National Public Radio's *All Things Considered* may not overlap much with the target audience of reality TV. Still, the show's producer and distributor expected that more than a few new viewers would tune into *Amish Mafia* just to see what the fuss was about. In fact, according to the producer, Eric Evangelista, "Mary Haverstick was, for a fact, the reason we got a fourth and final season. 100 percent."[13]

Another opportunity for the producers came in the form of story fodder. From the start, the producers of *Amish Mafia* had made hay with public controversy about the series. Entire episodes of the first and second seasons are devoted to cast members vociferously disputing critics who had denied the veracity of the show. The third season ends with a big blowup between cast and crew members supposedly stemming from criticism that cast members had received from their communities for taking part in a show that presents the Amish in a negative light.

Conflict is the backbone of story, as every TV producer knows. And here came another real-life conflict, ripe for the picking. Governor Tom Corbett was one of the nineteen Pennsylvania politicians who had signed Haverstick's statement calling for an end to the production and broadcast of *Amish Mafia*. "The governor wants to shut me down," Levi fumes, in the first episode of the new season. "He has no business with our Amish affairs!" In the third episode Levi tries to confront Corbett on a Lancaster campaign stop. In the sixth, he travels to the state capitol to sort things out "man to man." He is frustrated on both attempts to meet the governor, since the governor "hides behind his security team," as Levi puts it. So Levi goes on the stump in Lancaster, calling on the Amish to vote "for the first time" to end the governor's bid for reelection. The election takes place during the penultimate episode of *Amish Mafia*. Levi watches tensely as the results are announced on TV. Corbett loses in a landslide. "He thought he was going to shut me down—well, I guess *he* got shut down," Levi jubilates. "This is a great celebration for the Amish today, 'cause they don't have to worry about the government anymore!"

Exploitation TV

Reality TV is exploitation TV. There is no question about it. For one thing, the purpose of watching people bicker with housemates, get voted off an island, or gag on live worms is obviously not edification. It is sensation. For another, the so-called reality of reality TV shows is contrived to the core, and transparently so. Furthermore, reality TV builds entertainment on the backs of real people. It literally makes a public spectacle of them, with consequences that often include humiliation. Finally, the whole business of reality TV is to make money for producers and for media corporations like Discovery and Comcast. So even apart from the specific questions raised by Haverstick and her Respect Amish campaign, *Amish Mafia* is immersed to its elbows in exploitation. *All* reality TV is.[14]

Exploitation is a strong word. It is typically used to make people sit up and look around for villains. That is an excellent way to kick off ethical reflection; it is not a great way to pursue it to any depth. The concept of exploitation is simply not nuanced or discriminating enough. Consider this: every time you

turn on your TV, *you* are being exploited. You are being used by some corporation to make a buck: you're being sold to advertisers as a prospective
consumer or forced to pay for "services" you don't need. But you do not feel
used. You feel entertained. There is such a give and take in every discourse,
including reality TV and discussions about reality TV. There are complex,
ambivalent, and often contradictory interests and perspectives involved.

Take, for example, the perspective of *Amish Mafia* star Lebanon Levi Stoltzfus. Levi did not feel exploited; he was proud of his participation in the show.[15]
Nor did he regard himself as an exploiter of the Amish. In fact, he identified
himself as Amish, having grown up in an Old Order household and having
chosen to be baptized as an adult in an Amish-Mennonite congregation (which,
incidentally, permitted electricity, cars, and photography).[16] He saw himself
as doing a kind of service to the world by helping to puncture the false notion
that Amish society is pure, pristine, innocent, and conflict free. With respect
to the criticism that the show made things up, he shared the view of an Old
Order Amishman he had overheard: "If it's not the truth, then it shouldn't
offend us."[17] Lebanon Levi's answer to critics was this: "If these people don't
like *Amish Mafia*, why don't they just change the channel? Or better yet, why
not just turn off their televisions? The bishops would be thrilled, I'm sure, to
hear that they weren't watching any TV at all."[18]

The real exploiters of the Amish, Levi believed, were "self-appointed Amish
spokespeople" like Mary Haverstick, along with other Lancaster County busi-
nesspeople who made a lot of money by promoting a romanticized image of
the county and its Amish residents. Critics of *Amish Mafia* were motivated
more by self-interest than by any genuine interest in the Amish, Lebanon Levi
suggested. And they were the ones selling a "fairytale."[19]

There are indeed self-appointed protectors of the Amish. They often in-
fantilize the Amish, imagining them as simple and innocent children who
cannot protect themselves. To her credit, Haverstick is not one of these. "I
don't feel that I'm speaking for the Amish," she says. "They're adults. They can
speak for themselves."[20] Nor does she idealize the Amish. "Our group does
not advocate that the Amish are romanticized or perfect in any way. Of course
Amish people have flaws, like any other human being." And she has no personal stake in the tourist trade. Her only motive, she says, was to speak out
as a good citizen against a perceived injustice. "I'm doing this because we are
the creators and consumers of this media. Shouldn't we police ourselves as to
what's ethical and what's right?"

Nevertheless, Lebanon Levi has a point. Haverstick's Respect Amish campaign was itself a bit of "Amish-sploitation"—making a splash in the media by invoking the name of the Amish. And because it got Haverstick's name splashed all over the news too, it came off as a bit self-serving. I do not claim any moral high ground. I am guilty of having filmed Amish people myself, which so far as I know Haverstick has never done in her career as a filmmaker.[21] My point is that what seems like exploitation depends, at least in part, on where you happen to be standing.

Alignment of Interests

In chapter 1, I gave the example of a staged reverse-angle shot from Michael Moore's 2002 documentary *Bowling for Columbine* to illustrate a fairly typical filmmaking sleight of hand or "cheat" (fig. 1.5*A* and *B*). That particular cheat foregrounds Moore's righteous indignation toward NRA spokesman Charlton Heston. I observed that, for viewers sympathetic to Heston, the reverse-angle shot comes off as a cheap trick—the crowning touch on Moore's exploitation of the aging and infirm actor. But for the typical viewer aligned with Moore's political perspective, the staged shot seems perfectly appropriate—just good filmmaking.

One of the points of that example was that people are quite happy to overlook a bit of trickery if it suits their purposes. If it benefits them in some way—by helping to advance a viewpoint they agree with, for example—it is unlikely they will even notice it. If the trickery is pointed out to them, they will typically dismiss it as a legitimate means of conveying a deeper truth. My discussion of cooperative or collusive deception in chapter 5 makes the same point. The reason flattery, fairy tales, and magic acts are not perceived as lying is that their purpose is cooperative. Whenever the interests of the parties in a discourse are aligned, as when two people engage in gossip, any untruth or misleading representation is likely to be perceived as innocent or even beneficial rather than manipulative or deceptive. It is only when the interests of participants in a discourse are at odds that the specter of exploitation raises its ugly head.

The interests of Mary Haverstick and the producers of *Amish Mafia* are obviously at odds. Haverstick is evidently not a fan of reality TV, which she calls distasteful. But what really bothers her about *Amish Mafia* is not that it is tasteless. Nor is it the show's fakery or pretense—she is equally put off by idea of the fictional *Amish Haunting* show. What bothers her is that the negative depictions of the Amish in *Amish Mafia* hit close to her home. The neighborly feelings she has for Lancaster's Amish community cause her to take the show's false and unflattering depictions of Amish people as an almost personal affront. Haverstick observes that you would never see a show called *Jewish Mafia* or *Catholic Mafia,* but if there were such a show, it is unlikely that she would have launched a crusade to boycott it. Because of Haverstick's proximity to and familiarity with Lancaster's Amish community, she holds the Amish in special regard. She feels that others, including reality TV producers and audiences, ought to share that regard. The falsehoods and fakery of *Amish Mafia* bother her not so much because they are deceptive and misleading, but because they make the Amish look bad. If the show's fakery had the effect of making the Amish appear pious, peaceful, and good, Haverstick would probably have had no issue with it. But, as she points out, there would be no market for such a show.

Deception in human discourse—lying, counterfeiting, faking, misrepresenting, cheating—is perceived as a problem only when competing interests are involved. Of course, there are almost always competing interests involved. The whole point of lying, cheating, and counterfeiting is to gain some advantage over other people. One naturally supposes that would be true of the fakery in *Amish Mafia* as well: the producers are pulling one over on naive viewers and exploiting viewers' ignorance for their own financial gain. The most surprising and counterintuitive discovery from the audience research presented in chapter 4 is that, to the contrary, *Amish Mafia* fans are aware of but do not mind and often even enjoy the fakery in the show. They see it as beneficial to their own interests and purposes on the whole.

The reason for this, I have argued, is that what fans are looking for in a reality TV show is mainly the equivalent of good gossip fodder. The principle value of the so-called reality in *Amish Mafia* is not that it is factual or informative, but that it invites speculation by conveying the impression of truth while at the same time hinting that all may not be quite as it seems. The principle value of the fakery, on top of being something to speculate about, is that it allows producers to simultaneously deliver both the drama of fiction and the special emotional appeals of nonfiction. As I pointed out, for audience members who are primarily interested in the emotional payoff of their leisure-time investment, that twofer is a pretty sweet deal.

Wait a minute, Haverstick objects. What about the Amish? What do they get out of that deal? What they get is to be turned into so much grist for other people's gossip, most of which is demeaning and much of which is flat-out false. That's just not fair. It's insulting to the Amish. It may even cause some of them harm. What the Amish get, in short, is a very raw deal.

There Ought to Be a Law

American jurisprudence is largely a matter of protecting the rights of individuals. One of the most important of these rights is the freedom to say and do pretty much as you please as long as your words and actions do not harm others or infringe upon their rights. So if you happen to think *Amish Mafia* is a shameful piece of media dreck that spreads prejudice, harms good Amish folk, and contributes to the general degradation of our society, you have the right to say so—on the radio or even in print. It is your right to badmouth the producers on Facebook, organize a boycott against them, and even hire a private detective to follow them around—so long as your activities don't harm them or intrude upon their rights. That "so long as" caveat is crucial, however, since the most fundamental right of individuals, in our society, is to be safe from harm. The body of law that deals with tricky questions about what exactly constitutes harm in civil disputes and how particular harms ought to be remedied is called tort law.

Another crucial right, enshrined in American law, is the right to pursue a profit. That typically involves the exchange of goods and privileges. For example: "I'll agree to play a role in your reality TV show, follow your rules for the production, allow you to do whatever you want with my image, and excuse you from responsibility for any personal injury, emotional distress, and reputational damage I may experience as a result, in exchange for $1,500 per episode in which I appear." You can see how complicated and fraught any deal along these lines is bound to be. What if I break a leg during the production and have to go to the hospital? Who pays for that? What if I get fed up in the middle of production and want to quit? Am I allowed? What if you use my image in promotions for your show? Do I get paid extra? The questions could go on and on. Lawyers draw up agreements to try to cover all such contingencies in advance to avoid recourse to tort law. That is called contract law.

A third fundamental right under the law is the right to protect your property. Nobody can enter your home or borrow your car without your permission, since those are your personal property. Your money is your property too, obviously, as is your right to make money from things you own, by selling them, for example. Interestingly, by this rule, your face is your property. You don't own it exactly, since you can't take it off or sell it, but you do own the right to make a profit from it. If your face happens to be caught on camera during a news event, it can be shown on television without your permission since, in that case, you were in public and news is supposed to serve the pub-

lic interest. But if your face happens to be caught on camera during the filming of a reality TV show, the producers had better get a release (a permission
contract) from you before broadcasting it. Otherwise they are liable for using
your personal property for their own financial gain.

An idea can be your property too, if you spell it out. For example, if you
come up with a TV show called *Amish Mafia* about a make-believe Amish
gangster named Lebanon Levi, any profit potential in those names is yours. If
the actual Lebanon Levi wants to write a book and go on a book tour under
that moniker, he needs your permission. (That will typically involve a contract.) If a Lancaster County tour operator prints "As seen on *Amish Mafia*"
on a brochure, you can accuse him of stealing your intellectual property and
threaten to sue. (That would be a recourse to tort law.) The three kinds of law
described here—tort law, contract law, and property law (intellectual property
law, in particular)—are the pillars of American entertainment law.

It may seem peculiar to discuss legal matters like these, which clearly revolve around money and business, in a chapter on the kind of ethical questions Mary Haverstick raises about the reputation of and respect for a religious group. There are two reasons for bringing the law into it. The first is that
when questions of right and wrong are discussed in the abstract, as matters
of philosophical principle, the real world often gets left far behind. The purpose of this book, as I explained in the prologue, is to grapple with reality TV
in its real-world messiness. So instead of defining what reality means to reality TV viewers in abstract philosophical terms, I analyzed and explained what
it does for them in concrete, practical terms. The reason for that approach is
that TV viewing is always situated in the material world of causes and consequences.

Questions of right and wrong are always so situated as well. In the real
world of messy social interactions, these questions have to do not with absolute principles, like whether it is ever right to lie, but with navigating competing interests, like what to do when people disagree. In civil societies, competing interests are worked out through negotiation. The particular questions
Haverstick raises, about the right of a religious group to privacy and respect,
are public concerns that need to be worked out in the public arena. American
law is the end result, through a process of trial and error, of countless such
negotiations. If you want to understand what right and wrong mean to the
American public—not in some abstract philosophical sense but in concrete,
practical, everyday terms—then the law is the perfect place to look.

The second reason for looking at the law is an apparent peculiarity that requires some explanation. Haverstick maintains that the Amish are entitled to privacy and respect. In fact, she implies that this is their right, as a peaceful religious group that desires mainly to be left alone. That seems perfectly reasonable. As a matter of fact, however, under U.S. law the Amish as a group have no right to either privacy or respect.[22]

The simplest way to explain this is with a thought experiment. Imagine, instead of the Amish, a free-sex nudist pagan cult, living in a walled compound. Imagine that there are women in the group, possibly even children, who you fear are being taken advantage of sexually as part of the group's so-called religious practice. Are you required to respect the group's practices and leave it alone to do as it pleases? Of course not. For one thing, the right of individuals to be protected from harm is more basic than any other right, including freedom of religious expression. If you suspect that women and children in the group are being abused, you have a right, probably even an ethical obligation, to question the group's practices. Furthermore, if you find nudity and promiscuity to be immoral and repugnant—if they happen to offend *your* beliefs—you have every right to criticize and challenge those practices and groups that practice them. You are even free to make up silly and sensational stories about them.

By the same token, you have every right to criticize, challenge, and make up silly or sensational stories about the Amish and their practices. The fact that Haverstick and many others happen to hold the Amish in special regard does not entitle the group to special treatment. Justice does not play favorites. If some members of the group feel insulted or demeaned, like the Amish gentleman who phoned Haverstick, that is immaterial. The fact that somebody finds your words offensive does not give them the right to muzzle you. Remember, everybody has the right to do and say as they please in our society, so long as their words and actions do not harm somebody else. In the eyes of the law, feeling insulted does not rise to the level of harm.

But what happens if somebody tells scurrilous, defamatory lies about your group? Couldn't that damage your reputation? And couldn't that, in turn, negatively affect your livelihood? That would, indeed, rise to the level of harm in the eyes of the law. But there is a catch. The law treats your reputation, like your face, as property from which you can profit. If *you* do something that damages your reputation, that's on you. Anybody can say anything they want to about that. If somebody tells deliberate lies about you that damage your social standing with friends and acquaintances, that may hurt you, but even that does not rise to the level of harm in the eyes of the law. It is only when your ability to trade on your good name is damaged—when you take an economic hit, in other words—that you are likely to win a lawsuit. Even then, if the lies were spread only by word of mouth, you have no legal recourse, since word of mouth is just hearsay, and hearsay is almost impossible to prove. If, however, somebody prints a lie about you or puts it on TV, you can sue for libel, which is a kind of tort. You would of course need to demonstrate that what they said is an actual lie, not just an opinion that you dislike, and that the lie actually damaged your livelihood.

The situation is even more complicated if somebody tells a reputation-damaging lie not about you personally but about a group to which you belong. For example, imagine you are a careful and conscientious Amish dog breeder, with a dozen thoroughbreds that you treat lovingly as family pets, and that somebody starts to spread the story far and wide that all Amish dog breeding operations are puppy mills, in which dogs are kept in barns in stacked cages and removed only to breed. Imagine that the people who are spreading that story put up billboards and distribute pamphlets all over your neighborhood saying "Stop Amish Puppy Mills!" and that, as a result of all this bad publicity, your dog-breeding operation is driven out of business.

The Amish don't sue, as a rule, because they see that as a form of coercion. They believe in working out differences face to face as the New Testament instructs in Matthew 18: "If thy brother shall trespass against thee, go and tell him his fault between thee and him alone: if he shall hear thee, thou has gained thy brother." But imagine, for the sake of this thought experiment, that you were to sue those puppy mill protesters for having driven you out of business by damaging your reputation. The accused would naturally say, "We were never talking about *you*, since you didn't run a puppy mill. We were talking about *other* Amish people who do (or might) run puppy mills. Those are the folks you should be suing for damage to your reputation."

In the same way, if an Amish person were to sue Hot Snakes Media for making up reputation-damaging stories about a nonexistent Amish mafia, Hot Snakes Media could simply say, "If you are not an Amish gangster, then we weren't talking about you. We were talking about other Amish people who are (or might be) gangsters." It is for this reason that Hollywood movies typically end with the disclaimer "Any resemblance to actual persons, living or dead, or to actual events, is purely coincidental."

Obviously, Lebanon Levi in *Amish Mafia* does resemble an actual Amishman, and that's no coincidence. He's played by a guy who grew up Amish and claims to be Amish—as well as claiming to be a gangster and to be enacting (or reenacting) actual criminal behavior in the Amish community. But he's on contract to Hot Snakes Media and has specifically agreed not to sue for damage to his reputation. The same is true of other cast members. For good measure, *Amish Mafia* includes its own unusual disclaimer at the end of every episode: "Re-creations are based on eyewitness accounts, testimonials, and the legend of the Amish Mafia." That "legend" gives the filmmakers legal protection for making up any old story they wish about the Amish, from extortion rackets to demon exorcisms.

What about actual Amish people who feel disrespected by *Amish Mafia*, who believe the show harms the reputations of their community and their faith? Something similar happened when the feature film *Witness* was shot in Lancaster County in 1984. Even though *Witness* deliberately depicted Amish life in a sentimental and generally positive way, local Amish feared that they were being "misrepresented and mocked."[23] As far as the law is concerned, that's just their tough luck—it's the price they pay for living in the midst of a society that prizes freedom. They are free to practice their religion as they choose. In exchange, others are free to disrespect their religion and say whatever they want about it, including telling made-up stories full of unflattering misrepresentations. The Amish as a group have no legal right to be respected. No group does.

As individuals, the Amish do have a right to protect the reputation of their group. If they feel insulted or outraged by the depictions of Amish in *Amish Mafia*, they are free to do what Mary Haverstick did: write letters to news editors and congresspeople, go on the radio to complain, circulate petitions, and try to organize a boycott of the producers. These are all forms of civic negotiation that do not involve the courts. The insulted Amish could in principle take the matter to court too, but they would need to prove that the show caused them tangible harm, beyond distress and hurt feelings. That would be extremely difficult to do.

Calculated Risks

Chronic traumatic encephalopathy or CTE is a degenerative brain disease resulting from repeated impacts to the head. Its immediate effects are negligible, but years later it can cause or contribute to severe mental health problems, including cognitive deficiencies, impulse control issues, depression, and dementia. Anybody who plays a lot of American football is likely to wind up with some level of CTE because of the game's constant blocking and tackling.

Autopsies of more than a hundred former professional football players showed that nearly all of them had CTE.[24]

These facts have received a lot of press in the past few years. Most football fans are well aware of them. If you have the bad form to bring them up while watching Monday-night football with friends, your friends are likely to respond, "The players know the risks." According to this common way of thinking, if an adult wants to smoke cigarettes, ride a motorcycle without a helmet, or play tackle football, that is entirely up to them. Professional football players know the dangers of the sport. They have balanced these risks against the potential benefits to themselves, including money and fame, and made the informed decision to play. Fans of football are therefore not enablers of CTE. They are merely happy beneficiaries of players' rational choices, as are the businesses that make millions from the sport.

There are several problems with this line of reasoning. First, it is hard to apply it to the eighteen- to twenty-two-year-olds who play football in college with no financial compensation. I've spoken to a few of these. When I asked one whether he was concerned about CTE, he said, "I've had my bell rung a time or two and probably already have CTE. But I really love playing football, which is why I keep doing it." You can't argue with that. Still, it points to a deeper problem with the assumption that players know the risks, which is that the human brain is incredibly bad at assessing and responding appropriately to long-term risks, particularly when there are immediate rewards in view. That is one of the key findings of behavioral economics.[25] A lot of businesses besides football benefit from this deficiency in human reasoning, as you can easily see by counting the number of aisles in your grocery store dedicated to unhealthy snack foods.

A second problem with the "they know the risks" rationale is that, as recently as 2010, the NFL denied any link between repeated head impacts and long-term brain damage.[26] People can't possibly make good decisions if they don't have good information. For that reason, people who are asked to voluntarily take risks—in medical research, for example—are supposed to be informed of the dangers. This ethical norm is called informed consent. Because the NFL violated this standard by downplaying the danger of head injuries, they are paying settlements to retired former players that are expected to reach $1.4 billion.[27] Current players are precluded from suing for brain damage down the road, however, because now they supposedly know the risks.

Informed consent is the standard that applies to participation in reality TV, too—at least in theory. When people sign up to take part in *Survivor* or *The Bachelorette*, they know more or less what they are in for. There are real risks, to be sure. To drum up drama, producers routinely subject cast members to emotional stresses that some scholars have compared to torture.[28] The internet is full of stories of behind-the-scenes reality TV horror stories, including numerous deaths while filming and at least twenty-one suicides.[29] However, *Survivor* and *The Bachelorette* have been around for a long time, and they follow a formula. Potential participants go through an intense audition process, which includes mental health screening, and they sign a contract that outlines numerous potential harms. So they ought to be aware of the risks.

Amish Mafia is different. In contrast to *Survivor*, *Amish Mafia* is not a formula show. In fact, it's quite novel. At first even the producers could not have known entirely what to expect during filming. Even so, since the show is largely fake, the risks could be controlled. In *Survivor*, the producers hold all the cards and can treat cast member more or less however they please (isolating them, humiliating them, withholding sleep and food, and so on). In contrast, *Amish Mafia*'s concocted dramas depended upon the continued willing collaboration of cast members, who were consequently treated well on the whole. It is true that, unlike *Survivor* participants, *Amish Mafia*'s ex-Amish participants could not have really known what they were getting into since they grew up with little exposure to TV, much less reality TV. But the actual risks to them from filming were minimal. There were no real physical dangers, since the barn fights and buggy races were just for show, although one cast member told me he did fall off a buggy and hurt his wrist quite badly. As for the risk of experiencing fallout from their Amish communities, the cast members, having grown up Amish, could well predict that.

In sum, even though *Amish Mafia*'s cast members could not have known exactly what they were in for, they did know they were taking a risk—the risk of harming their reputation with friends and family at the very least. To that extent, they walked into the show with their eyes open. They were by no means tricked into taking part in some dangerous activity. They chose to participate, they faced minimal risk of physical or economic harm, and they got paid for it. They certainly didn't feel taken advantage of by the producers, at least not at first. But for one of them, at least, that changed.

Actual Harm?

Merlin Miller had a good run with *Amish Mafia*. Playing the crazy boss of the Ohio branch of the Amish mafia, he was one of the show's stars for the better part of all four seasons. Miller also worked as a de facto assistant producer for the show, finding other potential cast members, scouting locations, and helping to plan and organize shoots.

Unlike most Amish people, whose education ends at eighth grade, Miller earned a GED at his public high school. He is unusually outspoken and self-assured, particularly for an Amish person, which made him a natural fit for *Amish Mafia*. What drew him to reality TV in the first place, he says, was the money. (He mentioned the figure of $2,500 per episode.) He also enjoyed appearing on television. But what he was really hoping for, in the long run, was a professional career with a regular salary and job security, built upon his special background, skills, and interests. He saw working as a producer for Amish-themed reality TV as a perfect career choice and Hot Snakes Media as the perfect stepping stone. Unfortunately, after *Amish Mafia* was canceled, the regular work dried up, along with much of the income. Hot Snakes Media hired Miller to do additional work for its other Amish-themed show, *Return to Amish*, but Miller grew increasingly angry and frustrated at the way he saw himself and other ex-Amish employees being treated, and in April 2016 he quit, cut all ties to Hot Snakes Media, and turned his back on reality TV.

Miller was angry about three things. First, he felt he was poorly treated professionally. He never received credit for all the work he had done for *Amish Mafia* as a fixer and producer. The producers couldn't give him a credit in the show, since that would have burst the illusion that he was a genuine Amish mafioso. Nevertheless, Miller felt that Hot Snakes Media had held out to him the prospect of moving into a full-time job as a producer and never followed through on it. He was also never paid a salary, instead receiving daily or weekly wages. This is standard practice for cast and crew in the reality TV business. Still, after all the full-time work he had done behind the scenes to make *Amish Mafia* a success, Miller thought he deserved a full-time job.

Second, Miller believed the producers had repeatedly tricked him into taking part in representations of the Amish that were false and defamatory. For example, the producers once asked him to pray on camera in front of an altar. He found the use of the altar odd since the Amish do not have altars. When he asked about it, the producers told him, in effect, Don't worry about it—it's the praying we're interested in. Since Miller prays regularly, as do the Amish, he went along. When the episode appeared, he was surprised to discover that it depicted demon worship. He felt terribly guilty afterward, less because of how he himself had been portrayed than because he had unknowingly taken advantage of others by persuading them to be involved in the scene.

Third, Miller thought that he and other ex-Amish employees were simply not treated with the respect and care they were due. When he had ideas for the show or concerns about depicting made-up things like Amish witchcraft, those were dismissed or ignored. When a young female cast member was sexually abused by somebody not directly involved with the show, Miller says he was forbidden from talking about it or helping the woman seek legal recourse because the producers were concerned about bad press. Worst of all, Miller says, he and other ex-Amish cast and crew members were routinely lied to, manipulated, and played off against each other. Furthermore, in his role as a fixer, he was often put in the position of having to lie to and manipulate other cast members, for which he still suffers pangs of conscience. The constant stress of feeling manipulated, disrespected, and taken advantage of resulted in ongoing health issues.

Miller could easily have quit earlier, particularly when his contract was renewed for the fourth season. Other cast members did, but he didn't. By then he knew exactly what he was in for. Still, he carried on. In view of this, it would be hard to argue that he was unfairly exploited, even if he sometimes felt badly treated.

Mary Haverstick suggested, in her Respect Amish campaign, that the exploitation took place at a deeper level: that Amish young adults like Miller would have been better off had they not been enticed by the prospect of participating in reality TV in the first place and had instead remained in their Amish communities. There is no evidence that this is true. In fact, as I pointed out in earlier chapters, all of the supposedly Amish participants in *Amish Mafia*, including Merlin Miller, had either already left the church or were well on their way out the door. Besides, even if Miller had decided to remain in the Amish church, who is to judge whether he would have been better off? That's not Haverstick's call. It's Miller's, and he made it.

A litmus test for whether a person is actually Amish is whether he or she stands to be shunned by the church for bad behavior. None of the regular "Amish" cast members of *Amish Mafia*, including Merlin Miller, stood to be shunned for the simple reason that none were members of the church. In fact, in all the casts of all the Amish-themed reality TV shows, I found only one major character who appeared to actually be Amish: Mary Schmucker, the elderly woman in *Return to Amish*. She could have been shunned for appearing in a reality TV show. I wondered, Did she know what she was in for when she agreed to take part in the show? Did she suffer any actual harm beyond what she could have easily predicted, like being shunned by her church? Might she have been taken advantage of by the producers? Through an intermediary, I asked to interview her. To my surprise, she said yes. She told me she always enjoys talking to fans of *Return to Amish* who manage to track her down.[30]

Schmucker seemed not quite to grasp my question about whether she was taken advantage of, even though I asked in numerous ways: Do you have any regrets? Would you do it again? What hardships did you suffer? Her answers were, basically: No, I have no regrets. Yes, I probably would do it again. There were some very unpleasant experiences, like shooting in the winter in a filthy house with no heat, but the only real long-term suffering I experienced was at the hands of my church, through their shunning. As far as being taken advantage of, the producers would sometimes make us do things for the show that the Amish never do. I didn't take those seriously—*Return to Amish* is just a show—still, I would love to have my own hour-long special to set the record straight.

When Schmucker was first approached about appearing on reality TV, her family was in dire straits. Her husband couldn't find work, one of her sons was in trouble with the law, and the farm was facing foreclosure. For her, the income from reality TV was a lifeline. In fact, it saved the farm. She thought her participation was a one-time deal—that she would be filmed for a few weeks, shunned for a few months, apologize, be reaccepted by the church, and get on with her Amish life. And in the first year, that is exactly what happened. She says she was surprised when the producers returned to ask her to be part of the ongoing series. She had to weigh the costs of being shunned, which she says are terrible (another of her sons, who has remained Amish, barely spoke to her and wouldn't allow her to talk to his children), against the benefits of being able to help support the family, with the income from reality TV. She appreciated the affirmation and attention she received while filming, but that lasted for only a handful of weeks during the year whereas the shunning took place year-round. She opted for reality TV. Her participation in *Return to Amish*, and her shunning by her community, lasted for six years, from 2012 to 2018. In the 2018 season Schmucker announced her decision to return to the Amish community for good. She told me at the time that she expected the Amish community would take her back when she turned away from reality TV for good.

Probably Schmucker's biggest regret, looking back on those years, was getting her husband, Chester, involved for one season. She more or less bribed him to do it, she says. The experience was awful for him—he hated having to say and do things that he would never do in real life. He also suffered in the community by being shunned for a year. For her own part, though, she found the reality TV experience quite satisfying. She says:

> I never regret doing what I did, because the experience I had, the things I did. . . . like I drove a car, went to the fashion show, had a makeover. . . . I did so much I would not have been able to do. And it gave me a good experience about the English and how they work and everything. I don't think I'd ever give up my Amish ways—I like being Amish—but I also liked the freedom [to experience these other things].

It is fair to assume that most of the ex-Amish people who appear in *Amish Mafia* found themselves in over their heads, embroiled in something they did not understand, regardless of how they feel about it now. Miller says, "We were very naive, gullible and innocent in a lot of ways, like sheep being led to the (emotional) slaughter!"[31] No doubt they were treated badly from time to time in the ways Miller describes. No doubt they were exploited in a sense too, since most of them didn't have lawyers or managers to fight for their interests. Nevertheless, having spoken to a number of *Amish Mafia* cast members, I conclude that none of them was actually harmed in the making of the show, beyond the usual stresses and strains of television production, for which they willingly signed up. Whether or not they got what they wanted or expected in the end, they did give their informed consent to be involved, and they got paid for it. Some of them may pay a price in the long term. (Some of the clearly troubled cast members of *Return to Amish* seem to be in far more danger of this than those who took part in *Amish Mafia*.) Still, like professional football players today, who know about CTE but continue to play, that is part of a trade that they willingly made.

Truth or Consequences

When my children were small, my wife used to chastise them for climbing on the furniture or licking their dinner plates by asking, "What if everybody did that?" That is a child-friendly version of philosopher Immanuel Kant's famous dictum, "Act only according to that maxim by which you can at the same time will that it should become a universal law."[32] For Kant, this was not a matter of etiquette; it was a duty. Accordingly, he maintained that one should never lie, regardless of the consequences.

In an influential 1978 treatise, *Lying: Moral Choice in Public and Private Life*, ethicist Sisella Bok drew the same conclusion but on pragmatic grounds. We should never lie, not because lying is categorically wrong but because the smooth working of society depends upon trust, and once that trust erodes as a result of lying, society begins to break down.[33] We are seeing symptoms of this breakdown in the United States today, with the spread of lies and fake news in the political arena.

In an elegant little monograph entitled *On Bullshit*, moral philosopher Harry Frankfurt suggests that the casual bullshitter is even worse than the outright liar because of his total disregard for facts. "His eye is not on the facts at all, as the eyes of the honest man and of the liar are, except insofar as they may be pertinent to getting away with what he says. He does not care whether the things he says describe reality correctly. He just picks them out, or makes them up, to suit his purpose."[34] Frankfurt might be describing *Amish Mafia* here. The problem with such discourses, Frankfurt argues, is not that particular truths get lost in the shuffle; it is that all concern for truth goes out the window. The nonchalance with which viewers accept *Amish Mafia*'s bullshit seems to support Frankfurt's argument.

In *Simulacra and Simulation*, French cultural theorist Jean Baudrillard argues that in our highly mediated culture we are so surrounded by images and stories that those in effect become our reality.[35] The danger is that, when images become our reality, we become indifferent to the material foundation of those images, including their social and political consequences. Indeed, what *Amish Mafia* fans care about is the characters on the show and their travails. They are not concerned about actual Amish people. In terms of how they think about the world, the difference between simulated Amish people and actual ones has ceased to make a difference.

Confronted by the recent spread of fake news on Facebook and elsewhere, media commentator Brooke Gladstone expresses a similar concern: "It is not the lies that post the existential danger to democracy. It's the lying, the kind of thoroughgoing lying that gives rise to a whole new reality or, better still, to no reality at all."[36] If people don't know what to believe, she fears, they might wind up believing anything or, worse, nothing.

The thread that connects all these philosophies is the idea that lying does not just degrade the liar; it spills over on others to create a society of liars. We might call this the contagiousness-of-dishonesty hypothesis. Dan Ariely and his team of behavioral economists did a whole battery of experiments to see if this hypothesis holds. Their finding, in a nutshell, is that it does indeed. Dishonesty is contagious, in ways you would never guess.

In his most straightforward experiment, Ariely had a roomful of subjects do his standard cheating test—a time-consuming arithmetic task after which subjects tallied up their own correct answers to be paid for them. In this version of the experiment, he had a confederate stand up after just a few minutes, claim to have solved all of the problems correctly, and walk out with an envelope of cash. This raised the level of cheating in the room by 60 percent.[37] In another experiment, Ariely rigged up a candy-vending machine to return people's money along with their candy. Most people helped themselves to free candy two or three times. Nobody did it more than that. Four times would presumably have made them feel guilty. But more than half of the subjects also looked around for friends to invite them to help themselves to free candy from the machine.[38]

Dishonesty doesn't just spread between people, Ariely's experiments show. Like a virus, it can also trigger a cascade of symptoms within the individual. Ariely found that a dishonest act as trivial as wearing a pair of counterfeit designer sunglasses can make people much more prone to cheat. He gave a group of women some stylish Chloé sunglasses to try on. He told a third of the women that the sunglasses were genuine (which they were), he told a third that they were counterfeits that looked exactly like the real thing, and to the last third he said nothing about the sunglasses. He asked all of the women to walk around for a while with the sunglasses, looking out windows and at posters. Then he asked them to see how well they did on a boring arithmetic task, still wearing the sunglasses. The task was his cheating test. Forty-two percent of the women who had been told nothing about the sunglasses cheated—this was the level of cheating he had come to expect. Thirty percent of the women who had been told they were wearing genuine Chloés cheated—substantially fewer. But of the women who thought they were wearing fake Chloés, a whopping 74 percent cheated.[39] When Ariely followed up with a questionnaire, he found that the subjects who had been told their sunglasses were counterfeit gauged other people as far more likely to cheat than the subjects in the other two groups.[40] Wearing "fake" sunglasses changed not just their behavior but also the way they viewed others around them.

The likeliest explanation for Ariely's findings is the normalization of cheating. The subject subconsciously thinks, "The guy running the experiment told me the sunglasses were counterfeit, so that must mean he is okay with a little cheating." (Or, conversely, "The guy made a point of saying that the sunglasses were genuine, so he must put a premium on honesty.") Any instance of conspicuous deception sends the social signal that deception is to some degree normal, expected, and acceptable, which makes it easier for others to justify it to themselves. That is what happened when Ariely's confederate claimed to have completed all of the arithmetic tasks correctly in an impossibly short time. It prompted others to think, "If that person isn't ashamed to cheat, then I guess I needn't be either." *Amish Mafia* sends the same kind of signal by presenting viewers with a barrage of subtle and not-so-subtle clues about its fakery. This tells viewers, "Don't worry about the fakery. There's nothing wrong with it. It is perfectly *normal* to make up fake facts and tell lies—at least if it's done in fun."

The more normal we find deception to be, the easier it is to justify, both when we see it and when we do it. The main thing that keeps us honest, Ariely says, is that we want to feel good about ourselves. The flip side is that we don't want to feel bad about ourselves. We don't want to feel guilty. Guilt and its emotional correlates—shame, embarrassment, and the fear that others will think badly of us—are evolved self-censorship mechanisms that help keep us from doing things that will put us on the outs with other people. These feelings are triggered whenever we do something that we suppose the people around us would judge as bad or wrong. But if we observe other people unashamedly doing such things and getting away with it, we assume that maybe those things are not so socially unacceptable after all.

That is what *Amish Mafia* does: it sends the signal that fakery in reality TV is just fine. It tells us that, instead of expecting truth from reality TV, we should expect bullshit. If we come to expect bullshit, we are less likely to mind it. And if we don't mind it on reality TV, we are less likely to mind it when our political leaders spout it. We might well infer that everybody lies and cheats, at least a little. And if we suppose that, we will feel a little bit more justified in lying and cheating ourselves, which will in turn send the signal to others that we find lying and cheating acceptable. The result is a vicious cycle. Ariely puts it this way:

> Passed from person to person, dishonesty has a slow, creeping, socially corrosive effect. As the "virus" mutates and spreads from one person to another, a new, less ethical code of conduct develops. And although it is subtle and gradual, the final outcome can be disastrous. This is the real cost of even minor instances of cheating and the reason we need to be more vigilant in our effort to curb even small infractions.[41]

That is a very scary conclusion, particularly in this era of "truth decay."

Could it be that the lies and fakery in Amish Mafia are not actually cheating? Maybe the typical viewer doesn't see them as any more dishonest or deceptive or antisocial than, say, a magic act. If that is the case, they will work nothing like those supposedly counterfeit designer sunglasses. The reason those led to more cheating was that Ariely's subjects knew counterfeiting is illegal and wrong. But fakery in reality TV is not illegal, and who is to say it is wrong? If reality TV fans see it as socially acceptable, it won't even cross their minds as a justification to cheat. In that case, it won't make them vulnerable to the "slow, creeping, socially corrosive" effect that Ariely describes.

Unfortunately, this is probably wishful thinking. The evidence presented in chapter 4 reveals that, in fact, fans of *Amish Mafia* do perceive the show's fakery as a kind of cheating. They know they are being taken for a ride. They don't care, because they enjoy the ride. It suits their purposes in much the same way that juicy gossip serves people's purposes. It's fun, it's engaging, and it may even feel fulfilling. Unfortunately, it also likely exposes them to the truth-decay bug.

Bad Gossip

One of the main takeaways of this book is that the peculiar pleasures of reality TV are rooted in the human propensity for gossip. In chapter 5, I discussed positive dimensions of gossip, ranging from the "gentle policing" of community norms and values to the affirmation and support of less powerful members of society. I argued that reality TV in general, and *Amish Mafia* in particular, might share in some of these social benefits. But it is crucial to acknowledge that gossip can have powerful antisocial effects too, some of which may very well rub off on reality TV audiences.

In his book *Gossip*, cultural commentator Joseph Epstein writes, "In its destructive aspect, gossip is about two things: the ruination of reputation and the invasion of privacy."[42] These are the effects of *Amish Mafia* that most concerned Mary Haverstick with respect to the Amish. They were also the main concerns of Lancaster County Amish bishops when the feature film *Witness* was filmed in their community in 1984.[43] But mass-mediated gossip has two other destructive aspects that are far more dangerous to society as a whole. One is the spread of misinformation, which cuts people off from reality. The other is the propagation of tribalism, which deepens and inflames social rifts.

Both of these dangers are abundantly evident in the spread of conspiracy theories and fake news on the internet and on political talk radio and television today, and the harmful consequences have included actual violence. An infamous example is Pizzagate. In the run-up to the 2016 election in the United States, bad actors on the internet and Twitter (it is still not completely clear who) began to pick up, piece together, and embellish, gossip-style, an elaborate tapestry of factual tidbits, speculation, and hearsay, much of which was invented, culminating in the "news" that Hillary Clinton was running a child sex ring out of the basement of a Washington, DC, pizza restaurant.[44] This story was elaborated further and circulated far and wide, in tones of high dudgeon, by right-wing politicos (including associates of Donald Trump's campaign) and websites (including Breitbart News and Infowars). On December 1, 2016, upset and angered by this story, Edgar Maddison Welch, a father of two from Salisbury, North Carolina, showed up at the pizza restaurant armed with a semiautomatic rifle and a handgun to investigate the story and, if it turned out to be true, to free the captive children. He searched the restaurant, shot open a lock, terrorized customers and employees, but found no captive children. The restaurant did not even have a basement.

While Welch's actions were clearly not normal, the man himself is quite ordinary, judging from interviews and reports—soft-spoken, religious, not particularly political, not unintelligent, certainly not psychotic.[45] After finding no captive children in the pizza shop, he immediately surrendered to police and apologized for what he called "an incredibly ill-advised decision."[46] He was simply swept up by the gossip and set out to investigate it for himself.

It may seem a stretch to compare the cynical, inflammatory, deliberately manipulative lying of Infowars with the entertaining fakery of *Amish Mafia*. Here is the connection. Welch was not psychotic, but the behavior he exhibited looks almost like a mirror image of psychosis: a disorder in which perceptions of external reality are so inaccurate that thoughts, emotions, and actions are seriously dysfunctional. In his case, this condition was brought about by false gossip. Any kind of false gossip, including the false gossip in *Amish Mafia*, may plant the germ of the same disease.

Gossip that is true is never dangerous in this way. Even if somebody finds it to be embarrassing, intrusive, or hurtful, it serves essentially the same purpose as news: it gives us information about our world, especially our social world, that allows us to navigate it better and more successfully. False gossip, no matter how trivial, gives us incorrect information about our world. Incorrect information leads to inappropriate thoughts and actions. Granted, few people will take the kind of extremely "ill-advised" action that Welch took, but there are doubtless many others who thought much like he did on the basis of the same false gossip.

The Pizzagate incident proves that fake news can have serious consequences. Still, what is the harm in falsely supposing, based on watching *Amish Mafia*, that there is an actual gang of Amish ruffians running about Lancaster

County, Pennsylvania, extorting money from local businesses? How will that negatively affect viewers' thoughts and actions, particularly if they never come into contact with any actual Amish people? Perhaps not much. Still, they will be carrying around nonsense in their heads, which may make them a little more prone to believe other nonsense. The particular nonsense that *Amish Mafia* conveys may also contribute to a worldview that sees violence as endemic and corruption as normal. Seeing the world that way helps to make it that way, in the same subtle but definite way that seeing cheating as normal helps to make it so. (In mass-media research, this phenomenon is labeled the *mean world syndrome.*[47])

The propagation of tribalism is the other big danger of mass-mediated gossip. The main purpose of the false Pizzagate gossip was to create suspicion and distrust of Hillary Clinton, as well as of the political establishment and the mainstream press, which were presumed to be complicit in the cover-up of Clinton's purported crimes. Some of the purveyors of the story, like Infowars, deliberately aimed to fire people up—not necessarily to turn up in restaurants armed with guns, but certainly to turn up at the polls to express their anger and suspicion of the status quo by voting against Clinton and her party.

In the mass media, false gossip is often used to breed strong tribal feelings, as in this case. Strong tribal feelings, in turn, make people particularly susceptible to false gossip that supports their views. The result is a vicious cycle, which helps to account for both the phenomenon of "truth decay" and the divisiveness of contemporary American politics.

Again, it may seem an awful stretch to compare Infowars' deliberate political rabble rousing to *Amish Mafia*'s entertaining fakery. *Amish Mafia* has nothing whatsoever to do with politics. Democrats and Republicans are equally likely to enjoy the show and fall for its deceptions. Still, part of the pleasure of the show (and of reality TV generally) lies in the fact that it makes audiences feel good about themselves by feeling superior to others. I wrote about this in chapter 4. This feeling is evident in one *Amish Mafia* audience member's unintentionally ironic tweet during an episode: "whoever watches Amish mafia and believes its real sorry to say but your really stupid ha." This is just good-natured trash talking, of course. Anyone who reads it will instantly put themselves in the smart, unbelieving group. But that is the point. Reality TV frequently invites viewers to judge, deride, and dismiss others—to divide the world into us and them, where "we" are moral, clever, and sophisticated and "they" are not. Needless to say, the "Amish" of *Amish Mafia* mostly get put in the "them" category.

Reality TV fans can be victims of this sort of thinking, as well as perpetrators. In defense of those fans, TV critic James Poniewozik writes:

> If *Madmen* or *Boardwalk Empire* depicts sexism, or violence, or self-destructive behavior, it's nuanced storytelling. But if a reality show does the same thing, it's immoral, misanthropic, or bigoted. We assume that the audiences of HBO or FX dramas (or for that matter, readers of *Crime and Punishment* or *Lolita*) can empathize with the protagonists without wanting to emulate them; we assume they can maintain a critical distance from the narratives and perceive ironies between the characters' words and their actions. Why? Because we assume that someone who watches *Breaking Bad* is smarter, more mature—better—than someone who watches *Jersey Shore*. Scratch a criticism of reality TV, and often enough you'll find a criticism of the reality-TV audience.[48]

I have taken pains in this book to avoid looking down on reality TV audiences. One reason is that the *Amish Mafia* fans I spoke to were smart, thoughtful, and interesting people. Another is that I regard it as bad form to disrespect people's entertainment choices. Just the same, we need to be aware that all choices have consequences. One of the consequences of watching *Amish Mafia*, stemming from its relationship to false gossip, may be that it cultivates disrespect not just for the Amish but for everybody who is "not like us."

Movies have the power to help us understand others, walk in their shoes, see the world from their perspective. That kind of understanding is the key to compassion. Reality TV can, in principle, foster this kind of understanding. For example, the first popular Amish-themed reality show, *Amish in the City*, tried to do this and even succeeded in the eyes of some critics—at least with respect to its "Amish" cast members.[49] (Some of its non-Amish participants were not treated so sympathetically.)

Amish Mafia does not bother to try to create this empathy. It is too caught up with sensation to be concerned with sympathy and too preoccupied with fake Amish to be concerned with real ones. The danger here is not the absence of compassion. Movies have no obligation to cultivate compassion. There are many perfectly fine movies that don't—satires, for example. But, like gossip, reality TV purports to be about the real actions of real people, living real lives. The danger in making those up, as *Amish Mafia* does, is that in place of inviting compassion, it invites and rewards condescension. And condescension breeds more condescension in the same subtle but definite way that cheating breeds more cheating.

If one is truly interested in reality—the reality of the Amish, of crime and violence, of human emotion, of politics, of popular entertainment, or of anything else—then two things to avoid are bad information and false prejudice. The first cuts us off from the world. The second fosters self-perpetuating falsehoods and binds people into opposing tribes. *Amish Mafia* is definitely guilty of the first and arguably guilty of the second, even though its purpose is simply to entertain, which is not a bad purpose at all.

The way to avoid both bad information and false prejudice is, first, to be assiduously dedicated to reality and, second, to try to see things from many angles. The first involves not making things up, obviously, but also attempting to be accurate and scrupulously honest in thinking through and reporting one's observations of reality. The second involves paying careful attention to the observations and ideas of others, of course, but also deliberately triangulating answers to questions by approaching them in different ways. These are the methods I have brought to bear in this book as I have tried to make sense of *Amish Mafia*, entertaining fakery, and the idea of "reality" in reality TV. My goal, as I explained in the prologue, is to understand *Amish Mafia* and reality TV generally in terms of the complex ecology of interests, habits, and forces that circulate around all human activities—a system in which actions, even actions as apparently inconsequential as watching a reality TV show, have ripple effects that subtly affect the wider society.

Epilogue

Fake Reality TV

In 2018, in celebration of the thirtieth anniversary of its annual Shark Week, Discovery Channel revisited its 2013 fake documentary *Megalodon: The Monster Shark Lives* (broadcast a half year after the debut of *Amish Mafia*). That fake doc had smashed the network's ratings record but was roundly denounced by critics for having deliberately deceived audiences. (See "Discovery Network and the New Humbug" in chapter 3.) At the time Discovery's response had been coy: "The stories have been out there for years, and with 95% of the ocean unexplored, who really knows?"[1] In its 2018 look back, *Megalodon: Fact vs. Fiction*, Discovery finally comes clean.

There is a curious ambivalence in its retrospective. On the one hand, there is practically gleeful celebration of the controversy that the show generated. It "sparked a lot of interest in what could have been the biggest shark that ever lived," says Joseph Schneier, Discovery's vice president of development and production. "And let's use that controversy to talk about how cool the megalodons were." On the other hand, there is acknowledgment that the show went too far with its fakery. "We're super cognizant of what happened," says Schneier. "The last thing we want to do is cause ill will toward sharks, towards the brand, or anything like that." The implication is that you will not see fake documentaries on Discovery Channel again anytime soon.[2]

In Discovery's reality TV lineup, however, fakery is still going strong—particularly in follow-along shows like *Gold Rush*.[3] Just the same, no 2020 reality show anywhere appears to go nearly as far in its fakery as *Amish Mafia* did, passing off ordinary folks as gangsters. The one that comes closest is probably Discovery's own *Moonshiners*, which presents regular people from rural Appalachia as distillers of illegal liquor. But a lot of that show consists of good ol' boys reminiscing about and reenacting the good ol' days, when liquor was actually illegal and needed to be made and sold on the sly. Today, it's easy to get a permit to distill alcohol, so even though *Moonshiners* characters pretend to be hiding their activities from the police, there is little in the show that seems actually illicit or risky.

Since *Amish Mafia*, no reality TV shows have been especially novel or groundbreaking. Discovery network's entire 2019 lineup of "new" reality shows consisted of spin-offs, revivals, and remixes of earlier shows, like *Man vs. Bear*, a show that pits humans against tame grizzlies in competitions like tug-of-war (a retread of a 2003 show, *Man vs. Beast*), *River of No Return*, about residents of an Idaho wilderness (a knockoff of *The Last Alaskans*, from 2015), and *Rob Riggle: Global Investigator*, in which an actor/ex-marine travels the globe exploring mysteries such as mammoth remains in Alaska and a lost pirate ship in the Caribbean (basically, 2015's *Expedition Unknown*, with a different star and a dash of humor). The 2014 and 2015 seasons did bring a spate of new reality shows focusing on people toughing it out in the wilderness, including Discovery's *Alaskan Bush People* and *The Last Alaskans*, but those are in many ways a throwback to the granddaddy of them all, *Nanook of the North*, from 1922 (see "Framing Reality on Film," in chapter 2).

In 2015 (*Amish Mafia*'s last year), *New York* magazine's West Coast editor, Josef Adalian, wrote a column declaring that the boom days of reality TV are over:

> The sheer tonnage of unscripted content produced in the past decade-and-a-half has left the people who make it—and, arguably, those who watch—struggling to recapture the excitement of a once-vibrant genre. "Reality seems tired. It seems derivative," says one former network chief who now works in the digital world. "There hasn't been a really loud, innovative reality show in a while."[4]

Adalian offered a handful of business-related reasons as well. In contrast to scripted shows, which can be resold and rewatched for years, reality shows have a limited shelf life. For that reason, he said, streaming services like Netflix were not buying many. It is far easier to make a scripted show that stands out as different and original. Since the debut of *Survivor* in 2000, a staggering 687 percent increase in first-run dramas and comedies was siphoning off audiences. Finally, distributors kept squeezing producers' budgets. (Indeed, in

2019 Discovery even stopped paying for the production of reality shows up front, instead requiring producers to take out loans.[5]) According to Adalian, the only reality shows likely to achieve long-term success were well-established franchises, like *Shark Tank* and *MasterChef*, with their spin-offs.

Four years later, in 2019, an article in the *Hollywood Reporter* comes to a very different conclusion.[6] The article reports that reality TV is has "entered a golden era" and is "enjoying a renaissance" in spite of the boom in big-budget TV drama. As the cost of dramatic series rises, driven by players like Netflix and HBO, it says, the traditional networks are doubling down on lower-cost nonscripted content. New prime-time network shows like *The Masked Singer, Love Island,* and *Press Your Luck* are ratings hits. Netflix and Amazon have also discovered the appeal of reality TV. Amazon streams many of the classics, from *The Real World* to *Keeping Up with the Kardashians.* Netflix has licensed a stable of reality shows with slightly higher-brow appeal, like *Pawn Stars* and *The Great British Bake Off,* and has commissioned new ones of its own, like 2019's *Blown Away,* a competition show about glassblowing. Reality TV, it now seems, can have a great shelf life: "Unlike drama, which is increasingly short-lived, . . . once a reality show is a hit, it can run and run."

With respect to the future of reality TV, the article quotes Rob Clark, director of global entertainment for the production giant Fremantle: "There are two very opposite trends . . . at the moment—the move towards extreme shows, shows that are complete fantasy, like *Masked Singer* and *Love Island* and, at the other end, shows like *Five Guys* that feel completely authentic and real." *Five Guys a Week* is a show in which a single woman invites five men to move into her home and live with her for a week, all at the same time. Needless to say, this hardly seems "completely authentic and real." In fact, all of the new shows mentioned in the article are "format" shows, which rely on well-established competition formulas for drama, in contrast to more naturalistic follow-along shows, like Discovery's *Amish Mafia, Moonshiners, Gold Rush,* and *Alaskan Bush People,* in which drama is far less certain and, ironically, for that very reason, the fakery quotient is always a great deal higher.

Since reality TV relies on drama, the kinds of fakery evident in *Amish Mafia* (described in detail in chapter 1) are bound to be around as long as the follow-along reality show is around. Given the continuing success of shows like *Gold Rush* and its spin-offs, that is likely to be a long time. Still, the extremely high level of fakery in *Amish Mafia* is probably not sustainable in any show, for the simple reason that if you are playing a role that has nothing to do with your real life or real activities, it is difficult to keep up the facade unless you are a professional actor. For an ex-Amish roofing contractor, Lebanon Levi did a remarkably good job of pretending to be a gangster. Still, by the second season of *Amish Mafia*, the pretense was breaking down, largely because of story lines that grew increasingly remote from the characters' actual lives.

Amish and the Media

Amish-themed reality TV appears to have run its course. Hot Snakes Media's *Return to Amish*, the last of the recent crop, aired the final episode of its eighth season in January 2019. Apart from Mary Schmucker (the show's elderly Amish mom, who announced her decision to return to the Amish church in the 2018 season), the principal actors in the show can scarcely be called Amish; they had left the church and were living "English" lives well before the series even began. Some of those, like Mary's son and daughter-in-law, Abe and Rebecca, had quit the show several years earlier and were replaced with other supposedly Amish ringers.

What drove much of the interest in Amish-themed reality TV in its early years was curiosity about the actual Amish. But what the shows have always delivered—starting with *Amish in the City* in 2004—is a far cry from glimpses into actual Amish lives. Instead, these shows have offered an endless stream of makeovers, travel to new or exotic locales, food experiences, and the like, garnished with soap-opera-like "revelations" of secrets from the past and hopes for the future, and sustained by endless interpersonal bickering. (According to Mary, it was the constant bickering, deliberately stirred up by the producers, that eventually drove Abe and Rebecca from *Return to Amish*.[7]) The problem for viewers is that all of this gets repetitive and old. In reality shows where participants face some actual risk, like Discovery's *Deadliest Catch*, or constant competition, like *Survivor*, there is always genuine drama. Absent these types of drama, a reality show needs to work especially hard to sustain viewer interest. That is precisely why *Amish Mafia* turned to made-up elements, like extortion, explosions, gang rivalries, and witchcraft. But even such devices can get repetitive and lose their luster after a while.

By now, there is nothing new to see on Amish reality TV. It is for that reason, more than any other, that Amish-themed reality TV has most likely come to its end. This does not rule out the possibility of actual documentaries, down the road, which deliver glimpses into actual Amish lives. But documentaries almost never have the draw of reality TV. Also, the documentary approach does not lend itself to ongoing series, which is what TV producers and programmers want.

As long as acting on reality TV was an option for disaffected Amish young adults, there were those who were drawn to it. The cast of *Amish Mafia*, however, has all moved on. Lebanon Levi has abandoned his old social media accounts and is staying out of the public eye. Esther Schmucker is giving talks about surviving sexual abuse to audiences consisting largely of Amish and ex-Amish women. (You can see one of these on YouTube by searching for her name.[8]) Alvin Lantz has moved to Florida. In his Facebook photos he looks happy, healthy, and definitely not Amish. Former Mennonite Jolin Zimmerman lives in Texas, where he moved after quitting *Amish Mafia* at the end of the third season. Among other things, he now represents a rifle company on its team of competitive shooters. Alan Beiler, who planted the seed for *Amish Mafia* while giving the producer a tour for a planned cooking show, still occasionally offers his services to TV producers interested in the Amish.[9] As for Merlin Miller, who once hoped to become a producer of "Amish television," he is now back home in Ohio, working as a driver for hire for the Amish, which he says feels like a return to sanity after his "soul-crushing" stint in reality TV.[10]

The Amish, on the whole, are just not that interested in television, apart from some young folks on rumspringa and some people who watch the occasional football game. They don't watch reality TV, so they don't care whether it is fake or not. Even the hoopla surrounding *Amish Mafia* in Lancaster County had little impact on them. The media technology that has really had an impact on many Amish young people in recent years—perhaps even on how they think—is the cell phone.[11]

Traditionally, Amish have not had phones in their homes. For most Amish, phones are a dispensable modern technology. Phone lines represent an unwelcome connection to the outside world, and the ability to talk to people far away undercuts face-to-face communication, which is the mainstay of Amish communities. Still, many Amish people run businesses that require regular contact with the outside world, like roofing, selling quilts, and running market stands. As a compromise, Amish who need them have been allowed to keep landline phones in office drawers, barns, or booth-like shanties shared by groups of neighbors.

Cell phones are obviously much more convenient. For the Amish, they have another even bigger advantage: they are discreet. You can carry one around in your pocket, set it to vibrate, step outside to make calls, and nobody even knows you have it. So quite a few Amish business owners in Lancaster County got cell phones. And as cell phones became commonplace with youth in the wider culture, quite a few Amish young people acquired them too, sometimes surreptitiously, sometimes with the permission of their parents, mostly to stay connected with their Amish friends.[12]

Cell phones today are not just phones. They are also cameras, internet-connected computers, and media devices. It did not take long for Amish cell-phone use, particularly among young people, to lead to YouTube clips, Google searches, Facebook, Instagram, selfies, posted videos, and everything else that young people do with their cell phones. Today it is not uncommon, in some parts of Lancaster County, to see Amish young people walking along with their eyes glued to their cell phones, just like everybody else.

There are those who argue that social media use has had a profound effect not just on our politics but also on our psychology—for youth, in particular. One of these is social psychologist Jean Twenge. In a 2017 book, *iGen*, Twenge argues that social media are making young people increasingly self-absorbed.[13] Young people on social media are constantly concerned about how they are coming across and comparing themselves with others. They spend a lot of their "socializing" time alone, with screens. The result is that they are becoming anxious, depressed, and delicate—more sensitive (a good thing, on the whole), but also less and less able to cope with the world's challenges (definitely a bad thing).

Fortunately for the Amish, they may be less vulnerable to this danger than the rest of us, for two reasons. First, they have an abiding suspicion of screens of all kinds. A put-it-away ethos remains strong among the Amish, even with young people. Some Amish youth groups even punish cell-phone use by suspending members for a few weeks.[14] Second, Amish society is still so dominated by face-to-face interactions, including gossip, that the Amish have little need to rely on media to fulfill their social needs and desires. This also helps explain why they have no use for reality TV.

Trump, TV, and Twitter

In 2012, when *Amish Mafia* debuted, if someone had predicted that, within half a decade, reality TV would play a significant role in dramatically transforming the political landscape in the United States, that prediction would have been met with raised eyebrows and snickers. Reality TV just isn't that important, people would have said. Five years later, when a reality TV star was elected president, partly on the basis of a fake reputation created on reality TV, partly through the deft use of reality TV tropes and tricks, including fakery, the notion that reality TV might reshape the political landscape was considered neither far-fetched nor funny.

By the fall of 2019, two and two-thirds years into Donald Trump's presidency, he had made 13,000 false or misleading statements and sent out 11,000 tweets, according to tallies by the *Washington Post* and the *New York Times*.[15] Trump chose to use the president's bully pulpit largely to spread gossip and lies. This was, for many, a deeply troubling transformation of the president's office. Yet Trump remained extremely popular with his base—that one-quarter or so of registered voters who in polls persistently "strongly approved" of the way he handled his job.[16] Again and again, journalists and critics wondered, Why? Don't these people care about the truth?

The simple answer is, no, they didn't care about the truth, at least not where Trump was concerned. A 2018 Pew survey on Trump's job performance asked, "What if anything concerns you most about how Trump is handling his job as president?"[17] Those who approved of Trump's performance expressed some concerns about his personality, his social media use, and his policies, but none questioned his honesty or trustworthiness. That was simply not an issue for them. Among those who disapproved of Trump's performance, however, it was a major concern.

What *did* Trump's supporters care about, if not truth? According to the Pew poll, what they liked most was his personality. They supported Trump for being Trump, regardless of his policies.[18] To figure out why, cognitive neuroscientist Bobby Azarian conducted an informal survey of the psychological literature and found fourteen possible explanations.[19] These included Trump's mobilization of fear and resentment, the desire for a strong authoritarian leader, the self-interest of the monied class, and the "mental vulnerability" of paranoid elements in society. Surprisingly, there was one likely explanation that Azarian did not consider: some people were so attached to Trump because siding with Trump made them feel good about themselves.

There are plenty of people in America today who feel powerless and put upon, often with good reason. For some of those—in particular, those who identify as traditional white Christians—standing with Trump and his "Make America Great Again" crowd made them feel like they were part of a group that is fighting back. What these people most wanted from their news on Fox and Facebook was social and emotional validation. In the words of media scholar Daniel Kreiss, they sought "a sense of identity, place, and belonging;

emotional, social, and cultural support and security; and . . . political and so-cial affiliations and beliefs."[20] In this regard, Kreiss says, the pro-Trump media served as a metaphoric family for their fans. In fact, I would say they served as mass-mediated gossip. Kreiss says fans of the pro-Trump media didn't care about information. In fact, I would say they cared about *socially useful* in-formation and *social* intelligence, just as participants in gossip do (and, as I argued in chapter 4, as viewers of reality TV do). But Kreiss's key point is that, precisely because fans of right-wing media care so much about issues of iden-tity, they care less about the kinds of verifiable facts that mainstream news sources like the *New York Times* are concerned with. That is certainly so.

In practice, the *New York Times* serves the same gossip-like function for its readers as Fox News does for its viewers. Most of the facts reported in stories in the *New York Times* are so remote from most readers' daily lives that they have no direct impact. The reason readers read them, absorb them, and like them (along with the opinions and reviews and everything else in the paper) is that it makes them feel good about themselves: in the know, part of the right crowd, and armed with ideas to gossip about. Furthermore, because reading the *New York Times* positions them among the well-educated social elite, they can look down their noses at the resentment-based journalism over on Fox and, by extension, at those who watch it. Fans of Fox News recognize this. It is little wonder that Trump got so much traction with his base when he com-plained about the "fake" and "failing" *New York Times*.

As I pointed out in the last chapter, the greatest dangers of mass-mediated gossip are its capacity to spread misinformation and propagate tribalism. That is exactly what has happened in recent years, carried out especially (but by no means exclusively) on the part of the right-wing media. Understanding that popular news functions much like gossip can help us understand the problem better—as well as to see the flaws in remedies that have been proposed.

One remedy that has been widely tried, and has widely failed, is to attempt to counter false facts with true ones. With news, just as with gossip, people attend to and accept "facts" that seem plausible, personally relevant, and so-cially affirming, and they ignore or discount those that don't. Thus the prac-tical effect of trying to debunk fake news, like false gossip, is mainly to call more attention to it.

A second widely proposed remedy for fake news consists of editorial con-trols on media channels to flag or filter out false and unfounded information. Twitter eventually went so far as to cancel Trump's account, which turned out to be an effective means of putting a lid on his public dissemination of lies.

The danger with this remedy is that it smacks of censorship. Clamping down on certain kinds of gossip is tantamount to clamping down on certain groups of gossipers. This feels oppressive and unfair, particularly to those who are clamped down upon.

The third widely proposed remedy is to train media audiences in critical thinking so they recognize bad information in the media and tune it out. I explained why this doesn't work in the discussion of *War of the Worlds* in chapter 2. Essentially, to the extent that critical thinking contradicts what people already believe or gets in the way of something that they want, like self-affirming gossip, people just don't do it, no matter how well educated they are. Besides, trying to teach those who find validation in Fox News to be suspicious of Fox News and turn to the *New York Times* instead is bound to feel like political indoctrination.

Gossip is collusive. It involves an implicit social pact between its authors and its consumers. That's exactly how the news works too, whether it comes from Fox or the *New York Times*. It revolves not around belief in particular facts but around trust in cooperative intent. The reason some people gravitated so strongly to Trump is that they perceived that he had their backs. Whenever people feel that their social standing is at risk—whenever they feel beleaguered or judged or controlled—they are liable to resort to this kind of tribal thinking. No amount of true information or training in critical thinking is going to change that. Anything that smacks of censorship will simply make it worse. The only real hope for fixing the problem of fake news in the long run consists of political and social changes that genuinely address the grievances of those who feel powerless and disenfranchised. The media can't make this happen. But they can help by paying more attention to those grievances instead of dismissing them, belittling them, or looking down upon those who feel aggrieved.

In the short term, unfortunately, the deliberate spread of falsehoods in the media may well have caused and continue to cause lasting social harm. Hoping for eventual social and political changes hardly seems sufficient to address this immediate problem. So what can we do?

Reality Is Recalcitrant

There is a well-known anecdote in philosophy referred to as the appeal to the stone. The eighteenth-century Anglo-Irish philosopher Bishop Berkeley maintained that material reality does not exist. When you see a tree or stub your toe, the sensation you experience is an idea. Ideas are not matter. They exist in consciousness, which is also not matter. Berkeley supposed, therefore, that our sensations must come from God, who is the author of true reality. If this is hard to wrap your head around, picture the Matrix (from the movie), where the Matrix is created by the mind of God instead of by a computer.

Writer Samuel Johnson (author of the first English dictionary), a contemporary of Berkeley, although a good bit younger, thought this was nonsense. He is supposed to have walked up to a large stone and kicked it, saying, "I refute it *thus*."

Logicians have pointed out that this is not a good argument against Berkeley's claims. If you stub your toe on a stone in the Matrix, it really hurts, even though the hurt is in your head. It is the same with stones in Berkeley's universe. Nevertheless, Johnson's "appeal" has this clear advantage: stones are stubborn. If you think a stone does not exist, or imagine it doesn't exist, or deny that it exists, the sheer persistence of the thing is a problem you are going to have to deal with or else you are going to continue to stub your toe. Recalcitrant is a better word than stubborn, since it has the Latin word for kick (*calcitare*) built right in. Something that is recalcitrant is going to kick back, when you kick it.

In the ecological framework espoused in this book, reality is recalcitrant. Even though our sensation of a stone is entirely in our mind, the stone exists independently of us, which gives it the power to impose itself on our experience. In other words, if you fail to see a stone, or see it as something it is not, like a pile of leaves, you are likely to stub your toe on it. Within this philosophical framework is a kind of implicit faith that any falsehood that repeatedly flies in the face of material reality will eventually be exposed. The truth will out, as they say—hopefully before the untruth has caused too much damage.

Earlier, I observed that the kind of extreme fakery evident in *Amish Mafia*, particularly in the first season, was not sustainable. Another way of saying this is that *Amish Mafia*'s fakery eventually ran aground on the shoals of recalcitrant reality. There really is no Amish mafia, just as there is no living megalodon and there was no Pizzagate conspiracy. For that reason, attempts to "prove" otherwise were bound to eventually come apart at the seams. In the same way, the lies of self-serving politicians and their media lackeys are bound to eventually come apart at the seams.

But what should we do in the meantime?

If reality-based entertainment is indeed a form of mass-mediated gossip, as I have argued in this book, then when it propagates lies or misrepresentations or prejudice or discord, the best thing we can do, as consumers or potential consumers, is to treat it the same way we ought to treat false gossip. Trying to ban or boycott it just calls attention to it, as we saw with the Respect Amish campaign. Trying to prove that it's false won't change the mind of anybody who has their own reasons for liking or believing it, as we saw with fans of *Amish Mafia*. It certainly does no good to question the intelligence or the motives of people who participate in it. For one thing, that's usually not fair, as I hope the conversations with producers and consumers of *Amish Mafia* in this book have convinced you. For another, that kind of judgmental attitude drives people deeper into their social bunkers.

When we are confronted with false gossip, the best thing to do is to become part of the recalcitrant reality that both the deceivers and the deceived need to deal with. What that means, in practical terms, is simply to stubbornly persist in pointing out the truth and calling out the liars. That is probably the best thing to do when confronted with falsehoods in the media too.

ACKNOWLEDGMENTS

I'm grateful to Donald Kraybill, the former editor of this Johns Hopkins se-ries, for twisting my arm to write this book. Without his urging, I probably would not have touched the topic—my specialty is *real* nonfiction television, not reality TV—but I find, in retrospect, that what I learned by researching and writing this book has tremendously deepened my understanding of all kinds of nonfiction. What Don had in mind when he invited me to tackle this topic was a book about how reality TV shows about the Amish depicted and affected the Amish community, but my project soon morphed into something else: a study of the peculiar appeals of the "reality" in reality TV, using *Amish Mafia* as a case study. I am grateful to both Don and Steve Nolt, his successor, for supporting this shift in subject and scope. Both Don and Steve gave me a great deal of useful feedback on specifics as well.

I want to give credit for a lot of the legwork in the initial years of my re-search to four especially smart and energetic undergraduate students: Rebecca Gant, David Kime, Daisy Mase, and Sarah Reynolds. The unusual reception experiments described in chapter 4 were the product of a genuine collabora-tion among the five of us. I also wish to thank Ben Riehl, who was my main guide to Lancaster's Amish community, and Eric Evangelista, *Amish Mafia*'s principle producer and showrunner, who on several occasions carved time out of his busy schedule to explain his work to me.

A handful of *Amish Mafia* cast members, crew members, and producers took a risk by agreeing to talk to me, even though they were bound by non-disclosure agreements. Without their help, I would not have been able to see through a lot of *Amish Mafia*'s tricks and tradecraft, so I am deeply grateful to these individuals. I also wish to acknowledge the numerous reality TV fans who talked to me at length about their *Amish Mafia* viewing experiences. I won't name them because I told them I wouldn't, but a great deal of what I know about how and why people enjoyed *Amish Mafia*, I owe to them. Of course, I'm grateful to the many scholars, correspondents, and interviewees named in the book for what I learned from them. I wish to give particular thanks to Carl Plantinga, Catalin Brylla, and three anonymous readers of this manuscript for their helpful and insightful comments and suggestions.

Last but definitely not least, I received a great deal of support, of many kinds, from my employer, Franklin & Marshall College, and even more from my wife, Myrna. I thank them from the bottom of my heart.

Prologue

1. Dates and distributors of TV programs and movies will be included in the text where they are relevant. Otherwise, you can find them in the alphabetical list of programs mentioned in the references.

2. Oxford Languages, "Word of the Year 2016."

3. Collins, "Collins 2017 Word of the Year Shortlist."

4. Kavanagh and Rich, *Truth Decay*.

5. NBC News, "Conway."

6. Merlan, *Republic of Lies*.

7. Vosoughi, Roy, and Aral, "Spread of True and False News Online."

8. I borrow these terms from Donald T. Campbell, who was the first to show how Darwinian principles could explain creative thought and cultural change. Campbell, "Blind Variation and Selective Retention."

9. Geertz, *Interpretation of Cultures*.

10. Cinema scholar David Bordwell, one of the chief architects and advocates of this shift, describes it in more detail in "The Part-Time Cognitivist."

11. Nanicelli and Taberham, *Cognitive Media Theory*.

12. Zunshine, *Oxford Handbook of Cognitive Literary Studies*.

13. Hogan, *Cognitive Science, Literature, and the Arts*.

14. Anderson, *The Reality of Illusion*.

15. Zunshine, "Reality TV."

16. Hill, *Reality TV*; Ouellette, *A Companion to Reality Television*.

Chapter 1 · Enquiring Minds Want to Know

1. Gombrich, *Art and Illusion*, 332 ff.

2. Gombrich, 333.

3. Gombrich, 222.

4. A particularly nice explanation is offered in the clip "Inside NOVA: Change Blindness," YouTube, March 13, 2011, https://www.youtube.com/watch?v=VkrrVozZR2c.

5. Worth, "Pictures Can't Say Ain't."

6. Kelly and Greenhill, "How Bear Grylls the Born Survivor Roughed It."

7. Ordine, "7 in Pagans-Amish Drug Ring Are Sentenced."

8. Eric Evangelista, telephone conversation, March 17, 2016.

9. I have pieced together many details about the production of *Amish Mafia* in part because some cast and crew members were willing to talk to me off the record.

10. Hambright, "Amish Experience Halts 'Amish Mafia Tour.'"

11. Politifact, "The Principles of PolitiFact, PunditFact and the Truth-O-Meter."

12. Kraybill, Nolt, and Weaver-Zercher, *Amish Grace*, 52.

13. George, "'Amish Mafia.'"

14. Stoltzfus and Henican, *Amish Confidential*. It is clear that this book was written by a skillful and experienced author, not an ex-Amishman with an eighth-grade education, but it does convey Levi's point of view and experience, so I credit the stories and quotes to him.

15. Hot Snakes Media, accessed March 7, 2016, http://hotsnakesmedia.com/team.html.

16. Ogunnaike, "Quiet on the Fake Set."

17. Eric Evangelista, telephone conversation, March 17, 2016.

18. Hatmaker, "'Amish Mafia' Creator Responds."

19. Hatmaker, "'Amish Mafia' Cast Member Mary Troyer Speaks Out."

20. Kraybill, *Renegade Amish.*

21. Kraybill, *Riddle of Amish Culture*, 101 ff. Quote from p. 101.

22. Stoltzfus and Henican, *Amish Confidential*, 222.

23. Kraybill, 106 ff.

24. McCarty, "Ohio's 'Amish Bernie Madoff' Gets Prison Term"; Henriques, "Broken Trust in God's Country."

25. Steven Breit, interview, March 15, 2016. Throughout this book, statements in quotation marks are verbatim, often edited slightly for neatness or economy. Statements not in quotation marks are paraphrased.

26. Stoltzfus and Henican, *Amish Confidential*, 99.

27. Stoltzfus and Henican, 108.

28. Stoltzfus and Henican, 109.

29. Stoltzfus and Henican, 175.

30. Stoltzfus and Henican, 174.

31. Haidt, *Happiness Hypothesis*, 55.

Chapter 2 · *The Roots of Reality Entertainment*

1. Eric Evangelista, interview, March 16, 2016.

2. Harris, *Humbug.*

3. Harris, 23.

4. Harris, 23.

5. The details of this account are from Harris, 62 ff.

6. Harris, 65.

7. Harris, 67.

8. Eric Evangelista, interview, March 16, 2016.

9. Wilson, *Mathew Brady*, 167.

10. Hirsch, *Seizing the Light*, 105.

11. Leyda, *Before Hollywood*, 100–101.

12. Springer, "The Newspaper Meets the Dime Novel."

13. Fielding, *American Newsreel, 1911–1967*, 43.

14. Green, "This Reality Which Is Not One."

15. Quotes from a publicity poster reproduced in Gaines and Renov, *Collecting Visible Evidence*, 9.

16. Corliss, "Robert Flaherty: The Man in the Iron Myth," 234.

17. The ideas in this paragraph and the next are treated in more depth in Eitzen, "Reel Amish," 45 ff. Some of the wording of the following paragraph is drawn from that essay.

18. TLC, "I'm an Eskimo at the Beach!"

19. Jon Sechrist, quoted in Hawks, "Is TLC's Escaping Alaska Fake?"

20. Details are recounted in Schwartz, *Broadcast Hysteria.*

21. Gosling, *Waging the War of the Worlds,* 78ff.

22. Gosling, 218.

23. Cantril, with Gaudet and Herzog, *Invasion from Mars.*

24. Cantril, 55 ff.

25. Pooley and Socolow, "The Myth of *The War of the Worlds* Panic."

26. Cantril, *Invasion from Mars,* 115, table 7.

27. Bulger and Davidson, *Promises, Challenges, and Futures,* 12.

28. Kahne and Boywer, "Educating for Democracy."

29. Cantril, *Invasion from Mars,* 159–60.

30. West, Meserve, and Stanovich, "Cognitive Sophistication"; Sanchez and Dunning, "Overconfidence among Beginners."

31. O'Connor and Weatherall, *Misinformation Age.*

32. Ward, "Inventing Objectivity," 139.

33. Quoted in Schiller, *Objectivity and the News,* 79.

34. Schiller, 80, quoting Pray, *Memoirs of James Gordon Bennett.*

35. Quoted in Ward, "Inventing Objectivity," 140.

36. Ward lists six standards in "Inventing Objectivity," 142. I reduced the number by combining similar standards.

37. Cohen, "Business of International News," 74, quoted in Fielding, *American Newsreel,* 146–47.

38. Fielding, 148 ff.

39. Fielding, *March of Time.*

40. Fielding, *American Newsreel,* 231.

41. Buchanan, *Film and the Future,* 38 and 42, quoted in Fielding, *March of Time,* 247–48.

42. Parrish and Nauss, "NBC Admits It Rigged Crash."

43. Roig-Franzia, Higham, and Farhi, "Within NBC, an Intense Debate."

Chapter 3 · A Chronicle of Contrivance

1. This and other scenes can be seen at Thirteen, "An American Family."

2. Gilbert, "Reflections on An American Family, II."

3. Gilbert, "Reflections," 303.

4. Barnouw, *Documentary,* 235ff.

5. Blake, "*The Real World.*"

6. Rose and Hunt, "Reality TV Pioneer Jonathan Murray."

7. Hill, *Reality TV,* 49–50, 77.

8. MTV's *Jackass* (2000–2002) is the quintessential example of a reality TV show in which cast members deliberately put themselves in harm's way for the entertainment of viewers.

9. Kavka, *Reality TV,* 83.

10. Quoted in Hill, *Reality TV,* 73.

11. For elaboration, see Eitzen, "Documentary's Peculiar Appeals."

12. Kavka, *Reality TV.*

13. Kavka, 99.

14. Ted Magder details the new business model in "The End of TV 101."

15. Kompare, "Extraordinarily Ordinary."

16. Kompare, 108.

17. Telephone interview with reality TV writer Troy DeVolld, April 18, 2016. See also his guide to the reality TV writer's craft: DeVolld, *Reality TV.*

18. Gillan, "From Ozzie Nelson to Ozzy Osbourne."

19. Hill, *Reality TV,* 153ff.

20. See, for example, The Age, "Ozzy's Outburst Was Faked."
21. Greck, "MTV announces."
22. DeVolld, telephone interview.
23. Animal Planet, *Mermaids: The Body Found* (video).
24. Animal Planet, "Mermaids: The Body Found" (press release).
25. Dr. M, "RIP: Science on TV."
26. Mikkelson, "Mermaids: The Body Found."
27. National Ocean Service, "Are Mermaids Real?"
28. Dr. M, "RIP."
29. Dr. M.
30. Futon Critic, "Animal Planet Slays."
31. Hibberd, "Mermaid Hoax ."
32. Spector, "70% of People Still Believe Megalodon Exists."
33. Black, "Idiocy, Fabrications and Lies."
34. Walsh and Benzine, "15 Years."
35. Hendricks, *A Curious Discovery*, 235.
36. Hendricks, 297.
37. Epstein, "No More Megalodon."
38. Davidson, "Discovery Channel Provokes Outrage."
39. Hibberd, "Discovery Boss Vows Change."
40. Merlin Miller, telephone interview, May 3, 2016.
41. Steven Cantor, telephone interview, May 3, 2016.
42. Walker, "*Devil's Playground*."
43. Walker.
44. Laikind, "My Producer's Article."
45. Randy Stoll, telephone interview, May 4, 2016.
46. Laikind, "My Producer's Article."
47. Laikind.
48. Laikind.
49. Miller, telephone interview.
50. Eitzen, "Reel Amish."
51. Eitzen, "Hollywood Rumspringa."
52. Morrissey, "Arrests, Divorces, and Secret Children."

Chapter 4 · *The Pleasure in Being Deceived (and Its Limits)*

1. Interview, June 6, 2016.
2. Interview, May 23, 2016.
3. The psychological literature in support of these claims is too extensive to cite, but if you are skeptical or wish to learn more, I refer you to two excellent, accessible overviews: Eagleman, *Incognito*, and Kahneman, *Thinking, Fast and Slow*.
4. Dan McDonald, telephone interview, May 20, 2016.
5. Hall, "Perceptions of Media Realism."
6. Hall, 429ff.
7. Hall, 429.
8. Levine, "Truth-Default Theory"; Levine, *Duped*.
9. Hill, *Reality TV: Factual Entertainment*.
10. Winston, *Lies, Damn Lies and Documentaries*; see in particular ch. 4 ("Regulation," 87–112).
11. Hill, *Reality TV* (2004). See also Hill, *Restyling Factual TV*.
12. Hill, *Reality TV* (2004), 64.

13. An American study of responses to *Survivor* drew the same conclusion. See Crew, "Viewer Interpretations of Reality Television."

14. WNYC Studios, "La Mancha Screwjob."

15. YouTube, "Bret Hart vs. Shawn Michaels"; YouTube, "Vince Russo."

16. Barthes, *Mythologies*, quoted in Shoemaker, *Squared Circle*, 16.

17. Sloan, *I Watched a Wild Hog Eat My Baby*, 218.

18. Alliance for Audited Media, "AAM: Total Circ for Consumer Magazines."

19. Bird, *For Enquiring Minds*.

20. Bird, 120–21.

21. Perel, *Bat Boy Lives!*

22. Perel, "Hillary's Hot Nights" story dated September 25, 2001, pp. 166–67; "Saddam and Osama" story dated October 7, 2004, pp. 171–74.

23. Bird, *For Enquiring Minds*, 122.

24. Bird, 123.

25. Bird, 123.

26. Stoltzfus and Henican, *Amish Confidential*.

27. Bird, *For Enquiring Minds*, 204–5.

28. Frey, *A Million Little Pieces*.

29. YouTube, "Oprah Winfrey Show."

30. Smoking Gun, "A Million Little Lies."

31. YouTube, "Oprah Winfrey Show."

32. See Comedy Central, "Colbert Report."

33. Oprah, "Oprah's Questions for James."

34. YouTube, "Oprah Winfrey Show."

35. Hylton, "Oprah vs. James Frey."

36. Kottke, "James Frey's A Million Little Pieces Fiction?" All of the following quotes in this section are from this source.

37. Anderson et al., "Can I Make Stuff Up?"

38. This American Life, "Retraction."

39. *Amish Mafia*, "Shepherds' End."

Chapter 5 · Gossip and Lies

1. Stoltzfus and Henican, *Amish Confidential*.

2. Hostetler, *Amish Society*, 362.

3. Merry, "Rethinking Gossip and Scandal."

4. Stoltzfus and Henican, *Amish Confidential*, 170.

5. Epstein, *Gossip*.

6. Epstein, xiii.

7. Epstein, 13ff.

8. Stoltzfus and Henican, *Amish Confidential*, 168ff.

9. Epstein, *Gossip*, 3ff.

10. Epstein, 37.

11. Foster, "Research on Gossip."

12. Foster, 86.

13. The terms "information," "intimacy," and "influence" are gossip researcher Ralph L. Rosnow's. See Rosnow, "Rumor and Gossip in Interpersonal Interaction and Beyond."

14. Foster, "Research on Gossip," 87.

15. Foster, 85.

16. Foster, 85.

17. Dunbar, *Grooming, Gossip, and the Evolution of Language*.

18. Dunbar, 79.

19. Dunbar, 79.

20. Dunbar, 60.

21. de Waal, *Chimpanzee Politics*. The first edition of this book came out in 1982. A few years later, in *Machiavellian Intelligence*, primatologists Richard W. Byrne and Andrew Whiten developed the evolutionary hypothesis that Dunbar designed his research to elaborate and test.

22. Dunbar, *Grooming*, 40.

23. Dunbar, 20–21.

24. Max-Planck-Gesellschaft, "Benefits of Social Grooming."

25. Dunbar, *Grooming*, 123.

26. Dunbar, 175.

27. *The Young and the Restless*, July 20, 2018 (season 45, episode 225, minute 37), CBS.

28. Mumford, *Love and Ideology in the Afternoon*, 41.

29. Mumford, 51, 49.

30. Dunbar, *Grooming*, 200.

31. Julie Porter, "Hanging On by a Common Thread."

32. Porter, 222.

33. The ratings numbers in this paragraph come from Wikipedia, s.v. "List of U.S. Daytime Soap Opera Ratings," accessed March 9, 2021, https://en.wikipedia.org/wiki/List_of_U.S._daytime_soap_opera_ratings#cite_note-Encyc_ratings-1. This source conveniently compiles the data from Nielsen reports.

34. Ford, De Kosnik, and Harrington, "The Crisis of Daytime Drama."

35. Mumford, *Love and Ideology*, 9.

36. I lay out this argument more fully with respect to documentary in Eitzen, "Documentary's Peculiar Appeals." Some of the wording here is borrowed from Eitzen, "Duties of Documentary in a Post-Truth Society."

37. Dunbar, *Grooming*, 199.

38. de Waal, *Chimpanzee Politics*, 195.

39. de Waal, 178.

40. Spacks, "In Praise of Gossip." See also Spacks's subsequent book, *Gossip*.

41. Stoltzfus and Henican, *Amish Confidential*, 175.

42. This paragraph glosses the central argument of Kevin Glynn's *Tabloid Culture*. Glynn bases this argument largely on the work of John Fiske, who wrote widely and influentially on the democratizing potential of popular culture. See, in particular, Fiske's accessible and illuminating volumes *Understanding Popular Culture* and *Reading Popular Culture*.

43. Putnam, *Bowling Alone*.

44. Feldman, *The Liar in Your Life*, 11–16.

45. Byrne and Whiten, "Thinking Primate's Guide to Deception."

46. Byrne and Corp, "Neocortex Size Predicts Deception Rate."

47. Eco, *Theory of Semiotics*, 7.

48. Trivers, *Folly of Fools*.

49. In a 2018 podcast, writer Malcolm Gladwell defends Brian Williams by pointing out, quite correctly, that because of the nature of memory, all of us genuinely misremember facts in self-serving ways. Gladwell, "Free Brian Williams."

50. Bateson, Nettle, and Roberts, "Cues of Being Watched Enhance Cooperation."

51. Ariely, *Honest Truth about Dishonesty*.

52. Ariely, 27.

53. Ariely, 187.

54. Bailey, *Prevalence of Deceit*.

55. Bailey, 35.

Chapter 6 · Rights and Wrongs

1. Knapp, "Amish Horror Series on Tap."

2. Mary Haverstick, telephone conversation, January 28, 2016.

3. Haverstick, "Smart Talk: Amish Being Exploited on TV?"

4. Haverstick, "Smart Talk."

5. Haverstick, "Smart Talk."

6. Haverstick, "Smart Talk."

7. Mathis, "Corbett Calls for Amish Mafia to End."

8. Press release from RespectAmish.org, August 5, 2014.

9. Haverstick, "Smart Talk."

10. DeKok, "Tourism vs. Reality TV."

11. Cusick, "Growing Backlash."

12. Haverstick, telephone conversation, January 28, 2016.

13. Eric Evangelista, email to author, November 18, 2019.

14. I discuss these issues at more length in Eitzen, "Hollywood Rumspringa." Some of the wording in this paragraph is borrowed from that essay.

15. Stoltzfus and Henican, *Amish Confidential*. This perspective is not stated in so many words, but it is evident in the chapter on gossip, where Levi talks back to his critics, as well as in the opening and closing chapters of the book.

16. Sheridan, "Patricia Sheridan's Breakfast."

17. Stoltzfus and Henican, *Amish Confidential*, 265.

18. Stoltzfus and Henican, 264.

19. Stoltzfus and Henican, 262 ff.

20. All the quotes in this paragraph are from Haverstick, "Smart Talk."

21. I filmed them for a public-television documentary entitled *The Amish and Us* (1998).

22. I am grateful to Kirk T. Schroder, prominent entertainment lawyer and coeditor, with Jay Shanker, of *The Essential Guide to Entertainment Law*, for helping me understand the issues involved here, in a phone interview on October 17, 2019. Any misunderstandings are, of course, my own.

23. Hostetler and Kraybill, "Hollywood Markets the Amish," 223.

24. Mez et al., "Clinicopathological Evaluation."

25. See Daniel Kahneman's *Thinking, Fast and Slow* for a particularly lucid overview and explanation.

26. CNN, "NFL Concussions Fast Facts."

27. CBS News, "Claims in NFL Concussion Settlement."

28. Blair, "Surviving Reality TV."

29. For example, see Plesa, "Behind-the-Scenes Horror Stories."

30. Mary Schmucker, interview, August 22, 2016.

31. Merlin Miller, email to author, November 17, 2019.

32. Kant, *Grounding for the Metaphysics of Morals*, 30.

33. Bok, *Lying*.

34. Frankfurt, *On Bullshit*, 56.

35. Baudrillard, *Simulacra and Simulation*.

36. Gladstone, *Trouble with Reality*, 47.

37. Ariely, *Honest Truth about Dishonesty*, 199–204.

38. Ariely, 194–195.

39. Ariely, 125–126.

40. Ariely, 131–134.

41. Ariely, 214.

42. Epstein, *Gossip*, 173.

43. Hostetler and Kraybill, "Hollywood Markets the Amish."

44. The details recounted here are from Robb, "Pizzagate."

45. Goldman, "Comet Ping Pong Gunman Answers Questions"; Haag and Salam, "Gunman in 'Pizzagate' Shooting Is Sentenced."

46. Haag and Salam, "Gunman in 'Pizzagate' Shooting."

47. Gerbner et al., "Growing Up with Television."

48. Poniewozik, "Foreword," xi.

49. Eitzen, "Hollywood Rumspringa."

Epilogue

1. Davidson, "Discovery Channel Provokes Outrage."

2. Yahr, "A Fake Shark Week Documentary." *Washington Post*, July 16, 2018, https://www.washingtonpost.com/news/arts-and-entertainment/wp/2018/07/26/a-fake-shark-week-documentary-about-megalodons-caused-controversy-why-is-discovery-bringing-it-up-again/.

3. Marie and Spindler, "Reasons Why Gold Rush Is Totally Fake."

4. Adalian, "The Boom Days of Reality TV."

5. Andreeva, "Discovery Puts Squeeze on Unscripted Producers."

6. Roxborough, "MIPCOM."

7. Mary Schmucker, interview, August 22, 2016.

8. Kuss, "Revelo 05—Esther Schmucker."

9. Most of the information in this paragraph comes from social media sleuthing in October 2019.

10. Merlin Miller, telephone conversation, November 12, 2019.

11. Jantzi, "Amish Youth and Social Media."

12. King, "Amish and Social Media."

13. Twenge, *iGen*.

14. King, "Amish and Social Media."

15. Fact Checker, "In 993 Days"; McIntire, Yourish, and Buchanan, "In Trump's Twitter Feed."

16. *Washington Post*, "Sept. 2–5, 2019 Washington Post–ABC News Poll."

17. Pew Research Center, "Trump has Met the Public's Modest Expectations."

18. Bump, "By a 3-to-1 Margin."

19. Azarian, "A Complete Psychological Analysis."

20. Kreiss, "The Media Are about Identity," 94.

Print and Digital References

Adalian, Josef. "The Boom Days of Reality TV Are Over." Vulture, September 23, 2015. https://www.vulture.com/2015/09/reality-tv-boom-days-are-over.html.

Alliance for Audited Media. "AAM: Total Circ for Consumer Magazines." Accessed July 14, 2016. http://abcas3.auditedmedia.com/ecirc/magtitlesearch.asp.

American Media. "National Enquirer." Accessed July 14, 2016. http://www.americanmediainc.com/brands/national-enquirer (no longer active).

Amish Mafia. "Shepherds' End," season 3, episode 8. April 9, 2014. https://www.youtube.com/watch?v=TRSCY9-crI0&index=8&list=ELyzXnc3EyhD4.

Anderson, Joseph D. *The Reality of Illusion: An Ecological Approach to Cognitive Film Studies.* Carbondale: Southern Illinois University Press, 1996.

Anderson, L. V., David Haglund, Natalie Matthews-Ramo, Jim Pagels, and Jen Chaney. "Can I Make Stuff Up? A Visual Guide." Slate, March 21, 2012. http://www.slate.com/blogs/browbeat/2012/03/21/mike_daisey_david_sedaris_david_foster_wallace_and_other_storytellers_who_can_make_stuff_up_.html.

Andreeva, Nellie. "Discovery Puts Squeeze on Unscripted Producers with New Series Financing Mechanism." Deadline, June 26, 2019. https://deadline.com/2019/06/discovery-puts-squeeze-on-unscripted-producers-new-series-financing-mechanism-1202638379/.

Animal Planet. *Mermaids: The Body Found*. Video. Accessed April 27, 2016. https://www.amazon.com/Mermaids-Body-Found-Extended-Cut/dp/B00D11VJYG/ref=sr_1_1?dchild=1&keywords=mermaids+the+body+found&qid=1635634866&s=movies-tv&sr=1-1.

———. "Mermaids: The Body Found." Press release. Accessed April 28, 2016. http://ekits.press.discovery.com/ekits/monster-week-mermaids/press-release.html (no longer active).

Ariely, Dan. *The Honest Truth about Dishonesty: How We Lie to Everyone—Especially Ourselves.* New York: Harper Perennial, 2013.

Azarian, Bobby. "A Complete Psychological Analysis of Trump's Support." *Psychology Today*, December 27, 2018. https://www.psychologytoday.com/us/blog/mind-in-the-machine/201812/complete-psychological-analysis-trumps-support.

Bailey, Frederick G. *The Prevalence of Deceit.* Ithaca, NY: Cornell University Press, 1991.

Barnouw, Erik. *Documentary: A History of the Non-fiction Film*, 2nd rev. ed. New York: Oxford University Press, 1993.

Barthes, Roland. *Mythologies: The Complete Edition.* New York: Hill and Wang, 2012. First published in 1957.

Bateson, Melissa, Daniel Nettle, and Gilbert Roberts. "Cues of Being Watched Enhance

Cooperation in a Real-World Setting." *Biology Letters* 2, no. 3 (September 22, 2006): 412–14. http://www.ncbi.nlm.nih.gov/pmc/articles/PMC1686213/.

Baudrillard, Jean. *Simulacra and Simulation*. Translated by Sheila Faria Glaser. Ann Arbor: University of Michigan Press, 1995.

Bird, S. Elizabeth. *For Enquiring Minds: A Cultural Study of Supermarket Tabloids*. Knoxville: University of Tennessee Press, 1992.

Black, Riley. "The Idiocy, Fabrications and Lies of Ancient Aliens." Smithsonian, May 11, 2012. http://www.smithsonianmag.com/science-nature/the-idiocy-fabrications-and-lies-of-ancient-aliens-86294030/.

Blair, Jennifer L. "Surviving Reality TV: The Ultimate Challenge for Reality Show Contestants." *Loyola of Los Angeles Entertainment Law Review* 31, no. 1 (2010): 1–24. https://digital commons.lmu.edu/elr/vol31/iss1/1.

Blake, Meredith. "*The Real World*: 'This Is the True Story. . . .'" AV Club, June 6, 2011. http://www.avclub.com/tvclub/the-real-world-this-is-the-true-story-57041.

Bok, Sissela. *Lying: Moral Choice in Public and Private Life*. Updated ed. New York: Vintage, 1999.

Bordwell, David. "The Part Time Cognitivist: A View from Film Studies." *Projections* 4, no. 2 (Winter 2010): 1–18.

Buchanan, Andrew. *Film and the Future*. London: Allen and Unwin, 1945.

Bulger, Monica, and Patrick Davidson. *The Promises, Challenges, and Futures of Media Literacy*. New York: Data and Society Research Institute, 2018. https://datasociety.net/pubs /oh/DataAndSociety_Media_Literacy_2018.pdf.

Bump, Philip. "By a 3-to-1 Margin, Trump Supporters Embrace His Personality over His Policies." *Washington Post*, August 23, 2018. https://www.washingtonpost.com/news /politics/wp/2018/08/23/by-a-3-to-1-margin-trump-supporters-embrace-his-personality -over-his-policies/.

Byrne, Richard W., and Andrew Whiten. "The Thinking Primate's Guide to Deception." *New Scientist* 1589 (December 3, 1987): 54–57.

———. *Machiavellian Intelligence: Social Expertise and the Evolution of Intellect in Monkeys, Apes, and Humans*. Oxford: Clarendon Press, 1988.

Byrne, Richard W., and Nadia Corp. "Neocortex Size Predicts Deception Rate in Primates." *Proceedings of the Royal Society of Biological Sciences* 271, no. 1549 (August 22, 2004): 1693–99. http://www.ncbi.nlm.nih.gov/pmc/articles/PMC1691785/.

Campbell, Donald T. "Blind Variation and Selective Retention in Creative Thought As in Other Knowledge Processes." *Psychological Review* 67, no. 6 (1960): 380–400.

Cantril, Hadley, with the assistance of Hazel Gaudet and Hertz Herzog. *The Invasion from Mars: A Study in the Psychology of Panic*. Princeton, NJ: Princeton University Press, 1940.

CBS News. "Claims in NFL Concussion Settlement Hit $500 Million in Less Than 2 Years." July 30, 2018. https://www.cbsnews.com/news/nfl-concussion-claims-hit-500-million -less-than-2-years/.

CNN. "NFL Concussions Fast Facts." Updated August 15, 2019. https://www.cnn.com/2013 /08/30/us/nfl-concussions-fast-facts/index.html.

Cohen, Emanuel. "The Business of International News by Motion Pictures." *Annals of the American Academy of Political and Social Science* 128, no. 1 (November 1926): 74–78.

Collins. "Collins 2017 Word of the Year Shortlist." Language Lovers blog, November 2, 2017. https://www.collinsdictionary.com/word-lovers-blog/new/collins-2017-word-of-the-year -shortlist,396,HCB.html.

Comedy Central. "The Colbert Report: James Frey's Truthiness." Video, January 30, 2006. http://www.cc.com/video-clips/vbdym4/the-colbert-report-james-frey-s-truthiness.

Corliss, Richard. "Robert Flaherty: The Man in the Iron Myth." In *Nonfiction Film Theory and Criticism*, edited by Richard Meran Barsam, 230–38. New York: E. P. Dutton, 1973.

Crew, Richard E. "Viewer Interpretations of Reality Television: How Real is *Survivor* for Its Viewers?" In *How Real Is Reality TV? Essays on Representation and Truth*, edited by David S. Escoffery, 61–77. Jefferson, NC: McFarland, 2006.

Cusick, Marie. "A Growing Backlash against 'Amish Exploitation' in Pennsylvania." NPR, August 24, 2014. http://www.npr.org/2014/08/24/342474911/a-growing-backlash-against -amish-exploitation-in-pennsylvania.

Davidson, Jacob. "Discovery Channel Provokes Outrage with Fake Shark Week Documentary." *Time*, August 7, 2013. http://entertainment.time.com/2013/08/07/discovery-channel -provokes-outrage-with-fake-shark-week-documentary/.

de Waal, Frans B. M. *Chimpanzee Politics: Power and Sex among Apes,* rev. ed. Baltimore: Johns Hopkins University Press, 1998.

DeKok, David. "Tourism vs. Reality TV: Exploiting Pennsylvania's Amish." Reuters, August 17, 2014. http://www.reuters.com/article/us-usa-amish-tv-idUSKBN0GH0DY20140817.

DeVolld, Troy. *Reality TV: An Insider's Guide to TV's Hottest Market.* Studio City, CA: Michael Wiese Productions, 2011.

Dr. M. "RIP: Science on TV." Deep Sea News, May 30, 2012. http://www.deepseanews.com /2012/05/rip-science-on-tv/.

Dunbar, Robin. *Grooming, Gossip, and the Evolution of Language.* Cambridge, MA: Harvard University Press, 1996.

Eagleman, David. *Incognito: The Secret Lives of the Brain.* New York: Vintage, 2012.

Eco, Umberto. *A Theory of Semiotics.* Bloomington: Indiana University Press, 1978.

Eitzen, Dirk. "Documentary's Peculiar Appeals." In *Moving Image Theory: Ecological Considerations*, edited by Joseph D. and Barbara Fisher Anderson, 183–99. Carbondale: University of Southern Illinois Press, 2005.

———. "Hollywood Rumspringa: *Amish in the City*." In Umble and Weaver-Zercher, *The Amish and the Media*, 133–53.

———. "Reel Amish: The Amish in Documentaries." In Umble and Weaver-Zercher, *The Amish and the Media*, 42–64.

———. "The Duties of Documentary in a Post-Truth Society." In *Cognitive Theory and Documentary Film*, edited by Catalin Brylla and Mette Kramer, 93–111. New York: Palgrave McMillan, 2018.

Epstein, Adam. "No More Megalodon: Discovery Channel Promises a More Scientific 'Shark Week' This Year." Quartz, July 6, 2015. http://qz.com/445516/no-more-megalodon -discovery-channel-promises-a-more-scientific-shark-week-this-year/.

Epstein, Joseph. *Gossip: The Untrivial Pursuit.* Boston: Houghton Mifflin Harcourt, 2011.

Eugene, Kim. "Busting One of Tech's Biggest Myths." Slate, October 3, 2014. http://www.slate .com/blogs/business_insider/2014/10/03/cellphones_at_gas_stations_mythbusters _debunk_one_of_the_biggest_myths_in.html.

Fact Checker. "In 993 Days, President Trump Has Made 13,435 False or Misleading Claims." *Washington Post,* updated October 9, 2019, https://www.washingtonpost.com/graphics /politics/trump-claims-database/.

Feldman, Robert S. *The Liar in Your Life: The Way to Truthful Relationships.* New York: Twelve, 2009.

Fielding, Raymond. *The American Newsreel, 1911–1967.* Norman: University of Oklahoma Press, 1972.

———. *The March of Time: 1935–1951.* New York: Oxford University Press, 1978.

Fiske, John. *Reading Popular Culture.* Boston: Unwin Hyman, 1989.

———. *Understanding Popular Culture*. Boston: Unwin Hyman, 1989.

Ford, Sam, Abigail De Kosnik, and C. Lee Harrington. "The Crisis of Daytime Drama and What It Means for the Future of Television." In *The Survival of Soap Opera: Transformations for a New Media Era*, edited by Sam Ford, Abigail De Kosnik, and C. Lee Harrington, 3–21. Jackson: University Press of Mississippi, 2011.

Foster, Erik. "Research on Gossip: Taxonomy, Methods, and Future Directions." *Review of General Psychology* 8, no. 2 (2004): 78–99. http://dx.doi.org/10.1037/1089-2680.8.2.78.

Frankfurt, Harry. *On Bullshit*. Princeton, NJ: Princeton University Press, 2005.

Frey, James. *A Million Little Pieces*. New York: Anchor, 2005.

Futon Critic. "Animal Planet Slays with Best-Ever May in Network History." May 30, 2012. http://www.thefutoncritic.com/ratings/2012/05/30/animal-planet-slays-with-best-ever -may-in-network-history-143310/20120530animalplanet01/.

Gaines, Jane M., and Michael Renov, eds. *Collecting Visible Evidence*. Minneapolis: University of Minnesota Press, 1999.

Geertz, Clifford. *The Interpretation of Cultures: Selected Essays*. New York: Basic Books, 1973.

George, David. "'Amish Mafia': Amish Gone Wild?" *Salon*, January 16, 2013. http://www .salon.com/2013/01/16/amish_mafia_amish_gone_wild/.

Gerbner, G., L. Gross, M. Morgan, N. Signorielli, and J. Shanahan. "Growing Up with Television: Cultivation Processes." In *Media Effects: Advances in Theory and Research*, edited by J. Bryant and D. Zillmann, 43–67. 2nd ed. Mahwah, NJ: Lawrence Erlbaum Associates, 2002.

Gilbert, Craig. "Reflections on An American Family, II." In *New Challenges for Documentary*, edited by Alan Rosenthal, 288–307. Berkeley: University of California Press, 1988. Reprinted from *Studies in Visual Communication* 8, no. 1 (Winter 1982).

Gillan, Jennifer. "From Ozzie Nelson to Ozzy Osbourne: The Genesis and Development of the Reality (Star) Sitcom." In *Understanding Reality Television*, edited by Su Holmes and Deborah Jermyn, 54–70. New York: Routledge, 2004.

Gladstone, Brooke. *The Trouble with Reality: A Rumination on the Moral Panic in Our Time*. New York: Workman Publishing, 2017.

Gladwell, Malcolm. "Free Brian Williams." *Revisionist History* podcast, season 3, episode 4, 2018. http://revisionisthistory.com/episodes/24-free-brian-williams.

Glynn, Kevin. *Tabloid Culture: Trash Taste, Popular Power, and the Transformation of American Television*. Durham, NC: Duke University Press, 2000.

Goldman, Adam. "The Comet Ping Pong Gunman Answers Our Reporter's Questions." *New York Times*, December 7, 2016. https://www.nytimes.com/2016/12/07/us/edgar-welch -comet-pizza-fake-news.html.

Gombrich, Ernst H. *Art and Illusion: A Study in the Psychology of Pictorial Representation*. 2nd rev. ed. Princeton, NJ: Princeton University Press, 1969.

Gosling, John. *Waging the War of the Worlds: A History of the 1938 Radio Broadcast and Resulting Panic, Including the Original Script*. Jefferson, NC: McFarland, 2009.

Greck. "MTV announces the death of 'reality television' (Osbournes spoilers)." Straight Dope Message Board, August 2003. Accessed April 22, 2016. http://boards.straightdope.com /sdmb/showthread.php?t=204338.

Green, Jared F. "This Reality Which Is Not One." In Rhodes and Springer, eds., *Docufictions*, 64–87.

Haag, Matthew, and Maya Salam. "Gunman in 'Pizzagate' Shooting Is Sentenced to Four Years in Prison." *New York Times*, June 22, 2017. https://www.nytimes.com/2017/06/22/us /pizzagate-attack-sentence.html.

Haidt, Jonathan. *The Happiness Hypothesis: Finding Modern Truth in Ancient Wisdom*. New York: Basic Books, 2006.

Hall, Alice E. "Perceptions of Media Realism and Reality TV." In *The SAGE Handbook of Media Processes and Effects*, edited by Robin L. Nabi and Mary Beth Oliver, 423–38. Los Angeles: SAGE, 2009.

Hambright, Brett. "Amish Experience Halts 'Amish Mafia Tour' after Legal Threat." Lancaster-Online, May 9, 2013, updated April 8, 2014. http://lancasteronline.com/news/amish -experience-halts-amish-mafia-tour-after-legal-threat/article_0fff2a65-608f-56fe-bc92 -5558807b11f1.html.

———. "New Amish Mafia Character's Rap Sheet Includes DUI Crash with Horse and Buggy." LancasterOnline, May 14, 2013. http://lancasteronline.com/news/new-amish-mafia-char acter-s-rap-sheet-includes-dui-crash/article_c7bfd108-e01f-575c-aba1-cf6dfccc13b0.html.

Harris, Neil. *Humbug: The Art of P. T. Barnum*. Boston: Little, Brown, 1973.

Hatmaker, Julia. "'Amish Mafia' Cast Member Mary Troyer Speaks Out on Sexual Abuse and Being Shunned." PennLive.com, March 31, 2015. http://www.pennlive.com/entertainment /index.ssf/2015/03/amish_mafia_mary.html.

———. "'Amish Mafia' Creator Responds to What's Fake, What's Real on the Show ahead of Series Finale." PennLive.com, March 30, 2015. http://www.pennlive.com/entertainment /index.ssf/2015/03/amish_mafia.html.

Haverstick, Mary. Interview on WITF, "Smart Talk: Amish Being Exploited on TV?" August 4, 2014. https://www.witf.org/2014/08/04/smart_talk_amish_being_exploited_on_tv/.

Hawks, Asa. "Is TLC's Escaping Alaska Fake?" Starcasm.net, July 27, 2014. http://starcasm.net /archives/281361.

Hendricks, John. *A Curious Discovery: An Entrepreneur's Story*. New York: Harper Collins, 2013.

Henriques, Diana B. "Broken Trust in God's Country." *New York Times*, February 25, 2012. http://www.nytimes.com/2012/02/26/business/in-amish-country-accusations-of-a-ponzi -scheme.html.

Hibberd, James. "Mermaid Hoax Drowns Animal Planet's Ratings Record." Entertainment Weekly, May 28, 2013. http://www.ew.com/article/2013/05/28/mermaids-animal-planet -ratings.

———. "Discovery Boss Vows Change: No More Anaconda Stunts, Fake Sharks." Entertain-ment Weekly, January 8, 2015. http://www.ew.com/article/2015/01/08/discovery-anaconda -sharks.

Hill, Annette. *Reality TV: Factual Entertainment and Television Audiences*. New York: Rout-ledge, 2004.

———. *Reality TV*. New York: Routledge, 2015.

———. *Restyling Factual TV: Audiences and News, Documentary and Reality Genres*. New York: Routledge, 2007.

Hirsch, Robert. *Seizing the Light: A History of Photography*. Boston: McGraw-Hill, 2000.

Hogan, Patrick Colm. *Cognitive Science, Literature, and the Arts: A Guide for Humanists*. New York: Routledge, 2003.

Hostetler, John A. *Amish Society*. 4th ed. Baltimore: Johns Hopkins University Press, 1993.

Hostetler, John A., and Donald B. Kraybill. "Hollywood Markets the Amish." In *Image Ethics: The Moral Rights of Subjects in Photographs, Film, and Television*, edited by Larry P. Gross, Larry P, John Stuart Katz, and Jay Ruby, 220–35. New York: Oxford University Press, 1988.

Hylton, Hilary. "Oprah vs. James Frey: The Sequel." *Time*, July 30, 2007. http://content.time .com/time/arts/article/0,8599,1648140,00.html.

Jantzi, Charles. "Amish Youth and Social Media: A Phase or a Fatal Error?" *Mennonite Quar-terly Review* 91, no. 1 (January 2017): 71ff.

Kahne, J., and B. Boywer. "Educating for Democracy in a Partisan Age: Confronting Chal-lenges of Motivated Reasoning and Misinformation." *American Educational Research Journal* 54 (2017): 3–34. https://doi.org/10.3102/0002831216679817.

Kahneman, Daniel. *Thinking, Fast and Slow*. New York: Farrar, Straus and Giroux, 2013.

Kant, Immanuel. *Grounding for the Metaphysics of Morals*. 3rd ed. Translated by James W. Ellington. Indianapolis, IN: Hackett, 1993.

Kavanagh, Jennifer, and Michael D. Rich. *Truth Decay: An Initial Exploration of the Diminishing Role of Facts and Analysis in American Public Life*. Santa Monica, CA: RAND Corporation, 2018. https://www.rand.org/pubs/research_reports/RR2314.html.

Kavka, Misha. *Reality TV*. Edinburgh, Scotland: Edinburgh University Press, 2012.

Kelly, Tom, and Sam Greenhill. "How Bear Grylls the Born Survivor Roughed It—in Hotels." Mail Online, July 23, 2007. http://www.dailymail.co.uk/news/article-470155/How-Bear -Grylls-Born-Survivor-roughed--hotels.html.

King, Abigail. "Amish and Social Media." LNP, September 15, 2019. https://lancasteronline .com/news/local/amish-and-social-media-why-lancaster-county-teens-can-be-found-on -instagram-facebook-spotify/article_f419e046-91d5-11e9-8e8c-4ba919dccefo.html.

Knapp, Tom. "Amish Horror Series on Tap for Fall Season, from Makers of 'Amish Mafia.'" Lancaster Online, June 11, 2014. http://lancasteronline.com/entertainment/amish-horror -series-on-tap-for-fall-season-from-makers/article_46a103e8-f17d-11e3-8a6a-001a4bcf6878 .html.

Kompare, David. "Extraordinarily Ordinary: The Osbournes as 'An American Family'" In *Reality TV: Remaking Television Culture*, edited by Susan Murray and Laurie Ouellette, 97–166. New York: New York University Press, 2004.

Kottke, Jason. "James Frey's A Million Little Pieces Fiction?" Kottke.org, January 8, 2006. http://kottke.org/06/01/james-frey-fiction.

Kraybill, Donald B. *Renegade Amish: Beard Cutting, Hate Crimes, and the Trial of the Bergholz Barbers*. Baltimore: Johns Hopkins University Press, 2014.

———. *The Riddle of Amish Culture*. Rev. ed. Baltimore: Johns Hopkins University Press, 2001.

Kraybill, Donald B., Steven M. Nolt, and David L. Weaver-Zercher. *Amish Grace: How Forgiveness Transcended Tragedy*. 1st ed. San Francisco: Jossey-Bass, 2007.

Kreiss, Daniel. "The Media Are about Identity, not Information." In *Trump and the Media*, edited by Pablo J. Boczkowski and Zizi Papacharissi. Cambridge, MA: MIT Press, 2018.

Kruger, Justin, and David Dunning. "Unskilled and Unaware of It: How Difficulties in Recognizing One's Own Incompetence Lead to Inflated Self-Assessments." *Journal of Personality and Social Psychology* 77, no.6 (1999): 1121–34.

Kuss, Katerina. "Revelo 05—Esther Schmucker." YouTube, October 1, 2019. https://www.you tube.com/watch?v=feEVG08v9pA.

Laikind, Daniel. "My Producer's Article." *Blog of Mose J Gingerich*, May 1, 2012. http://www .amishinthecitymose.com/producer-article/ (no longer active).

Leslie's Illustrated Civil War. With an introduction by John E. Stanchak. Jackson, MS: University Press of Mississippi, 1992.

Levine, Timothy R. "Truth-Default Theory (TDT): A Theory of Human Deception and Deception Detection." *Journal of Language and Social Psychology* 33, no. 4 (2014): 378–92. http://dx.doi.org/10.1177/0261927X14535916.

———. *Duped: Truth-Default Theory and the Social Science of Lying and Deception*. Tuscaloosa: University of Alabama Press, 2019.

Leyda, Jay. *Before Hollywood: Turn-of-the-Century Film from American Archives*. New York: American Federation of the Arts, 1986.

Magder, Ted. "The End of TV 101: Reality Programs, Formats, and the New Business of Television." In *Reality TV: Remaking Television Culture*, edited by Susan Murray and Laurie Ouellette, 137–56. New York: New York University Press, 2004.

Marie, Tara, and Colin Spindler. "Reasons Why Gold Rush Is Totally Fake." Grunge, December 20, 2016, updated October 5, 2017. https://www.grunge.com/34777/reasons-gold-rush -totally-fake/.

Mathis, Joel. "Corbett Calls for Amish Mafia to End." *Philadelphia Magazine*, August 13, 2014. http://www.phillymag.com/news/2014/08/13/corbett-calls-amish-mafia-end/.

Max-Planck-Gesellschaft. "The Benefits of Social Grooming." Research news, January 23, 2013. https://www.mpg.de/6858847/oxytocin-social-grooming.

McCarty, James F. "Ohio's 'Amish Bernie Madoff' Gets Prison Term for Bilking Investors." *Plain Dealer*, June 13, 2012. http://www.cleveland.com/metro/index.ssf/2012/06/ohios _amish_bernie_madoff_gets.html.

McIntire, Mike, Karen Yourish, and Larry Buchanan. "In Trump's Twitter Feed, Conspiracy-Mongers, Racists and Spies." *New York Times*, November 2, 2019. https://www.nytimes .com/interactive/2019/11/02/us/politics/trump-twitter-disinformation.html.

Menand, Louis. "Nanook and Me: 'Fahrenheit 9/11' and the Documentary Tradition." *New Yorker*, August 9 and 16, 2004. http://www.newyorker.com/magazine/2004/08/09/nanook -and-me.

Merlan, Anna. *Republic of Lies: American Conspiracy Theorists and Their Surprising Rise to Power*. New York: Metropolitan Books, 2019.

Merry, Sally Engle. "Rethinking Gossip and Scandal." In *Reputation: Studies in the Voluntary Elicitation of Good Conduct*, edited by Daniel B. Klein, 47–74. Ann Arbor: University of Michigan Press, 1997.

Mez, Jesse, Daniel H. Daneshvar, Patrick T. Kiernan, et al. "Clinicopathological Evaluation of Chronic Traumatic Encephalopathy in Players of American Football." *JAMA* 318, no. 4 (2017): 360–70. https://doi:10.1001/jama.2017.8334.

Mikkelson, David. "Mermaids: The Body Found." Snopes, May 29, 2012. http://www.snopes .com/photos/supernatural/mermaids.asp.

Morrissey, Tracie Egan. "Arrests, Divorces, and Secret Children: *Breaking Amish* Is Nothing but Lies." Jezebel, October 5, 2012. http://jezebel.com/5949245/arrests-divorces-and-secret -children-breaking-amish-is-nothing-but-lies.

Mumford, Laura Stempel. *Love and Ideology in the Afternoon: Soap Opera, Women, and Tele-vision Genre* .Bloomington: Indiana University Press, 1995.

Nanicelli, Ted and Paul Taberham, eds. *Cognitive Media Theory*. New York: Routledge, 2014.

National Ocean Service, National Oceanic and Atmospheric Administration, US Department of Commerce. "Are Mermaids Real?" Accessed April 28, 2016. http://oceanservice.noaa .gov/facts/mermaids.html.

NBC News. "Conway: Press Secretary Gave 'Alternative Facts.'" January 22, 2017. https:// www.nbcnews.com/meet-the-press/video/conway-press-secretary-gave-alternative-facts- 860142147643.

O'Connor, Cailin, and James Owen Weatherall. *The Misinformation Age: How False Beliefs Spread*. New Haven, CT: Yale University Press, 2018.

Ogunnaike, Lola. "Quiet on the Fake Set; Cue the Unsuspecting Actor." *New York Times*, October 26, 2004. http://www.nytimes.com/2004/10/26/arts/television/quiet-on-the-fake -set-cue-the-unsuspecting-actor.htm.

Oprah. "Oprah's Questions for James." January 26, 2006. http://www.oprah.com/oprahshow /Oprahs-Questions-for-James.

Ordine, Bill. "7 in Pagans-Amish Drug Ring Are Sentenced." *Philadelphia Inquirer*, June 30, 1999. http://www.mapinc.org/drugnews/v99/n686/a08.html?9483.

Ouellette, Laurie, ed. *A Companion to Reality Television*. Hoboken, NJ: John Wiley & Sons, 2014.

Oxford Languages. "Word of the Year 2016." https://languages.oup.com/word-of-the-year /word-of-the-year-2016.

Parrish, Michael, and Donald W. Nauss. "NBC Admits It Rigged Crash, Settles GM Suit." *Los Angeles Times,* February 10, 1993. https://www.latimes.com/archives/la-xpm-1993-02-10 -mn-1335-story.html.

Perel, David, and the editors of *Weekly World News. Bat Boy Lives! The* Weekly World News *Guide to Politics, Culture, Celebrities, Alien Abductions, and the Mutant Freaks That Shape Our World.* New York: Sterling, 2005.

Pew Research Center. "Trump Has Met the Public's Modest Expectations for His Presidency." August 23, 2018. https://www.people-press.org/2018/08/23/trump-has-met-the-publics -modest-expectations-for-his-presidency/.

Plesa, Alexandra. "Behind-the-Scenes Horror Stories from Reality TV." Ranker. Accessed October 24, 2019. https://www.ranker.com/list/horrifying-behind-the-scenes-reality -television-stories/alexandra-plesa.

Politifact. "The Principles of PolitiFact, PunditFact and the Truth-O-Meter." Accessed February 25, 2016. https://www.politifact.com/article/2018/feb/12/principles-truth-o-meter -politifacts-methodology-i/.

Poniewozik, James. "Foreword: The Morality of Amoral TV." In *The Ethics of Reality TV: A Philosophical Examination.* Edited by Wendy N. Wyatt and Kristie Bunton, ix–xi. New York: Continuum International, 2012.

Pooley, Jefferson, and Michael J. Socolow. "The Myth of the *War of the Worlds* Panic." Slate, October 28, 2013. https://slate.com/culture/2013/10/orson-welles-war-of-the-worlds -panic-myth-the-infamous-radio-broadcast-did-not-cause-a-nationwide-hysteria .html.

Porter, Julie. "Hanging On by a Common Thread." In *The Survival of Soap Opera: Transformations for a New Media Era,* edited by Sam Ford, Abigail De Kosnik, and C. Lee Harrington, 220–24. Jackson: University Press of Mississippi, 2011.

Pray, Isaac Clark. *Memoirs of James Gordon Bennett and His Times.* New York: Stringer and Townsend, 1855.

Putnam, Robert D. *Bowling Alone: The Collapse and Revival of American Community.* New York: Touchstone, 2000.

Rhodes, Gary D., and John Parris Springer, eds. *Docufictions: Essays on the Intersection of Documentary and Fictional Filmmaking.* Jefferson, NC: McFarland, 2006.

Robb, Amanda. "Pizzagate: Anatomy of a Fake News Scandal." *Rolling Stone,* November 16, 2017. https://www.rollingstone.com/politics/politics-news/anatomy-of-a-fake-news -scandal-125877/.

Roig-Franzia, Manuel, Scott Higham, and Paul Farhi. "Within NBC, an Intense Debate over Whether to Fire Brian Williams." *Washington Post,* February 11, 2015. https://www .washingtonpost.com/lifestyle/style/within-nbc-an-intense-debate-over-whether-to-fire -brian-williams/2015/02/11/8e87ac02-b22f-11e4-886b-c22184f27c35_story.html.

Rose, Lacey, and Stacey Wilson Hunt. "Reality TV Pioneer Jonathan Murray Talks 'Real World,' Kim Kardashian Marriage Fallout." *Hollywood Reporter,* March 30, 2012. http:// www.hollywoodreporter.com/news/bunim-murray-25-years-the-real-world-jonathan -murray-306327.

Rosnow, Ralph L. "Rumor and Gossip in Interpersonal Interaction and Beyond: A Social Exchange Perspective." In *Behaving Badly: Aversive Behaviors in Interpersonal Relationships,* edited by Robin M. Kowalski, 203–32. Washington DC: American Psychological Association, 2001.

Roxborough, Scott. "MIPCOM: Reality TV Enters "Golden Era." Hollywood Reporter, October 14, 2019. https://www.hollywoodreporter.com/news/reality-tv-enters-golden-era-at -mipcom-market-1247324.

Sanchez, C., and D. Dunning. "Overconfidence among Beginners: Is a Little Learning a

Dangerous Thing?" *Journal of Personality and Social Psychology* 114, no. 1 (January 2018): 10–28. https://doi.org/10.1037/pspa0000102.

Schiller, Dan. *Objectivity and the News: The Public and the Rise of Commercial Journalism.* Philadelphia: University of Pennsylvania Press, 1981.

Schwartz, Brad A. *Broadcast Hysteria: Orson Welles's War of the Worlds and the Art of Fake News.* New York: Hill and Wang, 2015.

Shanker, Jay, and Kirk T. Schroder, eds. *The Essential Guide to Entertainment Law.* Huntington, NY: Juris, 2018.

Sheridan, Patricia. "Patricia Sheridan's Breakfast with . . . 'Lebanon' Levi Stoltzfus." *Pittsburgh Post-Gazette*, May 4, 2015. http://www.post-gazette.com/ae/breakfast/2015/05/04/Patricia-Sheridan-s-Breakfast-With-Lebanon-Levi-Stoltzfus/stories/201504270156.

Shoemaker, David. *The Squared Circle: Life, Death, and Professional Wrestling.* New York: Gotham Books, 2012.

Sloan, Bill Sloan. *I Watched a Wild Hog Eat My Baby: A Colorful History of Tabloids and Their Cultural Impact.* Amherst, NY: Prometheus Books, 2001.

Smoking Gun. "A Million Little Lies: Exposing James Frey's Fiction Addiction." January 4, 2006. http://www.thesmokinggun.com/documents/celebrity/million-little-lies.

Spacks, Patricia Meyer. "In Praise of Gossip." *Hudson Review* 35, no.1 (Spring 1982): 19–38.

———. *Gossip.* New York: Knopf, 1985.

Spector, Dina. "70% of People Still Believe Megalodon Exists after Watching Discovery Channel's Fake Documentary." Business Insider, August 7, 2013. https://www.businessinsider.com/majority-of-discovery-channel-viewers-believe-megaldon-exists-2013-8.

Springer, John Parris. "The Newspaper Meets the Dime Novel: Docudrama in Early Cinema." In Rhodes and Springer, *Docufictions*, 27–42.

Stevick, Richard. *Growing Up Amish: The Rumspringa Years.* 2nd ed. Baltimore: Johns Hopkins University Press, 2014.

Stoltzfus, "Lebanon" Levi, and Ellis Henican. *Amish Confidential.* New York: Gallery Books, 2015.

The Age. "Ozzy's Outburst Was Faked." November 29, 2002. http://www.theage.com.au/articles/2002/11/29/1038386295373.html.

Thirteen (WNET, New York Public Television). "An American Family." Accessed April 4, 2016. http://www.thirteen.org/american-family.

This American Life. "Retraction." Episode 460, March 16, 2012. http://www.thisamericanlife.org/radio-archives/episode/460/retraction.

TLC. "I'm an Eskimo at the Beach!" Accessed March 24, 2016. https://www.youtube.com/watch?v=9P13LhDdmo8.

Trivers, Robert. *The Folly of Fools: The Logic of Deceit and Self-Deception in Human Life.* New York: Basic Books, 2014.

Twenge, Jean M. *iGen: Why Today's Super-Connected Kids Are Growing Up Less Rebellious, More Tolerant, Less Happy—and Completely Unprepared for Adulthood (and What This Means for the Rest of Us).* New York: Atria Books, 2017.

Umble, Diane Zimmerman, and David L. Weaver-Zercher, eds. *The Amish and the Media.* Baltimore: Johns Hopkins University Press, 2008.

VanDerWerff, Emily. "750 Reality TV Shows Aired on Cable in 2015. Yes, 750." Vox, January 7, 2016. http://www.vox.com/2016/1/7/10728206/reality-shows-how-many-peak-tv.

Vosoughi, Soroush, Deb Roy, and Sinan Aral. "The Spread of True and False News Online." *Science* 359, no. 6380 (March 9, 2018): 1146–51. https://science.sciencemag.org/content/359/6380/1146.

Walker, Lucy. "*Devil's Playground*: Director's Notes." Accessed May 5, 2016. http://www.lucywalkerfilm.com/DEVIL-S-PLAYGROUND.

Walsh, Barry, and Adam Benzine. "15 Years: It's Been Real." *Realscreen* 16, no. 1 (September/ October 2012): 33.

Ward, Stephen J. A. "Inventing Objectivity: New Philosophical Foundations." In *Journalism Ethics: A Philosophical Approach*, edited by Christopher Meyers, 137–52. New York: Oxford University Press, 2010.

Washington Post. "Sept. 2–5, 2019 Washington Post–ABC News Poll." Updated September 11, 2019. https://www.washingtonpost.com/context/sept-2-5-2019-washington-post-abc-news -poll/d4e18b36-79bf-492d-91e3-d1c7a49d37e2/.

West, R. F., R. J. Meserve, and K. E. Stanovich. "Cognitive Sophistication Does Not Attenuate the Bias Blind Spot." *Journal of Personality and Social Psychology* 103, no. 3 (September 2012): 506–19. https://doi.org/10.1037/a0028857.

Wilson, Robert. *Mathew Brady: Portraits of a Nation.* New York: Bloomsbury, 2013.

Winston, Brian Winston. *Lies, Damn Lies and Documentaries.* London: British Film Institute, 2000.

WNYC Studios. "La Mancha Screwjob." Radiolab, February 4, 2015. http://www.radiolab.org /story/la-mancha-screwjob/?utm_source=sharedUrl&utm_medium=metatag&utm _campaign=sharedUrl.

Worth, Sol. "Pictures Can't Say Ain't." In *Studying Visual Communication*, 162–84. Philadelphia: University of Pennsylvania Press, 1981.

Yahr, Emily. "A Fake Shark Week Documentary about Megalodons Caused Controversy. Why is Discovery Bringing It Up Again?" *Washington Post*, July 16, 2018, https://www .washingtonpost.com/news/arts-and-entertainment/wp/2018/07/26/a-fake-shark-week -documentary-about-megalodons-caused-controversy-why-is-discovery-bringing-it -up-again/.

YouTube. "Bret Hart vs. Shawn Michaels Survivor Series 1997." Accessed July 25, 2016. https:// www.youtube.com/watch?v=OwMOtdNnWYY (no longer active).

———. "Oprah Winfrey Show—Interview with James Frey." Accessed July 27, 2016. https:// www.youtube.com/watch?v=eYRQ_ZY1YoA (no longer active).

———. "Vince Russo on the Montreal Screwjob Being His Idea." Accessed July 25, 2016. https://www.youtube.com/watch?v=EFXpkRWIo6A (no longer active).

Zunshine, Lisa, ed. *Oxford Handbook of Cognitive Literary Studies.* Oxford: Oxford University Press, 2015.

———. "Reality TV: Humiliation in Real Time." In *Getting Inside Your Head: What Cognitive Science Can Tell Us about Popular Culture*, 117–24. Baltimore: Johns Hopkins University Press, 2012.

Television Programs and Movies Cited

12 Years a Slave (feature film). Steve McQueen, 2013.

Adventures of Ozzie and Harriet, The. ABC, 1952–1966.

Alaskan Bush People. Discovery Channel, since 2014.

All-American Muslim. TLC, 2011–2012.

American Crime Story: The People v. O. J. Simpson. FX, 2016.

American Idol. Fox, 2002–2016; ABC, since 2018.

Amish at the Altar. National Geographic, 2010.

Amish Haunting. Destination America, 2014.

Amish in the City. UPN, 2004.

Amish Mafia. Discovery Channel, 2012–2015.

Amish, The. PBS, American Experience episode, 2012.

Amish: Out of Order. National Geographic, 2012.

An American Family. PBS, 1973.

Ancient Aliens. History Channel, since 2010.

Apprentice, The. NBC, 2004–2017.

Bachelor, The. ABC, since 2002.

Bachelorette, The. ABC, since 2003.

Big Brother. European franchise, since 1997; CBS, since 2000.

Birth of a Nation (feature film). D. W. Griffith, 1915.

Blown Away. Netflix, 2019.

Born Survivor. Discovery Channel, 2006–2011.

Bowling for Columbine (feature documentary). Michael Moore, 2002.

Breaking Amish. TLC, 2012–2014.

Candid Camera. Various networks, 1948–2014.

Cops. Fox, since 1989.

Cribs. MTV, since 2000.

CSI. CBS, 2000–2015.

Cutthroat Kitchen. Food Network, 2013–2017.

Days of Our Lives. NBC, since 1965.

Deadliest Catch. Discovery Channel, since 2005.

Dirty Jobs. Discovery Channel, 2003–2012.

Documentary Now! IFC, since 2015.

Duck Dynasty. A&E, 2012–2017.

Escaping Alaska. TLC, 2014.

Five Guys a Week, in production in 2019.

Game of Thrones. HBO, 2011–2019.

God or the Girl. A&E, 2006.

Great British Bake Off, The. BBC (Britain) and PBS, since 2010.

Hell's Kitchen. Fox, since 2005.

Here Comes Honey Boo Boo. TLC, 2012–2014.

Hotel Rwanda (feature film). Terry George, 2004.

Jinx, The. HBO, 2015.

Jon & Kate Plus 8 | Kate Plus 8. TLC and Discovery Health Network, 2007–2017.

Keeping Up with the Kardashians. E!, since 2007.

Love Island. ITV2 (UK), since 2015; CBS, 2019.

Masked Singer, The. Fox, 2019.

MasterChef. Fox, since 2010.

Matrix, The (feature film). Lana and Lilly Wachowski, 1999.

Megalodon: The Monster Shark Lives. Discovery Channel, 2013.

Mermaids: The Body Found. Animal Planet and Discovery Channel, 2012.

Mermaids: The New Evidence. Animal Planet, 2013.

Monster Garage. Discovery Channel, 2002–2006.

Moonshiners. Discovery Channel, since 2011.

Mythbusters. Discovery Channel, 2003–2018.

Naked and Afraid. Discovery Channel, since 2013.

Nanook of the North (feature film). Robert Flaherty, 1922.

Office, The. NBC, 2005–2013.

Osbournes, The. MTV, 2002–2005.

Pawn Stars. History Channel, since 2009.

Prank Academy. YouTube, 2016.

Press Your Luck. CBS, 1983–1986; ABC, 2019.

Princesses: Long Island. Bravo, 2013.

Real Housewives. Bravo, since 2006.

Real World, The. MTV, since 1992.
Return to Amish. TLC, 2012–2019.
River Monsters. Animal Planet, since 2009.
Shahs of Sunset. Bravo, 2012–2018.
Shark Tank. ABC, since 2009.
Sister Wives. TLC, since 2010.
Sisterhood: Becoming Nuns, The. Lifetime, 2014.
Startup.com (feature documentary). Jehane Noujaim and Chris Hegedus, 2001.
State Legislature (feature documentary). Frederick Wiseman, 2007.
Survivor. CBS, since 2000.
This Is Spinal Tap (feature film). Rob Reiner, 1984.
Voice, The. NBC, since 2011.